The Years of Blood

AMERICAN ENCOUNTERS/GLOBAL INTERACTIONS
A Series edited by Gilbert M. Joseph and Penny Von Eschen

The series aims to stimulate critical perspectives and fresh interpretive frameworks for scholarship on the history of the imposing global presence of the United States. Its primary concerns include the deployment and contestation of power, the construction and deconstruction of cultural and political borders, the fluid meaning of intercultural encounters, and the complex interplay between the global and the local. American Encounters seeks to strengthen dialogue and collaboration between historians of US international relations and area studies specialists.

The series encourages scholarship based on multi-archive historical research. At the same time, it supports a recognition of the representational character of all stories about the past and promotes critical inquiry into issues of subjectivity and narrative. In the process, American Encounters strives to understand the context in which meanings related to nations, cultures, and political economy are continually produced, challenged, and reshaped.

The
Years
of Blood

STORIES FROM A REPORTING
LIFE IN LATIN AMERICA

Alma Guillermoprieto

Duke University Press   *Durham and London*   2025

Project Editor: Livia Tenzer
Typeset in Portrait and Helvetica Neue
by Westchester Publishing Services

Library of Congress Cataloging-in-Publication Data
Names: Guillermoprieto, Alma, [date] author.
Title: The years of blood : stories from a reporting life in Latin America /
Alma Guillermoprieto.
Other titles: American encounters/global interactions.
Description: Durham : Duke University Press, 2025. | Series: American
encounters/global interactions
Identifiers: LCCN 2024025089 (print)
LCCN 2024025090 (ebook)
ISBN 9781478031390 (paperback)
ISBN 9781478028178 (hardcover)
ISBN 9781478060383 (ebook)
Subjects: LCSH: Political violence—Latin America—History—20th century. |
Latin America—History—20th century. | Latin America—Civilization—
20th century. | Latin America—Politics and government—20th century.
Classification: LCC F1414.2 .G776 2025 (print) | LCC F1414.2 (ebook) |
DDC 303.6097—dc23/eng/20241216
LC record available at https://lccn.loc.gov/2024025089
LC ebook record available at https://lccn.loc.gov/2024025090

Cover art: Pictures of missing students on the eighth anniversary
of their abduction from Iguala, Guerrero; National Palace, Mexico City,
September 26, 2022. © Guillermo Diaz/Sopa Images/Alamy.

Contents

PART III. MEXICO

Introduction

A Reporting Life in Latin America

I was living in Bogotá, Colombia, in November 1988 when news broke that a terrible massacre had occurred in Segovia, a small mining town miles away from just about everywhere but reachable by plane from the city of Medellín. Reports of the massacre took hours to travel to the capital, but then it burst all over the national news. We learned that in just an hour and a half of carnage, dozens of people had been murdered that long weekend. For days after the killings, the newspapers ran pages of photographs of mourners in the pouring rain, grieving over rows of coffins. But for all the scandal and commotion that week, I couldn't find an account in the Bogotá media that would help me understand how such a horror could have taken place.

I was appalled by the story and fascinated, too: the little town hidden somewhere in the crags and valleys of Colombia's rough geography; the fact that entire towns, and stories, and huge crimes could remain so out of view in the capital; the historical inability of ostentatiously well-educated presidents and ministers to take control of their country; the mythical quality of Colombia's history, so steeped in blood. And then there was the horror of the massacre itself, which reportedly was perpetrated by a couple of dozen men, none of whom the security forces could manage to identify.

Of course I had to go. I made my first trip to Segovia in March of the following year, and even then, months after the event, a claustrophobic atmosphere of terror came down on me like a kidnapper's blanket from the moment I left the airport. It felt like there was no oxygen in that hot air, and even though I was visiting under the pretext of writing a story about a local British gold mine, and was met by the manager and toured the mine, the skin all up and down my spine crawled with apprehension every minute of that trip.

I did a few interviews at the mine for a story I eventually wrote for the *Guardian*, and then I went into town—lawless, Wild West territory. People whispered to me that the organizer of the massacre was a man named Fidel Castaño: a cattle rancher, gambler, small-time drug trafficker, and owner of the local cantina, with a sideline smuggling Colombian emeralds into Brazil and Brazilian diamonds into Colombia. A decade earlier, people said, his father had been kidnapped by one of the many guerrilla organizations that plagued Colombia then. The Castaño family had paid a sizable ransom—which the guerrillas accepted, even though the father had already died of a heart attack while in captivity, so that what Fidel Castaño and his family received in exchange for their money was a corpse. Hence, the massacre.

On the night of November 11, while the commander of the local army battalion and his troops slept peacefully—or so they later claimed—masked killers went up and down Segovia's main street checking names off a list, and when they finished their work forty-six people had been murdered. I assume that most of the victims were suspected by Fidel Castaño and his siblings of collaborating with the guerrillas who had abducted their father. The town's suspicion that the killers had included freelancers from the army battalion would prove correct.

One version I heard of why the massacre had taken place so long after the kidnapping is that it had actually been sparked by the election of a young left-wing mayor from a political party allied to the guerrillas and by the guerrillas' recent rustling of an entire truckload of Castaño family cattle headed for market. I talked to the mayor, who was understandably taciturn; and later at some length to her much more simpatico, loquacious bodyguard; got out of town the next morning; then went back a second, even creepier time days afterward and got out faster.

A few weeks later, two colleagues from a major Bogotá newspaper went to do the same story; on their way into town from the airport they were forced out of their taxi, made to kneel in the road, and executed. I never went back, but nine months after the Segovia killings I found out that a handful of men had been arrested and accused of perpetrating the massacre. I learned the name of one of the prisoners and made a visit to a not particularly secure jail on the outskirts of Medellín, where he was being held.

I won't mention his name here; he may be out now, trying to lead a normal life. Perhaps he wasn't involved in the crimes he was accused of. Perhaps he's dead, or he got out and is still taking odd jobs as a hit man. I told him who I was and what I was doing, but I'm not sure how much he understood. His vocabulary was limited, and he seemed a little dim—but live-wire nervous, too; nervous not like someone about to fire a gun at you in a sudden rage but like someone who expects to have the living daylights beaten out of him at any moment. This anxiety made him eager to talk—not about the murders, which he denied any involvement with—but about his life. He was twenty-six years old, fair-haired, as I recall, and muscular but slight, and he sweated and jiggled throughout our conversation.

Néstor, let's call him. He worked as a freelance gold miner, he told me, which meant that, with a partner, he would go up a likely-looking hill and pick at the ground with a pickaxe. If they struck pay dirt, he and his partner would take turns guarding the site. On a decent day, the vein would produce a fistful of gold chips that could be exchanged for maybe a week's worth of food and supplies. In this case, Néstor's partner was one of his brothers. One day, after they struck gold, six men came up the hill and killed his brother, while Néstor hid behind a rock, praying for his life.

There was another, younger brother, whom Néstor always referred to as his *hermanito*. This *hermanito* was a junkie, and he hustled small amounts of *basuco*, a kind of crack cocaine, to pay for his habit. At some point—I was trying back then to make sense of Néstor's circling account, and I've been trying now to make sense of my own notes from that long-ago interview—the *hermanito* was blinded by rivals who took his eyes out with a machete. Néstor thought that this *hermanito* may have started selling drugs in an area he didn't know was controlled by a different guerrilla group from the one that killed Fidel Castaño's father. Both groups, in any case, funded their activities largely by patrolling areas where coca leaf was grown and sold to cocaine dealers for export. *Basuco*, the residual product from the manufacturing process, was sold locally, to a new generation of addicts. Whether selling *basuco* outside his turf was the motive or not, one day the guerrillas dragged Néstor's *hermanito* off a suburban bus and shot him to death in front of all the other passengers. Or maybe it was two different *hermanitos*, one blinded and the other shot to death, plus the one killed at the mine . . . who knows. When my allotted hour was up and I closed my notebook, I was so full of Néstor's mumbling despair that I couldn't really think.

But now I can see how Néstor, if someone had come up to him and handed him a machine gun and said, "Let's go shoot some terrorists and here's a little cash," might have said, "Sure, when do we start?" And I can see something also about the man who probably hired him, the small-time trafficker Fidel Castaño, who founded a paramilitary group at this time that, in collusion with much of the army and police and with funding from cattle ranchers and cocaine traffickers, terrorized the countryside and was responsible for a good part of the hundreds of thousands of murders that took place in Colombia between 1988 and 2001. What I understood was this: Colombia has been historically an isolated and poor country and tremendously elitist. Unlike many other Latin American countries, it had never had a revolution or major social reform, and its economy was until recently too small to propel it into true modern-day capitalism, with its accompanying benefits of opportunity and social mobility.

So crime became a principal means, perhaps *the* principal means, of social ascent. Fidel Castaño was a gambler, a cantina owner, and a smuggler, which gave him start-up capital. And then he became a killer and that gave him power, and he took that small allotment—his inheritance and seed money, as it were—and ran with it. First, in collusion with local ranchers, he started a paramilitary group for the *departamento*, or state, of Antioquia and established a pioneering working relationship with the local army garrison. Then he took that model and reproduced it all over northeastern Colombia, until under his brother, Carlos, this paramilitary movement became an army as powerful as the guerrilla forces it waged war against.

The Segovia massacre was among the first and largest of dozens of paramilitary massacres that followed throughout the next quarter century in Colombia, and writing about it was to have been my first effort for the *New Yorker*, but it never ran. Now I think that's because I wasn't able to communicate what lay behind my need to write the story: the fact that prohibitionist US foreign policy with regard to drugs has created a voracious illegal market and led to the violent death of a million or more Latin Americans—men, mostly, and most of them young—in the past fifty years. It all started in the mid-1970s: President Richard Nixon's polls were collapsing; popular despair was on the rise regarding the condition of returning combatants from the United States' adventure in Southeast Asia; Nixon's own disgust with the drug-happy culture of younger Americans fueled the inchoate anger that would bring him down; and the result of the mix was the puritanical, repressive, and carelessly racist War on Drugs. Its designers thought it would be a proxy war: foreigners in foreign lands would exterminate foreigners and so protect the American citizenry, this time not from Communists but from bloodthirsty purveyors of drugs. We know how the war worked out for minority communities within the United States: the devastation it caused in Black communities; the transformation of youth gangs in Latino neighborhoods; the escalating addiction figures in rich and poor white communities, but that is not my subject here.

For years now, Latin America has had the highest homicide rate of any region in the world. The figures fluctuate according to time and place, but at different moments in parts of Honduras, El Salvador, Venezuela, parts of Mexico, certain cities in Brazil, some regions of Colombia, and lately even in

Ecuador, that peaceful country, for each 100,000 of their citizens, there have been as many as 83 homicides. According to Mexico's Instituto Nacional de Estadística, Geografía e Informática (INEGI, National Institute of Statistics, Geography and Informatics), in the eighteen years since then-president Felipe Calderón fatefully involved the army in his country's drug wars, more than a half million of his fellow citizens have died violent, often atrocious deaths. And this figure does not reflect the total damage—the disappeared, the maimed, the traumatized, the orphaned, or the increasing number of families in which poor and frequently unskilled women struggle alone to bring up hard-working, God-fearing children, often by risking everything in order to transport them to safety in the United States.

A younger me must have imagined that Segovia was a story about evil murderers pitted against innocent civilians, and there were certainly plenty of evil men involved: the army and police commanders, Fidel Castaño, guerrilla leaders, drug lords. The most interesting and difficult part of the story was how victims and murderers were locked into one another's fates—the father killed by guerrillas, the father's son murdering other fathers of other sons—until the protagonists of this endless story became like those figures carved inside Chinese ivory spheres, rolling about in an endless struggle with no escape and no winners. Still, the roots of Segovia are planted in what may be judged in time as the United States' most reckless exercise of its immense power in Latin America. I remain deeply grateful to Néstor, who helped me understand this, but at the time I never managed to untangle the story and what it meant to me, so that I could make it understandable for others too.

People sometimes ask me why I like writing stories that can be terribly violent and cruel, and the answer is that of course I don't. This is not what I expected to do with my life. When I started out in journalism in 1978, reporting from Nicaragua about a popular uprising led by the Sandinista National Liberation Front against Anastasio Somoza, it soon became clear that the country was about to rid itself of a dreadful dictator. My colleagues and I who witnessed the Sandinistas' triumph never imagined that forty years later we would be writing about how Daniel Ortega, the Sandinista who was president from 1985 to 1990 and has been president again since 2007, has surpassed Somoza in sheer arbitrary evil. Or about how Ortega's vice president and spouse, Rosario Murillo, has acquired, in addition to great power, all the eccentricities of a dictator's wife—the crazy makeup, the spiritual séances, the crappy poetry readings, the offering of her own daughter for her husband's bed. We couldn't have foreseen that the peace treaty that ended El Salvador's long internal war in 1992 would not end the violence but would lead to criminal gangs springing up two generations later, in large part made up of the ten thousand young men born in El Salvador of parents who fled the violence for the United States and who were then deported by the Barack Obama administration back to a country they barely remembered, if at all. But I couldn't stop writing just because the stories that turned up weren't the stories that I would have wanted to write. I'd picked up the thread of this story in Segovia, started to understand something about it, and although it definitely wasn't my intention to spend the next twenty-five years watching expanding pools of adolescents murder one another, and watching the drug trade cause not only that disaster but the erosion of civic structures throughout the hemisphere, I could hardly avoid this task: I had ended up with a career in journalism, and I was trying to see my way through the murk.

Ground seeded with the dragon's teeth of illicit drugs and violence is not fertile ground for democracy, and if in the 1980s and 1990s many of us who were then observing events in the region had found reason to hope as dictatorships collapsed and elections became a routine part of political life, we were soon reminded that elections are but the end product of a democratic life. Democracy needs not only a level playing field and elections free of bribes and fear but also equality among its citizens. So it is not surprising that in the most unequal region in the world people systematically deceived by their governments—subjected to security forces that keep only criminals safe, cheated of a decent education, respect, adequate transportation, and tranquility—should feel cynical and desperate when called upon to exercise their vote. In a recent poll by Latinobarómetro, the organization that studies citizen attitudes about democracy and their world, it came out that less than fifty percent of Latin Americans think that democracy is the best form of government. In Mexico, "something more than a third [of the electorate] supports democracy, while another third supports an authoritarian option." Further, 42 percent would support a military government in lieu of a democratic one, "if things should get really difficult." In some countries, the citizens have already voted: for Jair Messias Bolsonaro in Brazil; Hugo Chávez in Venezuela and, endlessly, his clownish successor, Nicolás Maduro; and, of course, Nayib Bukele in El Salvador, who has many, many fans throughout the continent, wishing they had someone like him to vote for.

THE STORIES THAT FOLLOW were reported and written from Latin America and published in this first quarter of the twenty-first century in three magazines whose readership is principally in the United States. Almost all have subsequently been translated into Spanish. It is the third such collection of stories since 1995, but, naturally, its concerns are different, as the preoccupations of the time have evolved faster than it would have been possible to imagine thirty years ago. The first collection, *The Heart That Bleeds*, edited by my forever missed friend and mentor, the great Robert Gottlieb, brought together stories in the *New Yorker* that appeared in their polished form under the loving guidance of the irreplaceable John Bennet. Violence was the subject of a few—notably, the stories about Colombia, and one about Peru, then in the grasp of a great terror generated by the Shining Path armed movement. Nevertheless, there was, in general, a celebratory spirit running through the book: in South and Central America the great iron weight of dictatorship had recently been lifted, commodity prices were high, and the formalities of electoral democracy were being observed with pride and hope. In Mexico this was the time of the first free trade agreement signed between Mexico and the United States, and the big question tormenting the soul of my compatriots was whether it was possible to remain Mexican while becoming modern.

The second collection, *Looking for History*, consisted of stories written for both the *New Yorker* and the *New York Review of Books*. The generous welcome extended to me by Robert Silvers, the *Review*'s towering founding editor, gave me freedom to write more meditatively about the problems of democracy in Latin America, where the twentieth-century free-election festivities had ended, and there were, seemingly, only a few straggler countries left, swilling the leftover bubbly before the hangover kicked in. Drug violence was becoming institutionalized, threadbare education systems were collapsing, and democracy's main product seemed to be corruption. There was, of course, progress as well: Latin American economies have advanced and modernized, health care in many urban centers is almost adequate, and an emerging middle class has taken root. But industry has thrived at the expense of its workers, who do not often receive the kind of salaries conducive to social mobility. Statistically, if you are born poor you and your children are likely to stay that way, and so the great glacier of inequality has kept moving our societies further in the direction of corruption and violence.

Looking for History was full of questions whose answers many of us could not find our way through, the main one being, *how do we change*? After the failure of armed revolutionary movements, after the iron rule of dictatorships determined to achieve progress through order, after the stumbling failure of formal electoral democracy, after we've tried everything in our power and still remained too much the same, how do we change at last?

A few stories in this collection spring from the disbelief felt by some of us born in the mid-twentieth century. We look back on the dreams of change we failed so resoundingly to achieve and wonder, *What were we thinking?* What was it that guerrilla movements were supposed to achieve? The story about Daniel Ortega and Rosario Murillo provides no answers but seeks to describe, at least, the lay of that now devastated land.

Equally, the stories from Venezuela and Bolivia chronicle events in places that once filled many people with hope and are now, to varying degrees, disasters. When a peace agreement was signed in El Salvador in 1991, after long years of war between a murderous state and a utopian and harsh guerrilla movement, it was not easy to feel great enthusiasm—the country was physically, financially, and emotionally devastated—but along with many observers at the time I thought that at least, at last, there would be an end to decades of hair-raising violence. After an absence of nearly thirty years I wrote a story born of the shock I felt at what I found when I returned to El Salvador in 2010. More modest hopes surrounded the ascent of Evo Morales, who did not come to power in Bolivia through a utopian armed uprising but in the 2005 presidential election. His downfall was notable because, although his achievements were significant, he suffered from an enduring presidential vice: he could not bring himself to get off that chair.

This book is, then, to a large degree, the story of disillusion and broken futures, an attempt to fix this moment in a continent's history so that, perhaps, readers will find similarities with their own experience of our time and look for paths away from our present dilemma. But if life were always grim it would not be worth living and people everywhere find reasons to celebrate, and love, and contemplate beauty. I am endlessly grateful to my profession for the chance to spend time on stories that do not deal with death but with the great, bubbling-over, defiant life of Latin America, like one I was privileged to report for *National Geographic* magazine, about traditional Bolivian *cholitas* who are the queens of the wrestling ring.

I wish there were more stories in this collection like it. I wish this book did not have this title. I wish that what humor there is did not bite quite so hard. But I have felt the obligation to observe and describe, for the record, the triumph of violence as a form of political expression and the decline of democracy as an aspiration in this twenty-first century. I hope that in the not-too-distant future a much younger writer will be able to report and write the stories of how peace was consolidated throughout these lands.

NOTE

All translations in this volume are mine, unless otherwise noted.

Part I

———

South America

Bolivia's Tarnished Savior

DECEMBER 3, 2020

Flying over the Andes in the dead of night, you know you've reached Bolivia because towns and villages become visible: neat crosshatches of light, every street illuminated. The terminal at El Alto International Airport may not have the best design or the most punctilious construction standards, but in the freezing predawn of this high plateau—the Andean altiplano—one could weep with gratitude that it is heated. Thirty years ago, El Alto was not a city but a straggle of unpaved, unlit streets spreading out from a ramshackle improvisation of piled-up luggage and technology-free checkpoints. Visitors arriving to the shock of thirteen thousand feet above sea level gasped for air, stumbled into a taxi, and rattled their way down a pitted, hairpin road to the capital, La Paz.

El Alto today represents everything that the government of Evo Morales—known by absolutely all his countrymen as el Evo—achieved during its almost fourteen years in power, from 2006 to 2019. It is Bolivia's second-largest city, and from the new six-lane highway into La Paz you can admire one of the most visible signs of the transformation: the crisscrossing cable cars of the capital's spanking-new airborne transportation system, baptized Mi Teleférico. There are eight lines with 1,400 gondolas serving thirty-seven stations, all built in barely eight years. Three of the lines swoop down from El Alto to La Paz, a city of 800,000 set in a treeless, arid canyon. A bus commute could eat a couple of hours of a worker's day; a Teleférico ride takes minutes.

But in important ways, El Alto itself has hardly changed since December 2005, when Alteños, along with a plurality of other Bolivians, voted overwhelmingly to elect Evo as Bolivia's first Indigenous president since independence in 1825. Sidewalk vendors still sell everything from llama fetuses to fake diamond–covered cell phone cases. Water remains scarce. Traffic remains a nightmare. The older Indigenous women, or *cholas*, still dress in traditional layered skirts and bowler hats. They are Aymara, descended from the inhabitants of the southernmost part of the Inca Empire, and although a significant percentage of El Alto's nearly one million people are Quechua (another Andean ethnic group), mestizo, or even Chinese, this is an Aymara city in its identity, habits, and language—the only Indigenous city that comes to mind in all the Americas—and it is passionately pro-Evo, a fellow Aymara.

Yet when he ran for a constitutionally questionable fourth term in 2019 and claimed a possibly fraudulent victory, some of the fiercest battles between pro-Evo Aymaras and anti-Evo Aymara evangelical Christians took place here, while hundreds of other protests throughout Bolivia demanded, day after day, that he resign. Three weeks later, with the country ready to burst into civil war, he boarded a plane bound for Mexico.

New elections were held last month, and two contradictory things happened: the Movimiento al Socialismo (MAS, Movement for Socialism) party triumphed at the polls, but Evo—the former president who defined the party, transformed his impoverished country, and is regarded by so many, not least himself, as Bolivia's savior—was removed from influence. For the immediate future, at least, he will not be returning to power.

JUAN EVO MORALES AYMA was born in 1959 in the remote highland region of Orinoca, so poor that, as he told everyone during his first presidential campaign, he dreamed of being rich enough to ride in a bus and throw sucked orange halves carelessly out the window, as he saw passengers do when he walked into town with his father. When he was nineteen, fresh out of military service and ambitious, he and his family realized there was no future in the arid altiplano. They joined a growing stream of highlanders moving down to the steaming, fertile lowland strip of territory called the Chapare to farm coca leaf, which was being bought for stacks of money by flashy foreigners in a hurry. A traditional and legal Andean crop with religious associations, coca is chewed by Bolivian campesinos—poor farmers—as a mild stimulant and was used as an ingredient in Coca-Cola until well into the 1990s. But a ton of leaves can also be refined into about two pounds of cocaine base paste. In the 1980s, at the height of the United States' reckless affair with coke, farmers in the Chapare were able to earn as much as $14,000 a year, for them a staggering amount.

It was then that Evo joined a growing union movement among the coca farmers as sports secretary (he is a soccer fanatic), eventually becoming the combative head of the federation of the six coca-growing unions in the Chapare. Like many of his union brothers, he saw himself first as a campesino, not an Aymara, but always as a union militant. Those were tough times: Washington fantasized that it could eliminate the cocaine trade—run mostly by Colombian smugglers and US distributors—by persuading a succession of hard-line, right-wing rulers to fight a proxy war against coca growers. US-trained Bolivian special forces were helicoptered into the Chapare, men were killed, women were abused, farmers' houses were burned down, and Evo emerged from those years of confrontation with a vaguely Marxist, fiercely anti-US view of the world.

Together with other campesino leaders and leftist sympathizers, he took over the MAS—then a sketchy, semifascist party—in 1998 and was elected to Congress the next year. As a one-term congressman, Evo fought for the right of Chapare campesinos to grow coca. (Coca farming for local consumption as tea or leaves to chew remains unrestricted elsewhere in Bolivia.) Most importantly, he led violent street confrontations that led to the resignations of two successive presidents, Gonzalo Sánchez de Lozada in 2003 and his vice president and successor, Carlos Mesa, in 2005.

Before his successful 2005 run for the presidency, immediately following Mesa's overthrow, Evo appears to have realized that he could not win a national election as a poor, coca-growing, brawling, radical union leader. With somewhere near half of the population identifying with one of Bolivia's Indigenous communities, he gradually oriented his message toward them. Back then I heard a flower-wreathed Evo open a rally in Cochabamba with a couple of phrases in what may have been Quechua, and he referred as often as possible to the *pachamama*, the bountiful Andean earth mother. He talked about the Qullasuyu—the southeasternmost corner of the Inca Empire, which mostly overlaps with modern-day Bolivia. At his rallies, the *wiphala*—a multicolored flag that stood for racial tolerance, equal rights, and the Qullasuyu—was increasingly spotted.

Evo's opponents on the right mocked his Indigenous origins, while Indigenous leaders who didn't like him pointed out that he had never worn native dress and could barely speak Aymara. But his change of image meant a great deal to Indigenous voters and, eventually, to him. "I don't consider myself the first indigenous president," he told the journalist Raúl Peñaranda:

> I consider myself the first union President. But later, reviewing things, coming as I do from an *ayllu* [traditional community] in Orinoca, where there . . . is still no private property even today, I consider myself indigenous.

Particularly during the first decade of his presidency, Evo and his vice president, Álvaro García Linera, radically transformed Bolivia. (Despite his non-Indigenous origins, García Linera, pale-skinned and professorial, was in 1986 the cofounder of an Indigenous-rights guerrilla organization and eventually spent five years in jail.) In short order, Evo delivered on a promise to bring the Indigenous population to the forefront of the nation's politics. He called a modernizing constitutional convention at which slightly more than half the delegates were from the MAS, and mostly Indigenous. About a third of the delegates were women, in the short skirts and flat straw hats of the lowland Quechua or the bowler hats and long, layered skirts of the Aymara. In the luminous courtyard of a colonial building in Sucre where the convention was being held, I talked to many of those women as they went from one meeting room to another, brimming with ideas and filled with the seriousness of their task.

THE NEW CONSTITUTION, enacted in 2009, declared clean drinking water and sewage systems a universal right, granted Indigenous communities a wide range of authority in their territories, and guaranteed a minimum number of congressional seats for native representatives. Thanks to high international prices for the country's main export, natural gas—averaging $8 per thousand cubic feet—the economy purred along at nearly 5 percent yearly growth, and the government had room to experiment and innovate during its first ten years in power. ("I governed with gas at $1.70," Evo's predecessor, Carlos Mesa, says bitterly and often.) For a few months, at least, the minister of justice was a Quechua domestic worker who had come up through the ranks of the MAS while organizing other women like her. In Bolivia, where the brutal oppression of conquest was still felt by the Indigenous peoples, their newfound visibility and the constitutional reforms brought a great healing shift in racial relations. This was fiercely resisted by fearful whites and mestizos, and yet, keeping in mind that in the recent past Bolivia had five presidents in one year, businessmen were grateful for the new stability.

It was enough to make the flaws and brutalities of Evo's rule seem almost irrelevant, almost tolerable. There was, for example, the persecution of journalists and the media. The Evo government bought up newspapers and television stations and forced out critical journalists. For all its proclaimed Indigenous identity, it clashed repeatedly with native groups, particularly in the tropical lowlands, where the decision to allow Shell Oil and Brazil's Petrobras into a forest reserve led to months of confrontation with the inhabitants.

And there was Evo's decision to increase the amount of land that settlers were allowed to clear in the tropical lowlands using the traditional and more discrete slash-and-burn method. The new settlers were mostly impoverished highlanders who had never seen a forest or grasslands and had no idea how to clear land with fire. As a result, fires raged for nearly two months last year across the dry-forest Chiquitania region, leading to the irreparable loss of some eight thousand square miles of virgin forest and the destruction of fauna. (This year, fires have continued to burn through an even wider swath of the same territory.)

There were also monumental levels of corruption, like the MAS senator who received $800,000 for public works in a nonexistent town, Evo's refusal to negotiate with his congressional opposition, and his habit of harassing his opponents with trumped-up charges, keeping them busy in the courts. Then there was his grotesque side: his repeated references to his sexual prowess, for example. (He likes to joke that nine months after he visits a village, all the women give birth, proof of his slogan "Evo Delivers.") The stale sexism, anti-environmental policies, corruption, and love of power for power's sake may have left voters and members of his own party—particularly the younger ones—feeling that despite the tremendous excitement of Evo's early, innovative years in office, he was starting to look like the old-fashioned semidictators with whom Bolivians were already too familiar.

In 2016 Evo called a referendum on whether he should be allowed to run for office a fourth time. He lost that vote by a narrow margin and promised to abide by it. Nevertheless, in 2017 the Electoral Tribunal, a supposedly independent body heavily controlled by the party in power, ruled that it would be a violation of Evo's "human rights" to restrict his ability to run for office. "I don't want to, but I must do it for my people," a blushing Evo allowed. If he won the October 2019 elections, he promised, he would stay in office only through 2025.

THE VOTE WAS held last year on October 20. The top contenders were Evo and Mesa, a journalist and historian by profession and a temperate politician who seems to drag himself reluctantly to each election but runs anyway. At

7:40 p.m., with nearly 85 percent of the vote counted, Evo had 45.28 percent and Mesa 38.16 percent. This was troubling to the president and exhilarating to his opponents: under Bolivian law, when there is less than a ten-point difference between the top two candidates, a runoff must be held. Everyone understood that in a runoff, with all the opposition parties joining forces behind Mesa, Evo would lose. But no celebration was held because before the next announcement of preliminary results, vote counting was suspended. It wasn't until 6:30 p.m. the following day that another result was announced. It gave Evo an advantage of 10.14 points over Mesa.

It's entirely possible that Evo won by that margin, or he may have won by an even larger one. But by temporarily shutting down the count, he erased his credibility. On the evening of October 21, with no warning, altiplano and lowland whites by the thousands, university students, doctors, Alteño merchants, and, everywhere, evangelical Christians who proclaimed that Evo had brought Satan into the government palace came out to prevent him from taking office.

For the next three weeks, anti-Evo demonstrators jammed the streets and blocked traffic on the highways, demanding that he step down. It was astonishing even to them: the marches, the violent brawls between pro- and anti-Evo protesters, the rioting that terrorized what is normally not a terribly violent country, the electrifying energy of normally apathetic high school and university students staging around-the-clock watches at barricades all over La Paz. The expression of national outrage in Bolivia cut across social, regional, and ethnic divisions.

By November 8, a cascade of MAS governors, senators, and cabinet members had resigned, and Evo's alliance with the armed and security forces strained and then snapped. Police were filmed that day in La Paz tearing the *wiphala* symbol from their uniforms, and elsewhere they joined the demonstrators.

On November 9, rebellious crowds reduced Evo to governing, or attempting to, from the presidential airport hangar at El Alto. That afternoon General Williams Kaliman, head of the armed forces and a crucial Evo ally, announced that the army would "never confront the people we owe ourselves to," effectively cutting his ties to the president. At 3:00 a.m. on November 10, the Organization of American States' electoral monitors released a long-awaited report listing the election's irregularities, including the use of "hidden" servers that could be used to hack the vote-counting system.

That morning, the government asked the opposition if the head of the Senate, the MAS member Adriana Salvatierra, who was next in the line of succession, would be an acceptable replacement if Evo resigned. After Salvatierra was rejected, it wasn't clear who could replace him. (Everyone understood that Vice

President García Linera would go wherever his boss did.) Evo offered to call new elections, but it was too late. Around noon, the largest union confederation, the Central Obrera Boliviana, broke ranks with the government and asked the president to resign.

At 3:45 p.m., General Kaliman "suggested" that Evo step down, but by then he was already boarding a plane to his home base in the Chapare, in the company of García Linera. Once there, a haggard Evo announced that he was resigning in the name of peace. A "civic, political, and police coup" was responsible for his defeat, he said. Curiously, he did not include the armed forces among the *golpistas*. Two days later, a Mexican Air Force plane sent by President Andrés Manuel López Obrador flew him into exile.

Whether the events leading to Evo's flight to Mexico constituted a coup is a subject of some debate, but generally coups are designed not only to remove rulers but also to replace them. That was not the case this time. As night fell on November 10, Bolivians looked around their unruly, leaderless country and wondered what could possibly happen next.

That was when a weeping and mostly unknown senator, Jeanine Áñez, took hold of a microphone and, to general surprise, declared, between sobs, that she was the second vice president of the Senate and therefore next in the line of succession, and she would be in charge during a transition period and would call for new presidential elections. And she would not consider running for the job herself. In the following days, she was discovered to be a deeply religious and even more deeply conservative former television presenter from the impoverished department of Beni. She was also a racist who tweeted about Evo, "Poor *indio*! Grabbing on to power!" and about Aymara New Year's rituals, "Satanics! No one replaces God!" She marched to her inauguration holding aloft an enormous Bible, proclaiming that "God has let the Bible return to the national palace."

But there was chaos for days: nationwide, the police refused to report back for duty, pro- and anti-Evo demonstrators remained locked in raging confrontations in El Alto, the MAS was utterly demoralized, and at least nineteen more people were killed by army and security forces. Faced with the impending meltdown of the country, the remaining MAS leadership and its opposition brokered a political agreement, and by late November the streets were quiet once more. Áñez formed a new government, scheduled elections for May 3, acquired a team of advisers, a few pantsuits and softer makeup, and announced her candidacy for the presidency.

Devastating numbers of COVID-19 cases forced the election to be postponed twice. After months of mismanagement, Áñez withdrew from the race in September. The MAS nominated Luis Arce Catacora, Evo's longtime minister of the economy.

AN UNLIKELY CANDIDATE, Arce nevertheless won the election, in a comeback triumph for his party and for Evo. Seen from a certain perspective, one could credit Arce with many of the great achievements of the Evo era. He put an end to the recurrent cycles of hyperinflation that had often made daily life in the country a surrealist challenge. In contrast to Evo, with his strong Indigenous features and elegant alpaca jackets trimmed with pre-Hispanic motifs, Arce has an unmemorable appearance and private life—married, three kids, no scandals. Always discreetly in the background, he engineered the economy that financed Bolivia's transformation. Per capita income tripled and a new Indigenous middle class was born. The number of Bolivians in extreme poverty shrank from 38 to 16 percent of the population. Roads were built in an all-but-roadless country. Arce owes the bounty that enabled these changes to the steep rise in the price of natural gas, of course, but he could have chosen to spend it differently. There will be no such good times for President Arce: the collapse of fuel prices and the coronavirus pandemic, which hit Bolivia with devastating force, have seen to that.

Evo, who idolized the Venezuelan leader Hugo Chávez, had plenty of spare cash to spend on Chávez-like projects—a multimillion-dollar museum of Evo in the remote hamlet where he was born, an expensive presidential jet—and certain sectors of the MAS got away with bare-faced theft, but by and large Arce conducted the economy for the benefit of the vast majority of Bolivians. That and his nondescript persona made him a soothing choice for the electorate after a year of ceaseless trouble.

For the Indigenous base of the MAS, this mestizo needed only one qualification: he was *Evo's* choice. This makes it all the more remarkable that even as he was celebrating victory in his understated way, Arce stressed—not just once or twice—that neither Evo nor any member of his cabinet would have a position in the new government. "They have finished their cycle," he told an interviewer. "Now we need renovation." Other pro-renovation leaders of the MAS chimed in. "We don't believe that this is the right moment" for Evo to return to Bolivia, declared the MAS head of the Senate, Eva Copa, who added, in a tour de force of understatement, "He still has issues to resolve."

Among those issues is Noemí Meneses, Evo's pleasant, cheerful young companion in exile. She sends him passionate tweets and Evo appears to remain besotted with her, despite the fact that she is now all of nineteen and not a nu-bile fourteen, as she was when, according to all the evidence, they started their relationship. There are selfies and pictures of Evo and Noemí's interlaced feet in matching socks, his calves big and hairy, hers half the size.

Evo's affair with Noemí was no secret—Meneses has shown up in photo-graphs and videos at rallies, ever ready with a towel to wipe her hero's face after he finishes a soccer game, at the side of cabinet members, or on official visits to the Falkland Islands or Santa Cruz. But the short-lived Áñez administra-tion gleefully fastened on to the relationship because it is evident and inde-fensible. Meneses has charged in a written statement that she and her sisters were kidnapped by the police in July, held for twenty-four hours and threat-ened, and forced to state that the photos the officers had obtained were of her and Evo. (The confession and dozens of her selfies were subsequently leaked to the press.)

She says that her romantic relationship with the former president began only on May 24 this year. There is, reportedly, at least one other young woman who was involved with Evo and bore him a child at the age of sixteen. The girls give new meaning to his repeated wish to retire with a plot of land, a *charango*, or Andean guitar, and a *quinceañera*, or fifteen-year-old girl. It isn't a joke.

Most legal charges filed by the opposition against Evo—for terrorism, ille-gal enrichment, and pedophilia (that would be Meneses)—are being dropped. Consequently, he has announced his return to Bolivia on November 9, one day after Arce's swearing-in. He will, he told reporters, repair to his old base, the Chapare, but only after a brief triumphal tour of three provinces, according to the latest announcement. Once home, he will devote himself to union activities and to breeding a species of tropical fish. It is hard to imagine that this new life will keep him happy for long.

For the moment, what is left of Evo's rule is the party he built. It is impossible to overstate how tough the MAS militants are. They know how to bring down governments. Arce may be in charge of the country, but within his rambunc-tious party he represents a minority. He will have to take on the evangelicals, the right-wing separatists, white rabblerousers of the wealthy Santa Cruz prov-ince, and Mesa's middle-class and educated elite; reconcile with the military and police; and, perhaps most difficult of all, unify the party under his com-mand. He has some tough years ahead, but he won his election with five points more than Evo won his a year ago. Perhaps this time around, that 5 percent who didn't vote for Evo in 2019 were expressing their admiration for Arce's many vir-tues as minister of the economy. Or maybe it was just that, after all the turmoil and bloodshed, and after fourteen years of militant Evo, bland and boring looks pretty good.

POSTSCRIPT. At this writing, Luis Arce is still president, and a restless Evo Morales remains in rumbling, self-imposed exile in his Chapare power base. Former president Jeanine Áñez is in jail, sentenced to ten years for "nonfulfillment of duty" and "resolutions contrary to the constitution." The ongoing disappearance of Bolivia's glaciers has brought impossible scarcity to the campesinos of the altiplano, leading to growing migration to the river-blessed South and a heightening of tensions between the altiplano and the already rebellious, conservative, evangelical, and very angry South. Bolivia is not at peace.

NOTE

First published in the *New York Review of Books*, December 3, 2020.

In the Wrestling Rings of Bolivia

SEPTEMBER 2008

At the largest public gymnasium in El Alto, Bolivia, daylight is fading from the windows, and hundreds of people along the bleachers are growing impatient. They have been sitting for more than two hours now, jeering and whistling and yelling encouragement at the succession of *artistas* who have faced off in the center of the gym to match wits and perform dazzling feats of strength and skill. But it is growing late, and over the blaring disco music, foot-stomping and impatient whistles can be heard in crescendo: "Bring them on!" The music grows louder, the whistling too; there is a sense that rebellion may be about to erupt, but at last the houselights flash and dim, and the music shifts to the chunka-chunka beat of a modern Bolivian *huayno*. An announcer emotes into the microphone, the curtains leading to the locker rooms part, and "Amorous Yolanda" and "Evil Claudina," this evening's stars, make their longed-for appearance to ecstatic applause.

Like many of the women of Aymara descent in the audience, Yolanda and Claudina are dressed to the nines in the traditional fashion of the Andean highlands: shiny skirts over layers of petticoats, embroidered shawls pinned with filigreed jewelry, bowler hats. Their costumes glisten in the spotlights while they make a regal progress around the bleachers, greeting their public with the genteel smiles of princesses, twirling and waving gracefully until the music stops. That's the sign for the two women to swing themselves deftly onto the wrestling ring that has been the focus of this afternoon's activity. Swiftly they remove their hats, unpin their shawls, and . . . whap, whap, whap! Claudina belts Yolanda one, Yolanda slaps Claudina, Claudina tries to escape, but Yolanda grabs Claudina by her pigtails and spins her around, and WHAM! Claudina whirls through the air, petticoats and braids flying, and lands flat on her back on the mat, gasping like a fish. The audience goes nuts.

WELCOME TO THE delirious world of Bolivian wrestling. In the cold, treeless, comfortless city of El Alto ("high point"), thirteen thousand feet above sea level, there are one million people, most of whom fled here over the past three decades to escape the countryside's pervasive misery. The lucky ones find steady jobs down in the capital city of La Paz, which El Alto overlooks. Many sell clothes, onions, pirated DVDs, Barbie dolls, car parts, small desiccated mammals for magic rituals. The poorest *alteños* employ themselves as beasts of burden. All of them battle hopeless traffic, a constant scarcity of fuel and water, the dull fatigue of numbing labor, the odds that are stacked against them. When they're done working, they need to play, and when they want to play, one never knows what they will come up with. Lately, they've come up with the extraordinary spectacle of the *cholitas luchadoras*—fighting *cholitas*—which has given new life to Bolivians' own version of Mexican *lucha libre*, a free-form spectacle somewhere between a passion play, a wrestling match, and bedlam.

"Watch out!" the entire audience shrieks. Yolanda has been celebrating her victory, but Claudina, as proof of her evil nature, is about to lunge at her from behind. Yolanda spins too late; Claudina knocks her flat and clambers like a crazy person onto the ropes. "I'm the prettiest!" she yells at the audience. "You're all ugly! I'm your daddy! I'm the one the gringos have come to see!" Indeed, three rows of ringside seats are filled with foreigners, all pop-eyed, but they're actually irrelevant. It's their fellow Bolivians the *cholitas* are performing for.

Claudina, who is officially a *ruda*, or baddie, has taken a swig of soda pop and is spraying the public with it at the precise moment that Yolanda, a *técnica*, or goodie, pounces on her and drags her up to the bleachers, sending the spectators there scattering in blissful, screaming alarm. Yolanda wins! No, Claudina wins! No, Yolanda! But wait! The audience screams in warning again because a new menace has silently made his entrance: "Black Abyss"—or maybe it's

"Satanic Death" or the "White Skeleton"; it's hard to keep track—has leaped into the fray and has Yolanda in a ferocious leg lock. The situation looks hopeless, but no, here comes the "Last Dragon," out of nowhere, and he's carrying a chair! And he's whomping Black Abyss, or maybe the Skeleton, or maybe Yolanda, on the head with it! Even Claudina seems to have lost track of who's who: she's taking a flying leap at her own ally, the loathsome "Picudo." "He is destroyed forever!" the announcer yells frenetically.

Or almost forever: In *lucha libre*, no defeat is ever final.

"WHAT I WANT to make absolutely clear," says Juan Mamani, who fights as a *rudo* under the *lucha* name of "El Gitano" and who runs the show, "is that it was me who came up with the idea of the *cholitas*." Mamani is a tall, angular man whom it would be kind to call unfriendly. He cuts phone conversations short by hanging up, does not show up for appointments he has been cornered into making, and tries to charge for interviews. His *cholitas* are terrified of him. "Don't tell him you called me; don't tell him you have my phone number!" one of them begged.

I hunted him down near the El Alto gym, and after an unpromising start—he kept trying to duck past me—I said the magic words "Mexico" and "Blue Demon." The face of Juan Mamani, the ogre, was suddenly wreathed in smiles. "My greatest passion is *lucha libre*," he said. "And for us, Mexico is the example. Blue Demon is for me *lo mas grandioso.*"

Mamani's wrestlers all hold daytime jobs, and he makes a living from a small electrical-repair shop. But he has invested a good part of his life's earnings in a huge wrestling ring at home, where his group trains. He pays his wrestlers between twenty and thirty dollars a match and probably doesn't clear vastly greater amounts himself. "Here in Bolivia it's impossible to make a living from this great passion of mine," Mamani said. His dream was to create a Bolivian school of wrestling heroes to equal the feats of the great Mexican *lucha* legends—their daring leaps and backflips, their unique costumes and regal bearing. Had I seen Blue Demon fight? Really? He shook my hand as I left.

ABOUT SEVEN YEARS AGO, when he was fretting about the diminishing audience for the weekly *lucha libre* spectacle at the El Alto gym, Mamani had the inspired idea to teach women to wrestle and put them in the ring in *cholita* clothes. "Martha la Alteña," an outgoing *luchadora*, not remarkably muscular but very strong, was among the sixty or so young women who answered Mamani's open audition call. Like several of the eight or so who ended up staying, she comes from a wrestling background. "My father was one of the original Mummies," she said proudly, referring to one of the best loved, or most dreaded, of Bolivian *lucha*'s creatures.

Amorous Yolanda was also inspired by her *luchador* father, and even though her parents separated on unfriendly terms when she was an infant, she used to sneak into El Coliseo in downtown La Paz—long since gone—to watch him perform. "But a lot of times men don't believe in women," she told me. "Once I heard my father say that he wished he'd had a son instead of me, so he could follow in his footsteps as a *luchador*." When she heard about Mamani's casting call, Yolanda, then still called Veraluz Cortés, raced to audition, leading to a temporary rift with her father. Whether her *lucha* stardom also contributed to the breakup of her marriage is not clear.

Outside the ring, Martha la Alteña generally wears what is called the senorita style of dress—blue jeans and sweaters—and part of the glamour of her *cholita* costume is provided by turquoise-blue contact lenses. Yolanda, on the other hand, who is thin and very intense, wears a bowler hat and petticoats and skirts, even when she is knitting sweaters at her day job, and considers herself an authentic *cholita*.

"Sometimes my daughters ask why I insist on doing this," she said. "It's dangerous; we have many injuries, and my daughters complain that wrestling does not bring any money into the household. But I need to improve every day. Not for myself, for Veraluz, but for the triumph of Yolanda, an artist who owes herself to her public."

ESPERANZA CANCINA, FORTY-EIGHT, who sells used clothing for a living, has installed her large family and her ample self, in all her petticoats and skirts, in the choice ringside spot behind the announcer's chair, at a safe angle from the popcorn and chicken bones and empty plastic bottles the audience likes to pelt the fighters with. Ringside seats cost about $1.50 each, which is hardly cheap, but Señora Cancina comes faithfully to the show every other Sunday. "It's a distraction," she explains. "The *cholitas* fight here, and we laugh and forget our troubles for three or four hours. At home, we're sad."

Around us, the youngest members of the audience, including her grandchildren, are skittering around the edges of the ring in an adrenaline frenzy, trying out *lucha* leaps and swarming after a wrestler who has just been defeated, trying to hug him, touch his costume. The music is booming, and it's hard to conduct a conversation, but Señora Cancina is amiable and cooperative. She had twelve children, she says, but after a pause adds that six died. How? Her face takes on a distressing blankness. "Scarlet fever, diarrhea, those things . . . ," she murmurs, and has to repeat the answer over the noise. Would she have wanted to be a *luchadora* too? Definitely, she says. "Our husbands make fools of us, but if we were wrestlers we could express our fury."

OVER ON THE LONG side of the bleachers, in the prime chicken-bone-throwing area, Rubén Copa, a shoemaker from La Paz with an easy, friendly smile, is waiting impatiently for the afternoon's final match—one in which the "Mummy Ramses II" will take on *cholitas* yet to be announced. "Bolivian wrestlers aren't half bad, you know," he says with a touch of pride. Not even the women? He huffs and waves his hands in protest. "There's none of that anymore! Every kind of work is for everyone now." I want to know if it's true that men come to the lucha libre just to see the *cholitas'* (very modest) underpants. For a moment he looks offended, but then he smiles again. "Not at all!" he says. "I come to see them wrestle! You'll see for yourself how good they are."

And indeed a few minutes later the Mummy Ramses II is staggering around invincibly in a red-stained jumpsuit and a fright wig, dragging one *cholita* behind him while another one looks for something to set him on fire with, and the kids are screaming in delicious terror, and Señora Cancina is yelling things at the Mummy that cannot be printed in this magazine, grinning broadly as she does so. The Mummy is slamming his victim against the wall, and it looks tough for the *cholitas*, as the announcer warns us, in this *definitivo y final combate*—it looks very, very tough. But something tells me that you can't keep a *cholita* down.

Here comes Martha, flying through the air!

NOTE

First published in *National Geographic*, September 2008.

3

Don't Cry for Me, Venezuela

OCTOBER 6, 2005

On the reality show that Hugo Chávez, president of Venezuela, stages at irregular but frequent intervals for the benefit of his nation, he is the only star. Most Sundays, he can be seen on the all-day program *Aló Presidente*, which is obligatory viewing for anyone who might be interested in knowing what will be on the political agenda the following week, but there are also unscheduled interruptions to the evening newscasts and *telenovelas*, when the president takes over the networks to discuss whatever might be on his mind.

Television is his natural medium: articulate, artless, more than a little hefty, completely at his ease, open-faced and just-folksy even when he is denouncing the press or a laggard member of his own cabinet, Chávez is indisputably fascinating, and often even endearing, when he takes over the airwaves. On *Aló Presidente*, which tends to start around 11 a.m., he might reminisce about an episode of his past life, like the failed military *golpe*, or coup, that first brought him to public attention back in 1992, when he was an idealistic lieutenant colonel. (At times like this, he is likely to recite a poem or sing.)

The president also briefly shares the screen with the studio guests. He asks beneficiaries of a particular government program to describe their part in it. Visiting intellectuals and ambassadors are asked to greet the crowd. Members of his cabinet give an accounting of themselves. Front-row guests listen and applaud, and also, perhaps, think longingly about supper and the bathroom—for once admitted to a performance that lasts much longer than the Oscars, guests cannot leave—while Chávez discourses on politics, Jesus Christ, history, the week's events, baseball, and, at great length, himself. The Chávez show goes on forever, but, like any reality program, it never lasts quite long enough: Who will he rebuke, or dismiss, on the air? What will he say to his wife on the eve of Valentine's Day? (The correct answer is: "Marisabel, tomorrow I'm giving you yours.") And, since he has already persuaded the aging world-famous crooner Julio Iglesias to warble "O Sole Mio" along with Jiang Zemin, then president of the People's Republic of China, and himself, who will he sing with next?

When he takes over all the private television stations for a talk—forming a "national network"—he is usually on his own:

Hello, my friends! A very good evening to you. National network. No time limits. We've gone back to the original strategy. We'd made a change, a curveball on the outside corner for a few weeks with the Thursday national networks, but no, tonight we're going back to the original pitch; that is, whenever it's convenient, every time it's convenient. It could be one national network a week, or three or four a week, according to the dynamic of events. Or once a month. We'll see. We'll evaluate as we go according to what might be happening in Venezuela and the world. And also, no time limit. It's 9:15, and I think we'll end around midnight. We're going to talk about a series of topics which I'm greatly interested in explaining to you, in reflecting on with you, because we're living in times that require a great deal of reflection, a great deal of thought—and action, of course. We're living in a peak moment of Venezuela's history, and all *venezolanos* must be worthy of the peak of this supreme moment. Keep your eyes peeled. Alert. Careful, because there's many campaigns that try to disinform, every day. So we revolutionaries must be clear about this. We Bolivarians must be very clear. What is going on? What path is the revolution taking? How is the revolutionary process advancing? Every day with greater optimism. I have more optimism every day, more joyfulness every day: this morning I was singing, and this evening I was singing, some song or another. Perhaps I'll remember it later. Singing! Joyful! Taking care of people! Solving problems. Looking to the future.

Somehow, on the screen it all makes sense.

It's hard to imagine any other chief of state carrying off a performance like this week after week, for nearly six years. Fidel Castro is too inhibited, George W. Bush lacks the imagination, and virtually any other ruler who comes to mind lacks the power, but this the president of Venezuela has in plenty. Ten years ago, a failed *golpista* and retired military man, he was dependent on friends for pocket money and transportation. Today, at the age of fifty-one, he heads a state with one of the world's great cash flows, enjoys popularity ratings of 80 percent, faces a vehement but demoralized and perhaps terminally disorganized opposition, and appears to be a magnet to women. It has been a remarkable rise to power.

1.

Hugo Chávez was born into a dirt-poor family at a time when oil was making his country immensely rich. The Chávezes lived far from the provinces of the fantastic oil boom, in a village on the edge of Venezuela's vast grasslands. His father, Hugo Sr., finished sixth grade and eventually qualified as a rural schoolteacher, but he still didn't earn enough to keep his family. Accordingly, after Hugo was born, he and his older brother were sent to live in a small nearby town, Sabaneta, with their paternal grandmother, Rosa Inés. Chávez has told one of his biographers, Aleida Guevara, daughter of Che, that he was an active, happy boy, scampering around Sabaneta after school to sell the caramelized fruit sweets his grandmother cooked in a pot at home. An engaging raconteur, he talks about clambering up avocado trees for the fruit, sneaking off to the movies to watch Mexican comedies, and helping the woman he called Mamá Rosa water down the yard, while she chatted to the plants to help them grow and he sang to them. But there is also this:

> [After his younger brother Narciso was born, his parents also moved to Sabaneta] and my father built a little house . . . diagonally across from my grandmother's house, which was made of thatch. My parents lived there with the other children as they came along. . . . [Theirs] was a little house made of [cement blocks], a rural house, but it had an asbestos roof and a cement floor.

Chávez does not say what he thought of this arrangement, but although he has remained on perfectly cordial terms with his parents (his mother, Elena, is very much the matriarch of the Chávez brood), his loyalty and family love are reserved for the memory of Mamá Rosa.

Hugo Chávez Sr. seems to have passed his unquenchable desire to be someone, and his love of politics, to his son. The older Chávez would eventually become director of education for his home state of Barinas (he was state governor until 2008), but this had not yet happened when the younger Chávez, against Mamá Rosa's wishes but looking for his own way up through the world, decided to apply to the army academy in Caracas.

In their indispensable biography *Hugo Chávez sin uniforme: Una historia personal* (2004), Cristina Marcano and Alberto Barrera Tyszka provide an account of the future president as a backcountry cadet, shy and well mannered—no reckless escapades or wild drinking nights for him—constantly measuring his social possibilities against his ambition. He loves the army, feels at home in it, graduates eighth in his class. He plays baseball, the national sport, better than well, and his fellows are surprised to see him, the *provinciano*, emceeing a beauty contest—and not badly, one assumes. He is articulate and likable, and by the age of twenty-one, having obtained a degree in army engineering, with a major in communications, he is the star of his own radio program. Never an outstanding student, he is nonetheless full of ideas and soon is at the center of a group of youthful leftist conspirators in the army.

FOR NEARLY TWENTY YEARS, Chávez would foster his vague, romantic complot, inspired not by Marxism or any other ideology but by intellectual politicians and nineteenth-century fighters who were his heroes even before he became a cadet. Richard Gott usefully provides chapters on them in his biography *Hugo Chávez and Bolivarian Revolution* (2005). One was Ezequiel Zamora, a leader of the federal forces in the unending civil wars of the nineteenth century: he fought under the slogan "Land and Free Men, Popular Elections, and Horror of the Oligarchy." There was Simón Rodríguez, the wonderfully cosmopolitan thinker and political adventurer who signed himself "Robinson"—as in Crusoe—and was mentor to Simón Bolívar. And Bolívar himself, supreme: the daring, restless hero who liberated the Andean provinces one by one from the Spanish Crown and who realized too late that, once separated, the new nations of Venezuela, Colombia, Ecuador, Peru, and Bolivia would never coalesce into the grand union he had dreamed of.

Chávez worships Bolívar, memorizes his proclamations, makes it a point to visit his shrines: the hero's home in Bogotá, the sites of all his great battles, the tree under whose shade the Liberator used to rest. Marcano and Barrera point out that from an early age the future leader of Venezuela would make a point of tying all the founding moments of his own political life to Bolivarian dates.

Once in power, he would also amend the name of his country to "The Bolivarian Republic of Venezuela." But the unforgettable image is one that they report as rumor, told to them by one of Chávez's many disaffected mentors, who says he saw it happen: during the early cabinet meetings in Miraflores palace, the official residence, President Chávez would pull up an empty chair for Bolívar.

How in the world did he get to the palace? As they watch him sing and expostulate and scold on their living room screens, the members of Chávez's disconsolate opposition struggle to understand. Largely, he wanted to. He formed his first clandestine cell within the army at the age of twenty-three, worked constantly to expand it, traveled the country consolidating a core group of conspirators who dreamed with him of a better Venezuela and of their heroic role in creating it. They could change their homeland for the better, Chávez insisted, not quite sure how. He was good at hortatory speeches, both to his troops and in front of the students he ended up teaching history to at the military academy.

When he met Herma Marksman, a young, very pretty historian (his first wife, Nancy, and their children were back in Sabaneta), he told her right from the start that he couldn't marry her (partly because his mother would not give him permission to divorce Nancy) but that he wanted Herma to share his life and dreams. She did, for nine years, carrying messages around the country, taking notes at meetings, making the calls needed to keep the conspiracy going. Conspiracy to do what? Chávez seemed to be waiting for some inner voice to let him know. He contacted former guerrillas and leftist leaders, lived modestly, came up through the ranks. The country would need him; it needed saving. Oddly, he seems never to have thought of becoming active in politics.

2.

Chávez first acquired his political restlessness in a country that, like him, had already greatly improved its prospects. In 1935, after the death of the dictator Juan Vicente Gómez, Venezuela entered the modern era—entered, at last, the twentieth century, historians like to say. It had a population of barely 3.5 million then, a 90 percent illiteracy rate, no public health services to speak of, a threadwork of dirt roads in lieu of a highway system. Gómez, a monster with a kindly smile who would become the template for so many fictional tyrants, liked to run his country as if it were a hacienda. The approach worked well for him; he ruled for twenty-seven years and died in bed. Another dictator, General Marcos Pérez Jiménez, the last of a line of military tyrants who had ruled Venezuela for much of its independent history, was toppled in 1958, when Hugo Chávez was four years old. As he grew up he benefited from the stability and modernization provided by the civilian regimes that followed the Pérez military dictatorship.

The country's enviable political stability was made possible in large part by the abundance of oil that left its seaports in those years. Seven presidents, all survivors of the struggle against the dictatorship, succeeded each other in orderly fashion, rotating power between two parties—one, the Acción Democrática (AD, Democratic Action), a member of the International Socialist alliance; and the other, the Comité de Organización Política Electoral Independiente (COPEI, Social Christian Party), allied with the Christian Democrats. But the system bred self-satisfied administrators rather than statesmen. Political debate became a matter of pro forma electoral exchanges between the two parties, both more interested in preserving the privileges of the ruling elite than in restructuring an increasingly unfair society. There was a great deal of corruption, a great deal of waste, and, as the rural population migrated toward the oil territories and Caracas, a huge accumulation of urban poverty and a dearth of public policy to deal with the needs of the poor.

Not all the oil income was lost to corruption and profligacy, though: ambitious educational systems, highways, museums, dams, and health and housing programs were created for a population that multiplied too quickly. (The last census counted some twenty-five million people.) The last of the big public spenders was Carlos Andrés Pérez, who nationalized the oil industry and presided over the era of Venezuela Saudita. The oil bonanza kept the rate of exchange for the currency (the bolivar, of course) so high in those years that members of the new Venezuelan upper classes, on shopping sprees from Argentina to France, became known for the phrase "That's cheap. Give me two." Corruption became a way of life, and by the time Carlos Andrés Pérez left office in 1979, the two-party system in Venezuela seemed bankrupt. Despite the allegations of great personal corruption that have stuck to his reputation, CAP, as he is always called, was revered by the poor after that first presidency. He is remembered as the most charismatic and forceful figure in public life until the advent of Chávez, who staged his failed coup against him. Venezuela produces very little of export value other than oil. The state oil company, Petróleos de Venezuela, S.A., or PDVSA, accounts for 80 percent of export income, 27 percent of the gross national product, and 40 percent of the government budget. Those funds were insufficient to finance CAP's tireless spending; he left his successor to deal with the resulting inflation, crushing debt, high unemployment, and an empty treasury.

In 1988, the former president campaigned for, and won, a second term in office. A convert by then to the market approach known as the Washington consensus, CAP declared himself in favor of a currency devaluation, price hikes on all public services, and an end to government subsidies—a set of measures that were similarly enforced throughout the region, in the hope that the economy would, if not recover, at least become more attractive to US banks and investors. Three weeks later, the inhabitants of Caracas staged the first riot of the century. Descending from the steep hills to which they are normally confined, thousands of *caraqueños* set fire to entire city blocks and looted whatever they could find.

Dozens of people had already died by the time the president called out the troops and declared a state of siege. When it was all over, more than 250 people were dead, and Hugo Chávez was left with the feeling that, as he told Gabriel García Márquez, he had missed "the strategic minute": desperately poor people were in worse straits than usual and the government was failing them, imposing austerity measures when it was emergency aid that was called for and then shooting them when they rebelled. Politicians were corrupt, at the service of the rich, and incompetent to boot. The civilian two-party system Chávez had known all his life was exhausted. It was time for him to make his entrance, he thought, and he had missed his cue. He would make up for it.

Whatever his original intentions may have been on February 4, 1992, when he at last staged his coup attempt—to overthrow Carlos Andrés Pérez and install a caretaker government, or to make way for a junta that would convoke a constituent assembly—the uprising itself was a complete failure. His longtime coconspirators fought bravely in other parts of the country, but the army did not split, and in Caracas itself Chávez surrendered with barely a shot fired. Nevertheless, his fortune was made. On the morning following his surrender the army leaders allowed him to make a live televised statement about the failed coup, intending that he would discourage the remaining rebels. They did not insist he tape a prepared statement. He talked for less than ninety seconds, but it was enough for him to establish an emotional connection with his viewers so intense as to guarantee him a permanent place in national politics. "For now," the conspiracy had failed, he said, two words that might have earned an ordinary *golpista* an even more severe prison sentence. But the lucky man must have had good friends in the highest ranks of the military: he and his comrades were charged merely with "rebellion." Two years later, he was released from jail and granted an honorable retirement from the service. Four years later, in 1998, having decided to join the politicians after all, he put himself at the front of his movement and won 56 percent of the vote in the December presidential elections.

THE SIZE OF Chávez's victory is interesting because in the six years he has been in power he has held various sorts of elections (including one presidential election, one to elect a constituent assembly, and two referendums) and the percentage of his vote has never reached 60. In a country where his target audience of the poor and the very poor together made up around 68 percent of the population last year, nearly half the people who show up at the polls on election day still refuse to vote for him. And nearly three-quarters of the adult population has stayed away from recent elections. Chávez, who knows the voting results well, plays a high-risk game: he governs not as if he were the president of a divided nation but as if he had a national mandate to carry out his Bolivarian Revolution, as if he had taken over the presidential chair for keeps.

The definition of the president's ongoing Revolución Bolivariana under the Quinta República, within a system of *democracia participativa*, remains hazy. Like Bolívar, he would like to unify Latin America. In Venezuela he is the center of power: Chávez has said in various contexts and in several ways that he is not averse to the word *caudillo*. The revolution's first priority is the poor. It has some elements of socialism (although Chávez was not always so keen on Fidel Castro). Sometimes it is anticapitalist, and sometimes not: Chávez, who talks often of his own religious faith, has referred to capitalism as *el demonio*, but a great many businessmen have prospered under his rule, and he has made it clear that he sees a significant role for the private sector and, most particularly, for foreign investment. What there does not appear to be much room for is the opposition.

Within three months of his inauguration, the new president won a referendum authorizing him to call a constitutional convention, which replaced the "moribund" old charter with one that concentrates a great deal of power in his hands and threatens the very existence of an opposition: government financing of political parties' electoral campaigns is now outlawed.

In addition, the *chavista* majority in the National Assembly—which under the new constitution replaced the old bicameral legislative body—increased the number of judges in the high courts from twenty to thirty-two and made sure the new ones were pro-Chávez, thus virtually ensuring the president a majority. In the course of a lengthy, and a high-risk, confrontation with the state oil company, PDVSA, Chávez also replaced the old meritocracy with his own directorate. This has, essentially, allowed him to run a foreign policy based on oil sales to poor countries on highly favorable terms (and in exchange for their support in international politics) and to use oil income to finance his various domestic projects. Washington, in turn, is hampered in its foreign policy toward Caracas. Although the Bush administration appears to loathe Chávez and his pro-Castro policies, nearly 15 percent of the US oil supply comes from Venezuela.

3.

In downtown Caracas one afternoon, I sat in a comfortable, lived-in office, talking to Marcel Granier, owner of RCTV, the largest television station in Caracas. We had talked about the difficulties of running a profitable television station when it is subject to so many long and unscheduled interruptions of its programming by Chávez. Now Granier was recalling the time *chavista* thugs tried to set fire to the RCTV installations (with everyone inside). I glanced at the panel of screens in his office and saw on one channel a very agitated-looking man waving about the front page of *El Universal*, a principal Venezuelan daily. "Him?" Granier said. "That's just Isaías Rodríguez—the attorney general—going on about some article or another."

It seemed alarming to have a cabinet minister getting into a public lather about a newspaper article, but Granier didn't pay much attention; this sort of thing happens all the time, he said. Phil Gunson, of the *Miami Herald* and *Newsweek*, and Juanita León, of *Semana* magazine in Colombia, have also been startled to find themselves denounced on the air by high-ranking officials—León by Chávez himself, on a Sunday *Aló Presidente*—a distinction of sorts.

I later read the transcript of Rodríguez's press conference; his accusations were convoluted and confused, but I gathered that what he was lamenting was that his office was being systematically attacked by a scheming body of human rights lawyers and international human rights organizations, specifically Human Rights Watch. They were, he said, working in concert with the press and the US State Department, and the proof—or part of the proof, at any rate—was that *El Universal* had written an editorial charging that the administration of justice was corrupt, inefficient, and barely functioning under his command. This was not fair, this was straight out of the new CIA coup manual, and he would lodge a complaint before the Human Rights Commission of the Organization of American States (OAS), charging the plotters with harassment of the government.

Actually, Rodríguez has a faster recourse closer to hand. He could take the author of the offending editorial to court on charges of insulting, or staining the honor of, a public official. There is an old law that covers this offense, but it was rarely enforced in the past, and punishment consisted of payment of a fine. But thanks to a revision in the penal code by the National Assembly—in which *chavista* members now need only a majority of half plus one to pass legislation—if Rodríguez won his case against *El Universal* (the lower courts are also packed with professed *chavistas* these days), the author of the offending editorial could end up serving three to five years of jail time. But this isn't likely to happen; like other recent legislation on currency controls for individuals, for example, the law is designed to be enforced selectively and to intimidate.

Other attacks on those who oppose Chávez are more frightening but further from public view; in the army, punishment for opposition has become ruthless, and sometimes fatal. When five corporals were burned to death in their prison cells, a general went on the air to explain how it was possible that blowtorches might have been used to kill them. He was sentenced to five years in prison.

THE INSTRUMENT MOST frequently used by Hugo Chávez against his opponents, however, is not a law but something known everywhere simply as *la lista*—the list of signatures submitted in 2004 to demand a referendum on Chávez's recall. People on the list cannot get government jobs, qualify for many of Chávez's public welfare programs, or obtain government contracts. Its use was once surreptitious; officials asked for one's *cédula*, or ID/voter registration card, and the number was checked against *la lista*. But since December, when the list was put on the internet by a *chavista* member of the National Assembly, it is used openly. "The . . . list doubtless fulfilled an important role at a given moment, but that's over now," Chávez told his party's elected officials in April, possibly with a wink. A young doctoral candidate I met in July, who had gone to the National Library the previous week to do research, was asked for her *cédula* by the woman signing passes. Annoyed, my acquaintance asked why. *Ay, mi amor*, the woman replied. *Para la lista.*

It is too soon to judge how well the many ambitious social welfare and education programs launched by Chávez—they are known as *misiones*—have succeeded in redressing Venezuela's deep inequalities, but they suffer already from an essential flaw: as with everything else Chávez creates, their existence depends on him. This would seem to be a reflection of the president's apparent sense that everything that happens, that has happened—in Venezuela, and in this hemisphere as well—in some way relates to him. At a meeting with Uruguayan investors last July he noted that their national independence day was approaching. What a coincidence, he noted: in July also—on July 26, 1953—Fidel led his assault on the Moncada barracks. And on another July 26—in 1952—Evita, Eva Perón, died. "And just two days later," he said, "on July 28th [1954], *I* was born! Imagine!" There is the melodramatic flair, the flamboyant clothes, the generic love for the poor and the authoritarianism: one could actually think that he is Evita reincarnate, and Juan Perón, too, if it weren't for the fact that Perón died rather late (1975) for a proper transmigration of souls to take place.

Such are the hallucinatory terms in which one can easily find oneself discussing the state of Venezuelan politics. In Caracas today it often seems as if there were no issues, only bilious anger or unconditional devotion—or gasping bafflement—all provoked by the president, who takes up so much oxygen that there is no breathing room left for a discussion of, say, the merits of his neighborhood health policy, his relations with Cuba, or whether the chronically overflowing currency reserves should be used merely to guarantee the rate of exchange or to finance, as Chávez has, the multiplying *misiones*. How can one reasonably discuss whether the upper management of the oil company was involved in plotting a coup when the president is busy firing seven of those managers on *Aló Presidente*, saying "You're out!" and giving a blast of an umpire's whistle? And how can an interviewer, in this case Jorge Gestoso of CNN en Español, possibly discuss the merits of such an approach with Chávez when Gestoso must begin by insisting to Chávez that this event actually did take place? The official use of lies, the opposition's terrified rantings, the abandonment of civility by the press and television take place outside the realm of politics and do away with reason.

THE PROBLEM IS THAT all of this defies description, one observer has written:

> ... That is why the critics are so totally at a loss; they don't know what the weak flank of *chavista* politics is because it is an unheard-of combination of little-known things, with a totally new result. The populist element, the good-ole-boy element, the martial spirit, the willfulness, the Bolivarian delirium, the economic pragmatism, and the monarchic arbitrariness are known, along with the authoritarianism of the old [Caudillista] compadre. None of this is new, but the combination of it all (to which must be added his luck, of which he has too much) is what is incomprehensible.

Thus, in a convoluted, sometimes brilliant journal, the columnist Colette Capriles, who writes as if she had spent much of the last few years lying on her sofa in a state of mild depression, watching events unfold on the television screen.

Even after a visit of only a few weeks, one can start to feel claustrophobic in Venezuela, as if the people there were all living inside Chávez's head, with some making small squealing noises as they try to get out. But the president has no visible worries: the various *misiones*—in favor of ethnic culture, literacy, college equivalency, medical care in the barrios, in defense of street children—are thriving, in no small part because there are tens of thousands of highly skilled

Cubans who have been assigned by Fidel to staff them and because they are lavishly financed—in ways the health and education ministries could benefit from. Who knows, Chávez says, he might even remain in power through the year 2024, or even 2030.

And why not? In a country with an economy the size of the Czech Republic's, the value of Venezuela's currency reserves is now $30 billion. Oil prices are not expected to decline anytime soon. The Bush administration, for all its hostility to Chávez, does not seem able to hurt him seriously. There are local and national elections of various kinds scheduled every single year between now and 2013, and Chávez and his political parties (he has two) can reasonably expect to win in all of them. Best of all, he has no local politicians—certainly none in his own movement—threatening his popularity. He can smile and go forward, singing. Joyful. Solving problems. Looking to the future.

POSTSCRIPT. Long before there was a Nayib Bukele in El Salvador, or an Ortega-Murillo duo in Nicaragua, or even a Donald Trump in the United States, there was Chávez, the One and Only. When observers of the disastrous developments in this hemisphere wonder how we came to be stuck in a new era of populist dictators—outrageous rulers who avail themselves of social media and unfree, unfair elections to drape themselves modestly in the rags of democracy and then shamelessly assault every rule and tenet of democratic belief—it is Chávez (d. 2013) who pops up from his grave, grinning and pointing to the source: ME! ME! ME! In the midst of worldwide disenchantment with all political parties and the answers provided by both socialist and capitalist systems to this century's failures and bewilderments, Chávez found a way by making everything all about him. The eccentricities manipulated for effect, the overweening need to be loved, the theatrics, the instinctive understanding of media, the talent for shifting blame, the wiliness—Chávez held more cunning in his little finger than all his opponents together—and, above all, the magical ability to become the obsessive concern of each and every citizen are all talents his political descendants have sought to copy.

Luck traveled with him always. He ruled when the price of oil, Venezuela's only export, was at an all-time high, and he had the good fortune to die before the bill arrived for the havoc he wreaked on the economy: the destruction of the national oil company, the collapse of agriculture and cattle ranching, a precarious health system completely undone. With his death only days away, he went on national television to announce that his successor would not be his right-hand man Diosdado Cabello, chairman of the ruling United Socialist

Party, but the amiable, goofy-looking foreign minister, Nicolás Maduro. *Who? What?* Even his supporters scratched their heads. After the funeral, Maduro sat down in front of a camera to relate how Chávez, in the shape of "a little bird," had circled three times around his head that morning, before settling on a nearby perch to give him blessings and encouragement. As the abyss of the future opened before Venezuelans, Maduro's prompt political demise was predicted.

Ten years later, Maduro is still there, no longer amiable. He has presided over the absolute collapse of what was once one of Latin America's most prosperous economies and a concomitant rise in crime. Supermarket shelves and market stalls emptied, as parts of the country approached near-famine levels of hunger. With inflation at more than 65,000 percent by 2018, the bolivar—the national currency—was all but worthless. More than seven million desperate Venezuelans—one out of every four—have crossed the Andes and braved the Darien Pass, desperate to find refuge in any country where they can actually stay safe and make enough money to feed their families. We know of attempts to overthrow Maduro in elections and through a gang-that-couldn't-shoot-straight short-lived invasion. We are likely ignorant of many other, more serious efforts. Colombian guerrillas now operate freely in southern Venezuela, as do Colombian traffickers hungry for the gold that pick-and-hammer miners extract illegally in the region south of the Orinoco river. It seems to be the case that in order to survive, Maduro has thoroughly corrupted the military, which is also said to be deeply involved in clandestine gold trade operations. Unsurprisingly, the press is persecuted; opposition members are cornered, imprisoned, or sent into exile; and elections are a sham.

Lately, things have improved for Venezuelans and for Maduro as well. Thanks to the Russian invasion of Ukraine, the price of oil has gone up, and the United States is making friendly overtures to the Venezuelan government, looking anxiously toward its precious oil supplies. A large proportion of those Venezuelans who fled have now settled in their adopted countries and are in a position to send money back to their families, a dollar or one hundred every month. In Caracas the glitzy restaurants are back; there is money in circulation again and food to buy. The poor seem to have put on a little weight. Inflation is down to a paltry 400 percent. I wasn't there, but I could bet that the little bird's key piece of advice to Maduro was, no matter what happens, *do not ever back down!* Admitting mistakes is for wimps and cowards. God forbid Maduro should have decided to resign in the face of the hunger epidemic, turmoil, and riots that swept the country only a few years ago. He faced all that down by ignoring most of it, sent the army out to do whatever was necessary—kill here, mangle there—ignored international condemnation of his regime, cracked terrible jokes and tried to dance for his audience in his poor attempts to resemble the Great One, and generally made a scary fool of himself.

Under enormous pressure from the United States and Europe, Maduro agreed to hold presidential elections in July 2024, but imposed so many restrictions on the opposition, such as outlawing their principal candidate, as to make it almost impossible for them to win. Nevertheless, the Carter Center for Democracy, the only watchdog group allowed to monitor the election, was able to count 81 percent of the vote tallies reported at each voting station and declared that the opposition candidate, Edmundo González Urrutia, was the actual winner, with nearly 70 percent of the vote. But González was forced to flee the country and Maduro remains in power. In his own clumsy way, he has turned out to be a more surprising figure even than Chávez.

NOTE

First published in the *New York Review of Books*, October 6, 2005. Reviewed: Richard Gott, *Hugo Chávez and the Bolivarian Revolution* (New York: Verso, 2005); Aleida Guevara, *Chávez, un hombre que anda por ahí: Una entrevista con Hugo Chávez* (Melbourne: Ocean Press, 2005); Cristina Marcano and Alberto Barrera Tyszka, *Hugo Chávez sin uniforme: Una historia personal* (Caracas: Random House Mondadori, 2004).

4

Confrontation in Colombia

JULY 22, 2021

I came to Cali in late May, at the end of a month in which all of Colombia had been engulfed in antigovernment protests. No place had been hit harder by violence in the course of the turmoil than this airy, pleasant city of some two million people, traversed by a smooth-flowing river and shaded by enormous trees—ceibas, jacarandas, caracolís. Cali likes to style itself the salsa capital of the world and, more ambitiously, the "Branch Office of Heaven." Maybe, but on the morning of May 28 a minor government official, enraged because he was not allowed through a roadblock guarded by adamant teenagers, took out a gun and killed two of them point-blank. He was then beaten to death by the others. It was the thirty-ninth known violent death in Colombia since the protests began, and hundreds were missing.

May 28 was supposed to have been a peaceful day, even one, perhaps, in which festive marches could mark an end to the weeks of unrest. But hard on those first brutal deaths, demonstrators were attacked again by police and armed civilians, and by dawn the next day five more people lay dead. President Iván Duque, an ineffectual and generally despised conservative, in office since

2018, imposed a military occupation on thirteen of the main areas of conflict in Colombia, principally Cali and the surrounding Cauca region. In Bogotá, the capital, there was nervous talk in upper circles about whether former president Álvaro Uribe, the gray eminence of Colombian politics, was seeking to get rid of the man who was elected on the slogan "The One Uribe Wants." ("I am not a puppet," Duque told an interviewer recently.) Who would replace him has not been settled in the gossip, and such a violation of the democratic formalities would be unheard of in Colombian politics and is probably impossible. Still, the mood was as tense as anyone could remember.

What amounts to a nationwide state of confrontation started on April 28. A long-seething mood of dissatisfaction and frustration had caught fire a couple of weeks earlier, when Duque's finance minister presented a sweeping tax bill to Congress. Squinting hard, one could almost see why raising taxes at that particular moment might have seemed like a good idea to the president. Colombia, never a wealthy country, has been poleaxed by the COVID-19 pandemic, with more than 3.6 million reported cases and nearly 95,000 deaths in a population of some 51 million; it has been burdened with medical bills and income supplements for the poor even as the economy shrank by 6.8 percent last year. The government needed money, and Duque decided to get it by increasing taxes, mostly on the poor.

The bill vastly expanded the range of goods and services subject to an existing 19 percent value-added tax—which notoriously devours a far greater portion of the budgets of wage earners than of the wealthy—and promised to impose an income tax by 2023 on people earning as little as $715 a month. Having read its provisions, the novelist Juan Gabriel Vásquez noted the obscene irony, in a country with one of the highest COVID mortality rates in the world, of imposing a 19 percent tax on funerals.

THERE HAD BEEN large student marches against the Duque administration in 2018, much larger and angrier ones in 2019 to protest a wave of human rights violations, and more demonstrations in September 2020, in the midst of the pandemic. Following this year's announcement of the tax bill, trade union leaders called for a national strike on April 28. The strike committee members are predominantly old, white, and male: they were not prepared for the spontaneous, ungovernable, overwhelming outpouring onto the streets of citizens whose lives their organizations do not touch.

The demonstrations began first in Cali, where at dawn a small group of Misak Native people toppled a ghastly modern statue of Sebastián de Belalcázar, the Spanish conquistador of the region. Within hours, turbulent streams of protesters were flowing through the streets of seemingly every city and town in Colombia, demanding not just the rejection of the tax bill but also a whole new world: one with a working justice system; access to study and jobs for the young; an electoral democracy not corrupted by drug money; real enforcement of a peace treaty signed in 2016 with the Fuerzas Armadas Revolucionarias de Colombia (FARC, Revolutionary Armed Forces of Colombia), the country's oldest guerrilla group; an end to the systematic assassination of peace activists; a halt to the aerial fumigation of poppy fields that also destroys the food crops campesinos live on—the list was long.

By the following day, highways, main streets, and principal roads from the southern state of Cauca to northern Santander were crosshatched with road-blocks set up by the protesters. The strike committee included leaders of the national truckers' syndicate, but they do not represent the thousands of owners of rattletrap farm trucks who collect milk or onions or mangoes from small producers every day, deliver the goods to market, and park every evening in their backyards. Those were the trucks obstructing traffic on the highways.

It took only four days for President Duque to withdraw his tax bill, but by then no one was paying attention. Kids with perhaps eight years of schooling who would never be able to find a proper job kept marching, alongside youths with college degrees who couldn't find work either. Schoolteachers marched and so did nuns. It poured rain for days on end and the protests only grew larger. The kids set up roadblocks along city streets, and women organized to feed them and to collect rags and vinegar as a defense against tear gas. Everyone wore the national soccer team's bright yellow T-shirt or waved Colombia's yellow, blue, and red flag or painted a map of the country on their faces. In the cities, people who didn't march leaned out windows and banged on pots.

Those were the euphoric early days, but even then the dreadful human toll was mounting: tens of thousands of protesters have been tear-gassed or attacked with giant grenade launchers loaded with flashbangs and stingballs; hundreds have lost an eye or been otherwise wounded by the police—in some cases certainly on purpose.

NOWHERE HAVE THE MARCHERS been more enthusiastic or suffered more casualties than in Cali. One of the largest strongholds of the protests in the city is a sturdily working-class neighborhood renamed Puerto Resistencia, whose neat streets are lined with two-story apartment buildings with scrubby little front yards and exterior spiral staircases that lead to the second-floor units. It's a neighborhood of tradespeople and shopkeepers, and I had the tastiest meal of my stay at a storefront diner here—three dollars' worth of vegetable soup, white rice, fried plantains, grilled chicken, guava juice, all of it good. The road the little restaurant is on has five barricades indifferently guarded by lolling youths, and neighbors continue their lives undisturbed.

Or at least that's what I saw; stories of extortion are not rare, and the hardship caused by the roadblocks has been enormous. According to the government, looters and vandals, perhaps provocateurs, who operate on the margins of the national protest movement have caused some $3 billion worth of damage. Transportation systems, police stations, government buildings, and ATMs have been set on fire. Trucks carrying food or spare parts have been overturned. There was widespread scarcity and hunger for weeks.

In Puerto Resistencia there are smashed traffic lights and the remains of bonfires everywhere. Nevertheless, polls show that an overwhelming majority of nonwealthy *caleños* remain emphatic in their support of the protests, as is the city's archbishop, Monsignor Dario Monsalve, who pointed out that for fifty thousand "traditionally excluded" youth in Cali, "the barricades are the only means they have in their territory" to force the state to listen.

"You go into the poorer sectors of Cali and there's anarchy everywhere," said Alejandro Eder, heir to one of Colombia's biggest sugar fortunes and an aspiring politician. He knows his country and his region well, having worked for years in peace and reconciliation programs, but I thought he was only partly right. The traditional order has certainly broken down in places like Puerto Resistencia, and it's been replaced by strange forms of organization that are largely ungraspable by outsiders and not likely to last but are a form of order nonetheless. The version in Puerto Resistencia was enforced by dozens of very young men and a few women old enough to be—and who in a few cases probably were—their mothers. One tiny woman grabbed me by the sleeve and marched me over to a house used as movement headquarters and community kitchen, where a bunch of youths were getting hearty bowls of soup for lunch. An extremely large and imposing young man was reclining on a bench as we approached. "Get up," my guide told him. "Talk to her."

I asked him if he was a spokesperson, and he answered in a convoluted way that this was far too hierarchical a term, then delivered a discourse so confusing and larded with half-chewed Marxist, New Age, Third World, and identity politics that I found it impossible to take notes. But of course the discourse hardly mattered. He was an obviously bright university student who, like virtually every young person I met in the protests, had never been able to find work and lived in a single-parent home. ("Welcome," he said, "to the country where men haven't learned to take responsibility for their actions.") A slight young man who listened in on our conversation had joined the army in the hope of getting hired as a security guard or a doorman on his release and had never had a job either. They were both twenty-three.

The point was this: they lived in a society that made them feel like trash and offered them no hope at all. Overnight, miraculously, with virtually no guidance except whatever orientation the large young man might conceivably be getting from the equally clueless but dangerous urban and rural guerrillas who are part of Cali's environment, they had organized a bespoke world for themselves, one where every unemployed or woefully undereducated kid had a part to play, where there was at least one good meal a day for all, thanks to the neighbors' continuing generosity—with maybe the proceeds of a little extortion thrown in, or maybe not—and where they could shout their loathing for their heartless rulers 24/7, dreaming for once that they were free.

THE YOUNG MAN who said he wasn't a spokesman wouldn't talk about the late-night gunfire that was keeping people awake in the barrios, although Alejandro Eder, the peace negotiator, had an explanation. "In some of the poorer neighborhoods the small shop owners started to hire youths to guard their businesses overnight from looters," he said. "And someone"—I took him to mean guerrillas and drug traffickers—"is paying some other kids to go in and vandalize. So these kids are basically now hands for hire, and once this is all done we're going to have to put in a disarmament and reintegration process."

Eder and every other observer I talked to about the crisis here believe, with good reason, that different groups are taking advantage of what is a genuine rebellion, including the guerrillas of the left-wing National Liberation Army; dissidents from the FARC, which demobilized in 2016; what someone called "populist politicians pushing forward hate-based political strategies" (that would be former president Uribe, in the view of many); assorted well-armed drug-trafficking gangs; and former paramilitary leaders who live in the fancier parts of the city. There are, in addition, the conservative whites who sit atop a pyramid of the multicolored and dispossessed and who have supported Duque's efforts to destroy the hard-won peace accords with the FARC. The collapse of those accords has brought increasing violence, as disillusioned, demobilized guerrillas join the gangs that now plague the countryside around Cali.

In addition, the United States began pushing the War on Drugs on Latin America in 1973 and has maintained it up to now. In the late 1980s, three principal figures essentially controlled the export of cocaine to the United States and managed its attendant violence: Pablo Escobar in the city of Medellín and the Rodríguez Orejuela brothers in Cali. With US assistance, Escobar was killed in 1993. Under pressure from Washington, the Orejuela brothers were extradited to the United States a decade later. As a result, dozens, if not hundreds, of ever more murderous and uncontrollable drug gangs are trying to fill the void. They are fighting one another and the guerrillas and seeking to increase their foothold in Cali. They, too, are responsible for the gunshots in the dark.

Jorge Iván Ospina, the mayor of Cali, was in a rueful mood when I talked with him. In Cali, the mayor wears a uniform, and that unexpected fact, along with Ospina's unpretentious affability, led me to ask, as he ushered me into his office and offered a seat, whether the interview I'd requested with the head of the local government was actually with him. A fifty-five-year-old surgeon, he is the son of one of the many assassinated leaders of the M-19 guerrilla movement, a group long since disbanded and incorporated into the country's left-of-center politics. Relatively new to public life—he had earlier served one term each as mayor and in the Senate—he acknowledged easily that his career had gone up in flames as a result of the strike. "I've been dumped on by everyone," he said.

In truth he hardly figured in the rhetoric of the strikers; what he had earned was the anger and contempt of the Cali establishment, in part for his disastrous mishandling of the budget in the pandemic year but mostly for his failure to bring order to the city early in the protests. It's fair to ask whether anyone could have, but in his telling he reduced the violence with behind-the-scenes measures that persuaded the government not to end the strike by force. "Otherwise I believe we might be facing a civil war right now," he said. When the dimensions of the strike and the government's desire to destroy it became clear, Ospina said, he put a call out to the diplomatic community: on May 4 more than thirty ranking diplomats, mostly from Western Europe and the United States, showed up in Cali to express their desire for a peaceful de-escalation of the conflict. "That international protection provided some breathing space," he said.

Later that week, Duque's defense minister called Ospina to say that a delegation of Misak people traveling from their reserve to Cali should not be allowed into the city. Ospina pointed out that the right of citizens to travel freely anywhere in their country is guaranteed in the constitution and refused to comply. When the Misak arrived in the early afternoon of May 9, fighting broke out between white residents of a wealthy gated community trying to stop them from entering the city and a dozen or so of the younger members of the delegation. Some of the residents then filmed themselves going out on their motorcycles to shoot Misak; two were killed. In response, President

Duque called on the Misak to "return to their *resguardos* [reservations]" in view of the "citizenry's suffering."

The mayor felt the need to point out to me Cali's layers of complexity; it is home to guerrillas, industrialists, Indigenous peoples, a shaky middle class, Afro-Colombians—or, as he put it, a multiplicity of agendas. He seemed to think that dialogue was the way out of the city's present turmoil, but I couldn't see how the conflict could be the mayor's to resolve, given that Cali's gigantic problems are Colombia's. Nevertheless, Ospina held out hope that the diffuse ideals and dreams behind this moment of rebellion could contribute to a better Colombia. "If we can get through this the right way, it may be transformative," he said.

ON A BREEZY AFTERNOON, I took a taxi to the renamed Puente de las Mil Luchas (Bridge of a Thousand Struggles), avoiding roadblocks and taking in the multiplying protest murals placed theatrically along the city roads, until we reached a viaduct bridge at one of some twelve points in Cali where serious, cop-challenging barricades have been set up. Barely two dozen people were manning the post: one was handing out yo-yos and teaching a scattering of local residents how to use them; two or three women were relaxing next to a tiny, unpromising kitchen garden; half a dozen more had improvised a soup kitchen inside a blue plastic enclosure.

On the roadway behind them, a scene from an early movie by Federico Fellini or Emir Kusturica: a cluster of actors in makeup and costumes clearly improvised from flea-market findings. Theater in Re-Existence was their name, they said more or less in chorus, and they had come together to bring theater to the barrios during the strike. "All of us [Colombians] were tired and exhausted by the pandemic," one actor said—there were too many talking at once to keep track of who. "And then the movement just exploded," another added. "So we said, 'We're not going to stop striking!'" a third said happily. A professional theater director took on the role of a people's newscaster; an established actor impersonated a famous right-wing anchorwoman; an acting teacher of great natural majesty played the Motherland. Soon the troupe was out on the main road under the bridge, clowning and making an audience of twenty-five or so, who in all probability had never been able to afford a theater ticket, laugh and hoot and applaud wholeheartedly.

THESE ARE UNPREDICTABLE and often frightening days, and there is no denying the tension, but I was considerably cheered by the joyous performance.

The media most often show the antiriot squads in their Darth Vader getups, the beatings and the shootings and the tear gas bursting into the air in great clouds. What appear less often are the ecstatic marches that are also celebrations of being alive after a year of COVID fear and loss. Colombia has a great tradition of protest parades, and it has been on display for weeks. In Bogotá, open-air concerts are offered by the Revolucionaria Orquesta Sinfónica, conducted by Susana Boreal and made up of student musicians and members of the city's several symphony orchestras. Women's *batucadas*, or drumming collectives, are common, and stilt dancers always show up. The rebellion has lasted weeks and access to a phone camera is now universal; one result is a rich harvest of music videos for *la resistencia*.

Take, for example, the video "Policía No Me Mates" (Cop don't kill me), a modest local hit by the seven or so siblings and cousins who call themselves Cronic Gang, whose oldest member is seventeen. The group lives three hours from Cali in Colombia's principal port, Buenaventura, a predominantly Black and overwhelmingly poor city on the Pacific Coast. Roadblocks would not have allowed me to travel there, so we talked on Zoom, and I was startled by how vulnerable they seemed, how Black and young and polite and innocently patriotic.

The poverty of their surroundings was apparent even in their music video, in which the group stands in front of a concrete wall wearing yellow T-shirts and black face masks. Jean Pier Valencia, aka JMenny, seventeen, Elián González (TFP), fifteen, Junior Arley Medina (JWEIT), fourteen, and a friend, Julian Woodcock, eighteen, take turns imploring a policeman to remember that he is the same race as they are and suffers the same discrimination. "I kept seeing on social media how police kill innocent people who just come out to protest and I was filled with indignation," JMenny said, explaining the song's origins. "If the police were created to keep us safe, who will keep us safe from them?"

Like the singers, the song is hopeful even though the realities are bleak. Roadblocks have kept another group member, David Villegas, trapped in the countryside where he had gone to visit his grandmother. On the screen, I saw that she lives in a small bare-brick building. During the worst of the strike the family went hungry, David said; they could hardly find any food and it was too expensive. Still, he felt that the strike was an overwhelmingly positive thing: "It shows the world how we fight for our rights. We need health care, we want a better education. How is it that we are the main port and we can't even have running water twenty-four hours a day?"

Cronic Gang wants to be famous, but they can't get reliable access to water, much less a minimally adequate education. And a month's worth of strenuous effort by the protesters to change their unjust nation, to make it at least pay attention to them, is not likely to provide a remedy. The strikers have had monumental triumphs of sorts: they've forced the removal of the finance minister and overturned his tax bill. The use of grenade launchers against peaceful protesters is now forbidden. Duque announced that registration fees would be suspended for the fall term in public universities. A chastened private sector is busily inventing job programs for the young. Most importantly, the protests may have put an end to the Uribe era: his formerly unassailable standing in the polls is now 73 percent negative, while Duque's approval ratings have bottomed at 18 percent. Yet the government's grand indifference to the suffering of its citizens remains unchanged. Violence, a miserable education system, and an economy now doubly ruined by the pandemic and the weeks of protest are still the lot of most Colombians, and realistically not much can be changed in the landscape of a disaster it has taken years to create.

But the possibility of failure was evidently the last thing on the mind of thousands of *caleños* who gathered on the morning of May 28 at the foot of Siloé, the city's largest favela, in preparation for the march to celebrate the one-month anniversary of the protests. It was clear that the country needed normalcy and that the energy for mass street demonstrations couldn't last much longer, but those thoughts could wait until tomorrow. For now there were papier-mâché figures of politicians that would be joyfully smashed to pieces later on, and *salsa-protesta* music to be danced and flirted to. There was an ecumenical delegation of evangelical pastors and Catholic priests, a group of mothers demanding safety for their offspring, a hundred or so Misak, and thousands of skinny kids, impossibly young, yelling and leaping about, hooting cheerful insults at their rulers and preparing to set off once more across the city, full of hope. We have not seen the last of them.

POSTSCRIPT. On the wave of the general uprising in 2021, Gustavo Petro was elected president of Colombia and has served since August 7, 2022. In this deeply conservative country, the election of a leftist candidate was a historic first. Petro's complicated history includes a short stint as a member of the M-19 guerrilla movement (long-since demobilized and integrated into society), two terms as congressman, one term as senator for a left-wing party descended from the M-19, and another term as mayor of Bogotá. He was an excellent senator, whose muckraking investigations helped reveal the military's illegal actions, and the corruption and association with right-wing paramilitary organizations of former president Álvaro Uribe Vélez. His reviews as mayor are considerably less enthusiastic: he is by all accounts a poor administrator (although an honest one). His first months in office have been, to put it into the most understated terms possible, tumultuous. He has already replaced half his cabinet and lost both his chief of staff and his closest political advisor on the same day. He also broke with the centrist parties that made his election possible, which will probably make it impossible for him to pass his most ambitious legislation. He is not looked on with favor by the business sector, the military, or, to state the obvious, by the right. His place in history may ultimately be determined by the success or failure of talks to demobilize, at last, Colombia's oldest remaining guerrilla group, the National Liberation Army. But given the presence of multiple drug groups in the countryside, it is highly unlikely that he will be able to fulfill his campaign promise of bringing "total peace" to his country.

NOTE

First published in the *New York Review of Books*, July 22, 2021.

5

Colombia's Healing Begins

JANUARY 2018

From a distance the terrified family could not have guessed the full extent of what was taking place in El Salado, a prosperous town by rural standards, at the center of territory disputed between left-wing guerrillas and their paramilitary adversaries. The assault produced one of the most horrifying episodes in Colombia's five decades of brutal ideological warfare.

Villagers who hadn't had time to flee were rounded up in front of the church, in a field normally used for pickup soccer games. As their relatives were forced to watch, the victims, accused of sympathizing with guerrillas, were taken into the center of the field one by one, tortured, mocked, knifed, and then strangled or shot. The paramilitaries beat those who cried out at the sight. They raped young women before killing them. They raided the community center, and, in this region of northern Colombia where music and dance are a central part of existence, they took the local band's instruments and celebrated each murder with loud, drunken playing.

The killing in El Salado and nearby towns lasted six days, from February 16 to 21, 2000. By the end of it, sixty-six people were dead. Returning home with her family, the child Mayito recoiled from the sight of the charred houses and the lingering smell of death. This time no one in her immediate family was among the dead, but the family had already been traumatized: Mayito's father had been murdered years earlier, accused of being a guerrilla sympathizer. Her mother packed up the family belongings as other survivors gave their relatives a hasty burial in four mass graves. Within a week, all of El Salado's four thousand residents had fled, joining more than two million other internally displaced Colombians at that time who were robbed of their families, their homes, their livelihoods, and their peace.

What makes this story different from other episodes of horror and heartbreak in Colombia is that the people of El Salado came back. In a stubborn return to this most unlikely promised land, the Saladeros took back their town two years after the killings, clearing the tropical vines that had climbed across roads, up walls, and into every empty room, whitewashing the adobe houses, and replanting the tobacco fields that had provided a tolerable income not so long before. There was no school for the children, but Mayito Padilla, by then twelve years old, decided to start one on her own, including literacy drills and the multiplication tables, and a history course in which her thirty-seven students went over their own experiences so as not to forget the terrible events of the recent past.

Today, El Salado and Colombia are transforming their grim heritage. The girl now known as "Miss Mayito" worked her way through a degree in early childhood education and became the head of community relations in her hometown. And after half a century in which the war circled repeatedly in on itself, and after four years of painstaking negotiations, the country's oldest guerrilla group, the Fuerzas Armadas Revolucionarias de Colombia (FARC), turned over the last of its weapons in June 2017 to a United Nations team. By then the entire country had been reshaped by violence. Now a lasting peace will have to be won, inch by inch. El Salado, with its head start on reconstruction, has given people hope that the country too can heal.

THE REALITY IS THAT in the two centuries since it gained independence from Spain, Colombia has rarely been without violent conflict. Some would argue that the latest cycle of bloodshed began on April 9, 1948, with the assassination of an overwhelmingly popular leader of the traditional Liberal Party, Jorge Eliécer Gaitán. The murder sparked deadly riots in the capital, Bogotá, and a ten-year wave of partisan killings—La Violencia—in the countryside. But long before that, members of the Conservative Party had been slaughtering Liberals, and often enough, vice versa.

In 1957, an agreement to end the violence by rotating power between both parties led to a decade or so of relative peace, and in the cities not many people took notice of a few dozen Liberal campesino families who'd been radicalized by a forceful communist organizer. Among those who did were the army, the sitting president, and an archconservative senator who accused the campesinos of wanting to create "independent republics" inside Colombia. In 1964, a military operation involving thousands of troops overran the Liberal group's small, precipitous holdings in Colombia's Andean foothills. Further radicalized by being bombed, the campesinos adopted the FARC name and embarked on a guerrilla war against the state that was to last fifty-two years.

The small band of radical campesinos with no weapons to speak of and no proper military training little by little recruited neighbors and nearby villagers, until their numbers exceeded the most fantastical expectations. Then the FARC grew again, explosively, in the 1980s, thanks to a war on drugs that began in the United States and was largely fought in Mexico and the Andean countries, where coca is grown. Leaves from the shrubby coca bush are medicinal, sacred to the Native populations of the Andes. They're also the central ingredient in cocaine, a chemical compound first developed in Germany in the mid-nineteenth century. When growing coca was declared a criminal activity more than a hundred years later, Andean peasants simply moved what was by far their sturdiest cash crop to increasingly remote parts of Colombia's vast hinterland. After all, some bloodthirsty drug mafia or other was always willing to pay top dollar for the otherwise useless plant.

Given the never-ending demand for recreational drugs from New York to Shanghai, the drug war only served to force prices ever upward. The FARC sensed an opportunity and stepped in. In exchange for protecting the campesinos from ruthless traffickers and ensuring standard prices for the coca leaves they harvested, the FARC levied an export tax for every kilo of processed coca paste that left the territories under its control.

Soon FARC troops had standardized uniforms and boots—and standard-issue combat weaponry too. Their numbers swelled to an estimated twenty thousand. The guerrillas were awash in money, and the leadership inevitably became corrupt, vicious, and hungry for more. Hardly revolutionary, they extorted, kidnapped, and set off bombs. And because FARC guerrillas attracted the attention of paramilitary groups that sprang up to combat them, they inflicted great suffering on the very campesinos they lived among. It was the

FARC that the paramilitary killers in El Salado accused the villagers of sympathizing with, and it was the FARC that, backed into a corner militarily, finally signed a peace accord with the Colombian government on November 24, 2016, and turned over its weapons in June of last year.

From the peninsular Guajira Desert to the high Andean *páramos*, where it's possible to walk with one's head literally in the clouds; from the tropical plains along the Atlantic to the deep green jungles of the Pacific, this is a breathtaking country, with only forty-eight million people occupying a territory almost twice the size of France. Colombia has more varieties of hummingbirds, butterflies, orchids, frogs, and whatever other tropical living thing one can imagine than just about anywhere else on Earth.

Many people here are shockingly poor, which is particularly clear if you travel from the modern cities to, say, the Pacific region of Chocó, whose impoverished Indian and Afro-Colombian populations still navigate numerous broad rivers in canoes because there are so few roads. Visitors to the resort city of Cartagena are rarely told about an outlying barrio named after Nelson Mandela, where some forty thousand people, mostly refugees from the violence in places such as Chocó and El Salado, live in shameful conditions. Flying over the emerald-green country, you can see broad, gleaming rivers everywhere; steep valleys covered in a patchwork of coffee farms; lush pastures spreading like velvet cloaks toward the Amazon.

What you can't see are the land mines.

When a round of peace talks in the early 2000s broke down, the tide of the war turned against the FARC, which intensified its use of mines—technically, improvised explosive devices, since they're handmade—to obstruct the army's hot pursuit. They're bitter souvenirs of the guerrillas' fight, and eradicating them is a crucial task faced by the government. Too often a campesino steps on a mine somewhere that was planted long ago, leaving a child blinded by shrapnel or a farmer missing a leg or an arm and no longer able to feed his family. According to the HALO Trust, a worldwide mine-clearing organization, Colombia has consistently ranked behind Afghanistan as the country with the second highest number of mine victims in the world; mines have killed or wounded more than 11,400 Colombians since 1990.

"Land mines did more damage to campesinos than to the army," Álvaro Jiménez, a mine expert, told me. Jiménez is a former guerrilla himself (the organization he belonged to, the M-19, turned over its weapons to the government in 1990). Eighteen years ago, he became the head of the Campaña Colombiana Contra Minas (CCCM, Colombian Campaign Against Mines), which creates and sponsors harm-reduction programs in areas mined by the guerrillas. "Mines generate many fears," he said. "Like the fear of venturing out after dark to look for a doctor if someone is sick, taking children to school. Normally campesinos live in a harmonious relationship with their surroundings. Mines destroyed that."

Jiménez suggested I travel to the department of Nariño, a land of high rolling hills quilted in a patchwork of soft green fields and then a plunge to the untamed tropics of the Pacific coastline. In the remote town of Ricaurte, which like most urban clusters in Colombia is crowded and graceless and roaring with motorbikes, I was introduced to Cristian Marín, a member of the Awá Indigenous people who live in a jungle preserve not far away. Slight, cinnamon skinned, and just a little potbellied, Marín is one of the youngest leaders to be elected by the Awá to solve disputes and deal with the outside world.

Marín speaks in a murmur and relies on understatement, so it's hard to get a picture of the damage his community suffered without resorting to rude questioning, and it was only in response to one such interrogation that he told me about an army–guerrilla confrontation near his own family's compound in which, as usual, neither party emerged the winner.

"And as usual," Marín said, "the guerrillas mined as they retreated. So people decided not to leave their homes. They were afraid." Besieged by fear, unable to work their fields or travel to market for supplies, they didn't venture beyond their own yards for months, suffering accordingly. Marín didn't mention, until I asked, that he himself had lost four relatives to mines. He seemed to me as incapable of optimism as a tree might be of flight.

We spoke under the shade of a leafy ficus in a public square bordered by nondescript municipal buildings. Marín was working in Ricaurte as an Awá representative, recruited to receive training in human rights. "It's a political thing they want to do," he said, shrugging. "There's a budget for it—the Norwegians are giving money." Nevertheless, he acknowledged, the effort was helping Awá citizens obtain legal documents and file complaints about human rights violations. And as part of the accords signed between the government and the FARC, a joint program with army personnel and demobilized guerrillas is beginning the slow and risky process of mine eradication. The current combat-free era is a great advantage too, he said: it's easier now for Awá children to get at least the substandard schooling available to them. "In my school I was always behind," Marín said, "because I spent so much time hiding under a mattress from the fighting."

IN THE BOOMING CITIES, with their sophisticated restaurants and art galleries and designer buildings, people could forget that a war was on. Even now that foreign investment is turning from a trickle to a flow and traffic jams are world-class, it's hard to remember that this is a modest economy, with a government that runs on a painfully inadequate budget.

In Bogotá I talked with a prominent Colombian senator, Antonio Navarro Wolff, in a shabby office with a crowded waiting room barely large enough for a hermit and a phone system that looked like it was set up in 1980. Navarro Wolff, once a governor of Nariño, is something of an expert in *posconflicto*, given that he was a leader of the former M-19 guerrilla organization. His group demobilized successfully, and he has kept abreast of the many peace talks that have taken place over the years.

I asked him which postconflict task the government should take on first, in light of budget and personnel limitations: Land restitution to campesinos evicted from their holdings by paramilitaries? Education and resocialization for some seven thousand demobilized guerrilla troops? Exhumations and identification of Colombia's tens of thousands of "disappeareds"? Mine clearing?

"The principal, most urgent, question is only one," Navarro Wolff answered. "Who is going to occupy the land abandoned by the FARC? The government or the new criminal bands?"

Guerrillas and paramilitaries fought for control of remote territories ideal for growing coca and the kind of poppy used for making heroin. "The guerrillas may go, but the land remains," Navarro Wolff said. And so does the illegal drug trade—and the drug war. "What we need now is police. In the *posconflicto* the task will no longer be to kill criminals but to make sure that there are no new criminals. For that we need a security force, but right now we have barely ten thousand police" in rural areas, he explained.

In a great irony of this complicated war, the FARC may turn out to be by far the cheaper of two evils, compared with the cost of controlling the savage new drug-trafficking gangs taking over the territories where guerrillas and paramilitaries once fought for control. The government estimates that 5 percent of the guerrilla forces have refused to lay down their weapons and may eventually find their way into the ranks of the so-called *bacrim* (short for *bandas criminales*). Today these gangs are mostly involved in the drug trade, but they're slowly taking over old guerrilla and paramilitary sidelines as well: extortion, kidnapping, and human trafficking.

And as Marín had told me in the little plaza of Ricaurte, "At least with the guerrillas, they had a central command one could negotiate with," for things such as curfew hours. Not so with the new criminal bands. "They just say '*plata o plomo*,'"—silver or lead, meaning bribes or bullets—Navarro said. "And anyone with any brains at all will say, 'Oh, I'll take silver, because lead is far too heavy.'"

HOW WILL THE 23 percent of Colombians who live in the countryside fare now that there's peace? Over the course of half a century, more than seven million people left their homes in the rural areas most afflicted by guerrilla and paramilitary violence. The government's reconstruction and reparations efforts are focusing on these regions. Seventeen years after the massacre that emptied out the town, El Salado is a good place to look for first results.

Set a couple of hours inland from the Caribbean shore, the town still isn't much to look at: a gulch runs through the center, and an unrepaired aqueduct made water supply problematic when I visited. And yet for a cohort of its residents in exile, nostalgia for their place of birth proved strong enough for them to band together, two thousand strong, in defiance of death threats and their own dreadful memories, to reclaim it.

Luis Torres led the return campaign seventeen years ago, and when the first 130 people agreed to come back to El Salado, he raised the funds to hire the trucks that brought them home. An articulate seventy-one-year-old with a rugged face and a startling liveliness about him, he was employed when I visited as the primary intermediary between the town and the Semana Foundation, which for many years coordinated the effort to resurrect El Salado.

In the beginning, Torres had to negotiate permission for the residents to re-settle their town with a FARC detachment that then held sway over the region. He subsequently spent three months in prison, charged with "rebellion," and then went into a long exile in the Netherlands, Switzerland, and Spain before he felt it was safe to return. Now he glowed with a sense of accomplishment as he showed me the sights of his hometown: a cell phone tower that at last allows Saladeros to communicate with the outside world, a preschool, a hundred new houses for the community's poorest families, a couple of storefront groceries, an evangelical church, a street lively again with scampering children, neighbors waving hello.

"When people first came back here, their fears were wide awake," Torres remembered. "And they had a stigma chasing them. In the cities they say about us, 'They must have done something if they had to leave their homes.' No one wants to hire a displaced person. And for our part, we have a mistrust and fear that won't go away. It's only recently that people have started leaving their doors open."

Depending on who was taking stock of the improvements—Torres or, say, me—one could see either heroic achievements against all the odds or modest recovery to the tune of millions of donated dollars, without solving many of the town's most basic problems, including water, jobs, and education. And El Salado is just one small town out of thousands in similar straits. It was only two years ago that it acquired its most significant improvement: a twelve-mile stretch of paved road that reduced travel to the nearest major town and highway to thirty minutes, down from as much as four hours, depending on the rain. Perhaps the transformation of El Salado has simply allowed it to become one more community without adequate water, sewage, education, health care services—and where all too many campesinos lack title to lands they may have occupied for generations.

Luis Torres has an ultimate dream: he sees himself standing in the crowd and applauding as the ribbon is cut on a technical school in his hometown, one that will train the kids who now zip around so aimlessly on their motorbikes for something better than a dirt-poor life. "Once I see that ribbon being cut, I'll die in peace," he said.

AT THE CENTER of the new Colombia, the former guerrillas who played such a large role in creating the old one have grander dreams. "I want to help create equality not just for ourselves but for all the Colombian people and—why not?—for the world," said a young man whose nom de guerre was Alex. We were sitting on an overlook, taking in an expanse of valley, all green fields and golden light. Behind us was a bare-bones communal kitchen, and around us a new settlement—one of twenty-six built from scratch in the past six months—designed to accommodate three hundred or so demobilized guerrillas. The settlements are part of the 297-page agreement so laboriously negotiated between guerrilla leaders and the government. They're supposed to contribute to a smooth transition into modern-day consumer society for some seven thousand fighters, now that they have laid down their weapons.

Despite the ramshackle quality of the dormitories—one wallboard room per guerrilla or guerrilla couple, toilet and shower stalls across the way—Alex was truly pleased with his new surroundings. All of twenty-five, painfully shy of strangers and completely innocent of the ways of capitalism, he looked and acted more like a teenager, as if his real life had stopped when he ran away from his family to join the FARC at age fifteen. "No money, no work, no chance to study—my family was poor," he explained. He said he had never had a moment of regret, but one wonders how much his situation improved: during his ten years as a guerrilla fighter he never slept under a roof, saw his family, or used money. "Looking back, those were years of suffering and hardship," he said. Sleeping most often in a hammock protected from the rain by a plastic sheet, guerrillas observed bedtime at six every day lest a conversation, a giggle, a lit cigarette give away the group's location. Radios weren't allowed, because an infiltrator might easily place a microchip locator in one. Crisscrossing the country with hundred-pound backpacks, guerrillas relied on rice as their main sustenance. On his first day out of training, Alex said, his group ambushed a military post, and he saw three of his young comrades die.

"One feels the change most in the *tranquilidad*," he said. And then there are the dormitories: "Now we each have an opportunity to organize our little room as we like. Our bedtimes have changed, because some like to watch their telenovela, others their soccer game." He worried that a monthly government subsidy of about $300 per demobilized fighter would be hard to administer properly, but the money was being deposited into a nearby bank. "Now that we're civilians," he said, "we have to learn to manage ourselves, and we know that out there you need money for everything."

IF THE GOVERNMENT had been bolder, or richer, or less hemmed in by loud opposition to the peace agreement in Congress and among Colombians in general, each former combatant would have received a far larger amount of money—enough to set up a curbside *arepa* stand, or finish school, or in other ways help ensure that a person reentering society from the equivalent of Mars, with only the clothes on his or her back, would find legality more attractive than a job with one of the criminal bands now hiring. The monthly subsidy will end in July 2019, as will the demobilization territories, where the United Nations verification mission and the national police are ensuring safety and protection. It was almost unfair to ask Alex, still adjusting to the basics of his new life, how he saw the future after this transition period, but clearly it was something he and his mates discussed constantly.

"What I worry most about is security," he said immediately. In the mid-1980s, failed negotiations with the FARC included a truce, an amnesty, and the opportunity to create a political party, which was called the Unión Patriótica. Within the decade more than a thousand party militants had been assassinated, mostly in broad daylight and, instructively, in public spaces. Now the FARC is transforming itself into a new party, which is supposed to guide the ex-fighters, win elections, and lead Colombia into the new world Alex thinks his years of struggle have made possible. When he's speaking in what might be considered his heroic voice, Alex muses about a future of collective effort and collective joy, but caught off guard, he dreams aloud about the little farm he hopes FARC leaders will arrange for him and the nursing degree or baking certificate to which others in his group aspire. He'd like to study too, finish elementary school and get his high school diploma. On the farm? He hesitates. Life is complicated and uncertain for everyone these days, but who knows? It might all work out in the end.

NOTE

First published in *National Geographic*, January 2018. Sources: Adam Isacson, Washington Office on Latin America; UNHCR; UN Office on Drugs and Crime; NASA; Victims Unit, National Information Network, Colombia; Office of the High Commissioner for Peace, Colombia.

Confessions of a Killer

OCTOBER 10, 2002

1.

A remarkable book has been published in Colombia, the country of perplexing and endless fratricidal violence. First available in local bookstores nationwide for the 2001-2 Christmas season and now in its eleventh printing, it is the "as told to" autobiography of Carlos Castaño, the man responsible for organizing, executing, or inspiring a good part of the twenty thousand or so politically motivated murders that have taken place in Colombia over the last ten years.

In 1994, following the death of his older brother Fidel, Carlos Castaño took over a small regional death squad. The older Castaño had founded the death squad in 1981 to avenge the kidnapping and alleged murder of their father, Jesús Castaño, by guerrillas of the FARC (Fuerzas Armadas Revolucionarias de Colombia). The Castaño family patriarch owned a prosperous ranch with about six hundred head of cattle in the hill country of Antioquia, a sort of Wild West where mining, violence, cattle ranching, gambling, and heavy drinking are interconnected activities to this day. The family had friendly relations with the local FARC militants, who were often farmers or miners themselves; a couple of the Castaño boys even considered themselves leftist sympathizers and read publications like *China Reconstructs* admiringly.

Nevertheless, when the guerrillas decided to ambush Castaño Sr. at his ranch one night in 1979, they kicked him and called him a "sonofabitch oligarch," according to the ranch hands who witnessed the abduction. Carlos Castaño writes that the kidnappers initially demanded 50 million pesos in ransom money from Fidel. When Fidel, who ran the local bar in the town of Segovia and was a notably skillful cardsharp and smuggler, among other things, came up with the sum, the guerrillas demanded 50 million more. Then the father either died or was killed in captivity.

Although all dates and numbers involving the Castaño brothers are approximate, it seems that Fidel was thirty-one years old and Carlos fourteen when this traumatic event took place. By the time Fidel died in a guerrilla ambush, the organization he created to avenge his father's death had grown to some several hundred men. It was based primarily in the contiguous agricultural regions of Córdoba and Urabá but also in the Castaños' native *departamento* of Antioquia, where drugs are a notoriously big business (its capital is Medellín). From the beginning, the death squad found support among some parts of the military and the forces of public order. Credible rumor has it that in Córdoba Fidel Castaño was so popular among the troops that he used to land his helicopter on the roof of the local police garrisons. Notorious from its inception, the organization is always referred to in the press and even by its supporters as *los paramilitares*, or *paras*, but Carlos does not use the term in his book. He prefers *autodefensas* (self-defenders), as in Autodefensas Campesinas de Córdoba y Urabá, or ACCU, which became the nucleus of the coalition organization put together by Carlos Castaño some three years after he took over from Fidel.

This new, nationwide group, the Autodefensas Unidas de Colombia, or AUC, is currently said to be around ten thousand strong, extremely well equipped and well trained, and highly motivated. Both the AUC and the organization it was born to extinguish, the FARC, are amply financed by profits from the drug trade, which is entrenched in territories where the two enemy groups hold sway. In less than ten years, by means of terror, the AUC has effectively wrested control from the FARC in many parts of the country where the guerrillas used to be strong. Castaño's organization has proved immeasurably more efficient at this task than the Colombian army, under whose indifferent eye the FARC grew at a steady rate for decades.

THE KIDNAPPING AND DEATH of Jesús Castaño is the leitmotif threading together the account provided now by his son of his own remarkable life. Unlike his sworn enemy Manuel Marulanda, the elderly, laconic founder and surviving leader of the forty-year-old FARC, Carlos Castaño is anything but inscrutable. Not yet forty, voluble, volatile, self-obsessed, self-important, self-questioning, and remarkably shrewd, Castaño has turned into the author, and hero, of what is already one of Colombia's all-time best sellers. Because so many copies of the book are pirate editions, particularly those hawked on street corners, there is no way of knowing whether Castaño has outsold the living national monument, Gabriel García Márquez, or Deepak Chopra; if he hasn't done so yet, it may be only a question of time. Castaño's omnipresence on the Colombian political scene is unquestionable, and he is not likely to go away soon. Also, he is popular.

There is virtually no aspect of his book, as object or text, that is not fascinating. I have in my hands a copy of the first edition, which is a hardcover, a rarity in Latin America, where the market for books is small. It's an expensive edition, too, with a four-color, high-quality photo of the author on the dust jacket. And what a photo! A strong-jawed, determined man stares forthrightly out from the cover. He is wearing a camouflage uniform and a ranger hat; the national colors appear on the armband stitched on his sleeve. Standing against the backdrop of a breathtaking waterfall, his figure is framed by the enclosing jungle. When I showed the book to a young acquaintance of mine whose eyes sparkle whenever he hears the word *guerrilla*, he became immediately starstruck. He took the news hard that the glamorous figure in the picture was actually the man who has made it his business in life to kill as many guerrillas as possible before he gets killed himself.

The canniest aspect of the book's presentation may be the title: *Mi confesión: Carlos Castaño revela sus secretos* (My confession: Carlos Castano reveals his secrets). Whether Castaño or his writer, Mauricio Aranguren Molina, came up with it, it is a seductive and accurate description of the contents, for although Castaño tells a sordid story, in many chapters he appears to do so straightforwardly. He recounts his first murder in gruesome detail and gives a step-by-step account of how in 1990 he set up the assassination of Colombia's leading left-wing presidential candidate, Carlos Pizarro, in a "true patriotic action." People generally write a confessional book when they are undergoing some sort of spiritual torment. It can be a way of coming to terms with oneself and the world, often in the face of approaching death, and one is tempted to feel sorry for Castaño that his present effort is so characteristically determined and ultimately so unsuccessful.

How does a man who has with his own hands carried out the execution of possibly hundreds of what he calls "individual" or "multiple" "military objectives" console himself when his conscience keeps him awake at night, as it seems to do rather often? "You can't fool your conscience, which is the mirror of the soul," he says. "The exam I submit myself to isn't easy. But I still find relief when I conclude that the fault isn't mine; the blame belongs to those who kidnapped Dad." How does he see the principal differences between himself and his older, more impulsive, more pleasure-loving and adventurous brother? "I don't carry a grudge."

The book is full of similar assertions. He likes to sing but prefers to recite poetry, particularly the idealistic left-wing verses of Mario Benedetti. He refers to "my intellectuals," who provide him with advice and reading lists. He objects to reporters and human rights investigators who accuse his troops of hacking their victims to death or dismembering them with a chainsaw: his men have always respected the fundamental human right to die in a dignified manner, with a bullet. Whether "there are some bodies which are cut in two or are mutilated in their extremities as a result of a volley of machine gunfire" is another matter.

Of his brother Fidel, he says, "The war allowed him to do the two things he wanted most: attack the guerrillas and become a rich man." A fierce admirer of Israel, where he received military training, he says, "Golda Meir and my mother are for me, without any doubt, the women who represent the maximum in excellence of their sex." He takes issue with the cliché-ridden writing of tabloid journalists: "five minutes were enough to do away with the criminal" is what they always say, he complains, but "no, no, no! It took whole days of work and synchronization" to carry out a crime—in this case, the airport murder of a drug king who got on Castaño's bad side.

AND YET ONE RESISTS the impulse to laugh or shrug in disgust and toss the book aside, because along with the self-aggrandizing and twisted moral vision comes a good chunk of the secret history of Colombia, in which men like Castaño have always played a part, meeting in elegant hideaways with the country's most prominent businessmen and politicians, putting together deals or even hit lists with them; trading information and weapons with a guerrilla group and then turning on its leaders or on one's former allies; engaging in drinking bouts with high-ranking military officials; working out the details of a joint operation in which left-wing activists or impoverished peasant supporters of the guerrillas will be eliminated, with information provided by the army and acted on by the paramilitaries, or vice versa.

In this shadow history, readers of Castaño's book learn that the M-19 guerrilla group, now disbanded, had friendly relations with the legendary cocaine exporter Pablo Escobar. In 1985, they mounted an assault on the Palacio de Justicia, or Justice Ministry, in which more than one hundred people burned to death, including twenty-eight guerrilla commandos and twelve Supreme Court judges. The assault would prove their undoing; in its wake, the organization was morally shattered (following a general amnesty in 1989, some of the survivors are active in parliamentary politics). The attack was financed by Escobar, with some weapons provided by Fidel Castaño. Or so says Carlos, who claims to have been present at the meeting where the assault was decided on.

Castaño also says that in the early days of the death squad, the brothers gained experience and prestige when they were called upon by a "Group of Six," half a dozen eminent and prosperous Colombians who discreetly provided the killers with a list of useful targets. Carlos describes back-room meetings in which a series of important politicians invited him to participate in a coup against then president Ernesto Samper, whom Castaño claims to despise on account of "his decision to accept money from the drug trade to finance his campaign."

Whether or not the younger Castaño brother was in fact present at these meetings, or even if they never took place, Carlos has an uncommonly good ear for dialogue. His actual credibility is of course the central question. Castaño fails to mention a large number of civilian massacres with which the family name or his organization has been linked. He denies participation in those he does mention, although in many cases survivors and eyewitnesses have implicated him, his brother, or his associates. However, when he describes incidents that I have any knowledge of, his information seems sound—if partial, or misleadingly interpreted. For example, Castaño accuses the young woman who was mayor of Segovia in 1989 of being a guerrilla collaborator and of preventing him from transporting the family cattle across state lines and selling it without prior vaccination. I heard this story in the frightening town of Segovia from the mayor herself, when she was in the middle of the dispute with Castaño. Rita Tobón was a young and very beautiful woman. If she was not a guerrilla, she was certainly a sympathizer: she had run for office and been elected on the ticket of the FARC's official legal front, the Unión Patriótica.

Sitting in a greasy restaurant, flanked by armed bodyguards, picking at her barbecued chicken and understandably jumpy, she told me that Castaño would move his livestock out of Segovia over her dead body. Like many others I talked to then, she blamed the Castaños for one of the largest mass killings in Colombia's recent history, in which forty-five men, women, and children had been mowed down the previous year by a carful of masked men. (One of her bodyguards said that he was the survivor of an earlier Castaño-sponsored mass killing, presumably carried out as revenge against the entire territory in which the family patriarch had once been held in captivity.) Castaño denies any part in either of these atrocities in his book, but his curiously frank portrait of his older brother's early career as a small-time hoodlum coincides with what I learned about him in Segovia back then.

He also recalls in some detail the evening when his car overturned and he fractured his arm. He was in the company of a young woman who is the sister of an important FARC regional leader. She was at the time Castaño's kidnap victim but, as Castaño willingly admits, the two were having an affair. When I first heard this story from someone well acquainted with the inner workings of the *autodefensas*, it was more elaborate. All the details of the car accident were the same, with one important difference: in a sort of mutual Stockholm syndrome, Castaño had, according to my source, fallen hopelessly in love with his kidnap victim, and the two had decided to run away together. The car accident, which could conceivably have been engineered by subordinates who got wind of Castaño's plan, my source said, convinced the leader to return to his true destiny.

Significantly, a number of the leading characters of recent Colombian history mentioned by name in *Mi confesión* have not yet challenged the author's version of events. For example, Castaño describes how Gabriel García Márquez recruited the former Spanish prime minister Felipe González to help the former outgoing president, Andrés Pastrana, put together a peace plan that had Carlos Castaño's approval. (The plan fell apart when the FARC rejected it.) García Márquez has denied neither the general story nor its particulars, as he took pains to do when a dreadful poem attributed to him circulated on the Web last year.

Similarly, Pablo Escobar's backing for the assault on the Palace of Justice has been convincingly reported before, notably by the Colombian journalist Ramón Jimeno. (Whether the raging fire in which so many perished was started by the army or the guerrillas has long been debated. No one will ever know the answer, but both Jimeno and Castaño argue that Escobar took an interest in the attack on the Supreme Court because its organizers in the M-19 promised to destroy the records of drug lords wanted for extradition in the United States.) One of the more fascinating sections of the book describes in detail what has long been known: that Escobar died when Carlos Castaño finally had enough of his one-time business associate and devoted his full attention to the manhunt for Colombia's leading criminal. An ad hoc group he created, Los Pepes (short for Perseguidos por Pablo Escobar), led the chase, while Castaño himself, he states, regularly informed the police high command on what he could find out about Escobar's whereabouts.

2.

In July, the US Congress acted to ease restrictions on the use of nearly $1.7 billion in drug-combat funds for Colombia, in order to make them available for antiguerrilla and antimilitary operations. Additional small amounts have also been approved to "protect US investment," like the pipeline transporting oil to its export point in the Caribbean, which guerrillas have enjoyed blowing up for years. Mostly, the recent legislation means that seventy brand-new helicopters can now be used to transport armed personnel to take part in combat and in surveillance operations. From Carlos Castaño's point of view, however, the most important recent change in policy is the decision of the Justice and State Departments to file requests for extradition to the United States of both guerrillas and paramilitary leaders involved in drug trafficking. The first requests from Washington name a prominent FARC regional leader as well as one of Castaño's associates in the AUC. So far, nothing has been said about the extradition of Castaño himself, but one assumes this is not for lack of interest.

Castaño's book is thus, among other things, an ambitious attempt to fend off extradition by portraying himself as a politically motivated, morally concerned, patriotic freedom fighter who can also expound thoughtfully on the realities of the anti-insurgency struggle in Colombia. Yes, he says repeatedly, he and his organization financed their operations with money from coca grown and sold to traffickers in territory under the *autodefensas'* control. But look, there's a war on, and he's the only one who's really been fighting it.

Castaño has recently been engaged in a showdown with his regional commanders over issues of principle and leadership. During the past few months, he has been using the AUC's fancy website to reveal the tensions and disagreements among the different regional organizations. Having resigned last year from the national leadership in favor of a collegial high command, he used his remaining power to push for an official AUC commitment to human rights. He set up a complaints section on the national website and forswore civilian murders and "nonpolitical" kidnappings, that is, for ransom.

At first, there were those who thought that Carlos Castaño was polishing his image because he was considering running for president, but the realities of the new antiterrorist policy of the Bush administration have squelched whatever political ambitions the AUC leader may have had one year ago. Now he merely seems to be repositioning himself. In mid-July, Castaño and his military commander in chief, Salvatore Mancuso, announced that their local *autodefensa* was separating from the national umbrella organization Castaño created in 1997, the AUC. The split has since been mended but one of its causes, he declared repeatedly, was that "a few" of the AUC regional forces were "feudalized" by the drug trade (one detects here the hand of Castaño's intellectuals). He now understands, he says, that this was very wrong. Just as it was wrong for the police forces on both sides of the Venezuelan border to take part in an AUC-sponsored kidnapping of a rich Venezuelan businessman. With such comments, Castaño is plainly trying to confer some legitimacy on himself and his organization. He wants to negotiate with the government, just as the FARC did until last year. He wants the United Nations to have a part in those negotiations. He wants combatant status.

But above all, he wants to dictate the terms in which he will go down in Colombian history books. For a B-movie avenger like Carlos Castaño, the only fate worse than death would be serving out a life sentence in a dungeon somewhere in the United States or not getting to die like a hero, which amounts to pretty much the same thing. He made his case in a rambling editorial on the AUC website:

> Today, more than ever, [the *autodefensas'*] continued existence is vital. Our achievements in political and military matters against the guerrillas cannot be denied; they will negotiate with the government sooner rather than later, fundamentally as a result of the pressure . . . [of our] irregular organization. . . .
>
> [The national *autodefensas*] were a stage in the search for our essence, the discovery of our destiny. . . . Today we know that the time has come to strengthen, not disband them. . . . We are still searching for our essence, but today, thank God, we know that neither the drug trade nor terrorism will be a part of this meeting with our destiny.

There are, of course, several problems with such magnificent intentions. One is that, absent a drug income, the $3 million a month Castaño claims is necessary to finance his organization will be hard to come by. Another is that many of his colleagues could fail to be moved by his new moral purity. Castaño may yet find death as he helped death to find Pablo Escobar—through betrayal by all but his most intimate associates.

3.

In May, Álvaro Uribe Vélez was elected to the presidency by one of the largest margins in Colombian history. Uribe is only the eighth consecutive freely elected Colombian president since a singular agreement to rotate power between the Liberal and Conservative parties came to an end in 1974. This agreement was the formula devised by the political elite to stop the twenty-year cycle of near civil war known as La Violencia, which lasted between, roughly, 1945 and 1965.

The past twenty-five years of unrestricted electoral political life have coincided with the steepest rise in ideologically motivated violence since the 1950s, at the height of La Violencia. In 2001 alone, two thousand Colombians died fighting or, as with most of them, were murdered in politically dictated events. Uribe's predecessor, Andrés Pastrana, left office in near disgrace: his three-year effort to bring peace to the country led only to the bizarre interregnum in which the FARC guerrillas enjoyed free rein in a no-fire, no-flyover zone twice the size of El Salvador. In February, Pastrana suspended the no-fire zone and ordered the army to resume military operations against the FARC. Since then guerrilla territorial control has for all practical purposes remained what it was before and during the Pastrana years.

Given the Colombian government's extreme weakness, a first question is whether the new president can rein in the FARC, the now fragmented and chaotic paramilitary organizations, and the rogue sectors of the military by force or persuasion, no matter how much aid from the United States he might receive. There is little hope that Uribe will be able to negotiate successfully with the FARC, which managed to sabotage Pastrana's three-year negotiating effort. But if the new president decides to open another front in the war and take on the AUC, can he persuade the army and former police forces to point their weapons in its direction?

URIBE IS A MAVERICK Liberal Party politician with avowed conservative leanings and an obsession with *autoridad*. Having understood the depth of

Colombians' disgust with traditional politics, he resigned from the party last year and became the country's first independent candidate to be elected president. Throughout his election campaign Uribe faced insistent charges that he himself has favored or even sponsored Castaño's *autodefensas*, although no evidence has come up to support these accusations. During his campaign he stated his commitment to fighting *"los violentos* on both sides." One of his first acts in the presidency was to request the good offices of the United Nations in seeking dialogue with the guerrillas. But in his first days in office he has also made some risky decisions that could well end up fueling, if not the *autodefensas* directly, a type of vigilantism that may prove even harder to control.

Uribe's inauguration on August 7 was marked by the FARC's inept and bloody attempt to sabotage it. Guerrilla commandos launched poorly aimed explosives in the direction of the Palacio de Nariño, or government house. One volley damaged the grounds of the Palacio, including the building itself. Others hit wide of the mark and landed in a pathetic slum five or six blocks west. All in all, twenty men, women, and children were killed, mostly among the street people from the slum. This was a repeat of the brutal event at an impoverished backwater village last May, in which guerrilla troops, in hot pursuit of the *autodefensas*, lobbed explosives at a church in which the local population had taken refuge, with a death toll of 119, including 47 children. These attacks only increased support for Uribe's initiative, announced the day after his swearing-in, to create a nationwide network of one million informers who are supposed to feed the army and security forces with information about *los violentos*, to use Uribe's catch-all term. Some informers are supposed to receive weapons for self-defense, and the prospect of arming civilian populations in regions of Colombia already on the verge of civil war has generated alarm among human rights activists as well as many former government officials involved in earlier attempts to bring peace to Colombia.

Uribe has said repeatedly that he chose to run for the unenviable office of the presidency out of strong feelings of patriotic duty, and it has to be said that if any country ever needed a savior, Colombia would seem to fill the bill. But the FARC and Carlos Castaño, too, feel compelled to do their patriotic duty by Colombia, as do certain sectors of the police and military forces who have often been accused in court or in human rights reports of collaborating with the AUC. Whether Colombians can survive such fervor is a real question. For the moment, it does not seem likely that Álvaro Uribe will be able to convince either the FARC leadership or the author of Colombia's best-selling autobiography that patriotism requires the warriors to let the country find its way without them.

POSTSCRIPT. Carlos Castaño was killed by his own men in 2004. It is reliably said that his brother Vicente Castaño ordered the murder. Vicente's whereabouts are unknown. Some say that he was killed by his own men too, others that he is still alive and living abroad under a new name.

NOTE

First published in the *New York Review of Books*, October 10, 2002. Reviewed: Mauricio Aranguren Molina, *Mi confesión: Carlos Castaño revela sus secretos* (Bogotá: Editorial Oveja Negra, 2001).

Claudia Andujar

Witness to the Yanomami's Last Struggle

APRIL 17, 2019

All that is overwhelming about public space in São Paulo, Brazil's business capital—the noise, the teeming crowds, the endless stream of cars and buses—is exacerbated on the Avenida Paulista, a stretch of concrete lined end to end with shiny glass office towers. The tropical noonday sun bounces off in splinters from the towers, the evening rush hour turns the avenue's wide sidewalks into a mob scene, and, in short, everything about this urban landscape seems to confirm one's suspicion that present-day capitalism shrivels or denatures everything it touches.

It is with a sense of prayerful relief, then, that a traveler might find herself in a quiet exhibition space several floors above the Paulista, wandering through a visual forest of images of the upper Amazon basin's first peoples—a retrospective of work by the Swiss-born émigré photographer Claudia Andujar, titled *A luta Yanomami* (The Yanomami struggle), mounted at the Moreira Salles cultural institute. Andujar began documenting the Yanomami in 1971. Her black-and-white photographs—suspended from the ceiling at eye level—form a composite portrait of the Yanomami people, once fierce in their independence and isolation but currently fighting for survival. In this white-walled enclosure one is free to contemplate the infinitely strange and elaborate lives of human beings who, in the first of two large rooms, are shown living on what we could consider absolutely nothing.

No clothes, for one thing. Men tie their foreskins with a bit of string and then knot it to a second string around the waist, so that the penis points jauntily upward at all times. Women don a necklace of tiny beads and the smallest of aprons. A little face paint, a palm reed through your septum, a feather or two, and you're ready for the day.

The Yanomami communities in these images live out their lives mostly inside an enormous *shabono* (sometimes also called a *maloca*), a thatched, circular enclosure that is at the same time home to an entire clan, and a symbolic representation of the universe. Families live in assigned sections of the *shabono* with a pot or two for cooking and one mesh hammock per person. There are a few extras: reed arrows and hollow tubes for blowing hallucinogenic snuff into one another's nostrils (used by men only); pots for preparing poison for the arrow tips, hallucinogens, and medicines of various sorts; stools for the elders.

In the early photographs, the various trinkets and goods brought in by missionaries and anthropologists—machetes, mirrors, radios, shorts—are not in evidence. The community's daily routine portrayed here involves a small amount of hunting by the men, who are happy when they can bring a large monkey or a peccary home for dinner. The women tend to the plantain and squash crops beyond the *shabono*, and cook.

Andujar's images of this group culture are attempts to translate the intense spiritual life of the community into visual language, and they are extremely beautiful. Young men look like angels, their hair adorned for a feast day with snow-white down plucked, if I am reading the splendid catalog correctly, from the chest of vultures. On a glittering river, the brown skin of young girls resembles velvet. At night, the many bonfires in a *shabono* are photographed from the outside, so that the light glints and winks through flimsy reed walls, and the whole thing looks like a new galaxy surrounded by other stars.

Through this haze of enchantment, though, an uncomfortable question is hard to avoid: Are the photographs revealing a magical and now lost world, an alternate turn in the long road of evolution that we failed to take, to our sorrow, or do they hide a nastier, brutish truth? It depends on your sources. The Yanomami—an anthropologists' designation for the various tribes and clans that live in a designated homeland along the border between northern Brazil and southern Venezuela—number some twenty-five thousand people today. They occupy 130,000 square miles of the Amazon jungle, part of which was ceded to the groups living in Venezuela in 1991, and the rest by Brazil in 1992.

FIGURE 7.1. Claudia Andujar, *Untitled*, 1976. Courtesy of Galeria Vermelho.

FIGURE 7.2. Claudia Andujar, *Untitled*, from the *Identity* series, 1972–76. Courtesy of Galeria Vermelho.

Famously, an anthropologist named Napoleon Chagnon wrote a book in 1968 in which he described the various Yanomami tribes as living in a state of "chronic warfare." According to Chagnon, the Yanomami world was a machismo-made hell: intertribal conflict broke out most frequently over women, who were scarce thanks to the custom of infanticide of girl babies at birth. Thus, according to Chagnon, the rape and abduction of women had evolved into the primary cause of intercommunal fighting: men who killed the most enemies had access to the greatest number of women and consequently produced the most offspring, meaning that their genes were distributed most widely. The tribes, Chagnon wrote, had an irritating habit of demanding gifts in an unsubtle and insistent way. The "burly, naked, filthy, hideous men" stank, and were made particularly unsightly due to the green mucus that trailed from their noses following a session with the snuff blowgun.

How true is this picture? Well, some of it, yes, and some of it, no. Never mind about the snot; Chagnon, who wrote in take-no-prisoners style, was attempting an anti–Margaret Mead, whose *Coming of Age in Samoa* (1928) had been criticized as romanticizing the natives. Her upstart challenger aimed for a just-the-facts approach, but a certain bias crept in. To begin with, Amazon people are small, averaging only about five feet—so hardly "burly." Further, anthropologists who had been living with the tribes for far longer than Chagnon reported that war between them was actually a rare occurrence. A *contre*-Chagnon was published by another anthropologist, R. Brian Ferguson, in 1995. This was followed by a ferocious attack from the pro–Indigenous peoples activist Patrick Tierney, who spent years investigating Chagnon's passage through the jungle and wrote a book about it in 2000.

One of Tierney's initial accusations—that a measles vaccination campaign co-sponsored by Chagnon might have contributed to a measles epidemic that devastated the Amazonian communities—has been discredited, but it is hard to argue with his claim that Chagnon's research methods altered the communities he studied in highly damaging ways. Tierney denounced, for example, Chagnon's reckless practice of distributing machetes and other valuable items as bribes so that tribal members would surrender taboo information to him.

The bitter argument over Tierney's book and Chagnon's work was actually about a number of things, including the sanctity of academic research and the concept of the primitive, but one question not addressed was why women like Margaret Mead saw things so differently from their male colleagues. Why do Claudia Andujar's photographs show a world in which fathers are gentle with their children, everyone bathes with pleasure in pools and rivers, and feast days are explosions of joy for men and women alike? Why did she write, through the decades, of feeling calm and complete—at *home*—when she was among the Yanomami? Perhaps she, and Mead, were sentimental. Perhaps she approached her subjects differently and saw things others did not. She may have felt, also, that it was better not to publish anything negative about a fragile people so brutally under attack.

ANDUJAR WAS BORN Claudine Haas in Neuchâtel in 1931 into a strict family; her father, a prosperous factory owner, was Jewish; her mother was Protestant. Although her father and much of his side of the family died in Dachau and Auschwitz, Claudine was able to emigrate and went to live in New York with an uncle. While Claudine, now Claudia, met, married, and divorced a young Spanish immigrant, Julio Andujar, graduated from Hunter College, and took up painting, her adventurous mother went to live in Brazil with her Romanian fiancé. In 1955, Claudia went to visit her there and ended up staying forever.

A year into her new life in São Paulo, Andujar had become a professional photographer, taking pictures of the Karajá peoples in north-central Brazil. By the time she traveled to a Catholic mission in the heart of Yanomami territory, she had been crisscrossing Brazil and taking photographs of Indigenous communities for Brazilian publications for nearly fifteen years.

The people who appear in the second section of Andujar's retrospective, a floor below the first, are wearing clothes: filthy T-shirts or ripped shorts, rarely both. Flip-flops, sunglasses, sometimes a bra for the women, who are more often exposed in ways that don't seem right.

The photographer arrived in Yanomami territory at the precise moment when Brazil's military dictatorship, true to its motto of "Ordem e progresso" (order and progress), was driving a highway straight through the Amazon, in the hopes of making the jungle an agricultural Eden for landless immigrants from the rest of Brazil. That road remains unfinished forty-five years later, and there is no Eden. Instead, the opening of the Amazon brought lumberjacks, gold miners, bounty hunters, construction equipment operators, tavernkeepers, and land robbers, all of them vectors carrying diseases that would course through the Yanomami territory and leave it rich with corpses, suspended, according to the peoples' religious custom, in rope cages in the forest canopy.

There is only one image of an "air burial" in the exhibit, and one would never know what it is simply from looking at it. Nevertheless, it is right that this second section of the exhibit is staged a stairway down from the first because it describes a descent into the hell of modernization that has awaited all tribal peoples, from New Zealand to the Amazon. The tour presented here offers a familiarly bleak perspective, even if Andujar chose long ago to leave out the worst images of disease and death.

The cultural dislocation and physical suffering Andujar witnessed shocked her so, and appear to have put her so in mind of the genocide in Europe, that by the 1980s photography became a secondary concern for her. Together with a group of doctors, she started a health services and vaccination campaign in Yanomami lands. With the anthropologist Bruce Albert, Carlo Zacquini, a Catholic missionary and friend, and the Yanomami shaman, translator, and Indigenous rights crusader Davi Kopenawa, Andujar campaigned relentlessly for a designated homeland for the people she had come to love. It is thanks to her and her fellow activists that the Yanomami Indigenous Territory exists today. By protecting the Yanomami, it has also protected, thus far, the countless creatures and remarkable ecology of that small corner of the Amazon.

Now eighty-seven, Andujar is suffering from the effects of a rugged life. Malaria took its toll on her, but she also now suffers from arthritis and other ills. Even so, by means of a chartered flight, she managed to visit the Yanomami territories as recently as 2017, traveling two hours down a jungle path in a wheelchair pushed by her old friend Zacquini. She is unquestionably a woman of heroic stripe. Yet Chagnon was not wholly wrong in his observations about the role of violence in Yanomami culture, so one wonders whether Andujar failed to see, or decided to give no account of, the situation of the women, who, according to plentiful testimony, were indeed often subject to culturally approved rape, abduction, and abuse. Perhaps she took the ill-treatment of women for granted, as most people once did. In any case, one gleans from a book cowritten by Albert and Kopenawa that the source of violence among the Yanomami was most often generations-long feuds, which could start with some incident of disrespect to an elder or an ancestor, or calling someone by their forbidden name.

IN MANY RESPECTS, the old debates about identity and primitivism, once fought with so much passion, have run out of time, along with most of the tribal peoples that gave rise to such controversies. Even among the most delusionary romantics, it has long been understood that Aboriginal culture will inevitably vanish. The question has always been how traumatic change will come to isolated or uncontacted tribes and how much control these peoples will have over their transition to modern capitalist society—to what degree they will be able to decide what they want to retain of their culture and how to incorporate the new.

It is for this agency that Davi Kopenawa, Claudia Andujar, and Bruce Albert have fought over long decades. But Brazil's reactionary new president, Jair Bolsonaro, has brushed aside all such discussions. The areas of wilderness reserved for Native tribes have been one of Brazil's significant achievements, but these territories face constant pressure from an assortment of profiteers of all kinds, including agribusiness and big oil. "There is no Indigenous territory where there aren't minerals," Bolsonaro said in an interview last year, campaigning on a promise of no new land for Indians. "Gold, tin, and magnesium are in these lands, especially in the Amazon, the richest area in the world. I'm not getting into this nonsense of defending land for Indians." On taking power, he delivered the responsibility for Indigenous affairs to the Agriculture Ministry. Since his election, countless small budget cuts have destabilized the Yanomami's subsistence economy.

Of course, the Yanomami are not the only ones under threat from the new regime: we all are. The Amazon currently loses nearly three thousand square miles of jungle forest every year. It is terrifying to contemplate the impact that Bolsonaro's assault on the area will have on climate change over the next four years of his presidential term.

"In a very real sense, the damage Bolsonaro will do to the environment, he has already done," a Brazilian friend told me recently. Beyond the legislation turning over the Amazon and its Indigenous communities to the Agriculture Ministry, beyond the spending cuts and hostile decrees, beyond whatever legal predations are to follow, there is a new sense that any landowner or industrialist who feels like shooting an Indian or two, or clearing a few thousand acres for cattle ranching, may do so with impunity. Policing the Amazon demands enormous sums of money and unwavering political commitment. Under Bolsonaro, it's as though all the security cameras have been turned off.

A struggle for survival that has lasted half a millennium may be about to end: some of the last people on earth who look at the world and see a wondrously different reality from the one we perceive are all but defenseless under this new president. And it could be that soon all that will remain of their presence on this earth will be Claudia Andujar's glorious photographs.

NOTE

First published in the *New York Review of Books*, April 17, 2019. The exhibition *Claudia Andujar: A luta Yanomami* (Claudia Andujar: The Yanomami struggle) was at the Instituto Moreira Salles, São Paulo (IMS Paulista), from December 2018 through April 2019, and at the IMS Rio, Rio de Janeiro, from July 20 to November 7, 2019. The exhibition toured to the Fondation Cartier pour l'art contemporain, Paris, December 13, 2019, through May 24, 2020.

Works referenced: Napoleon A. Chagnon, *Yąnomamö, the Fierce People* (New York: Holt, Rinehart and Winston, 1968); R. Brian Ferguson, *Yanomami Warfare: A Political History* (Santa Fe, NM: School of American Research Press, 1995); Margaret Mead, *Coming of Age in Samoa: A Psychological Study of Primitive Youth for Western Civilization* (New York: William Morrow, 1928); Patrick Tierney, *Darkness in El Dorado: How Scientists and Journalists Devastated the Amazon* (New York: W. W. Norton, 2000).

Part II

———

Central America

8

Nicaragua's Dreadful Duumvirate

DECEMBER 16, 2021

Sergio Ramírez, the illustrious historian, novelist, and former vice president of Nicaragua, could well have been among his unfortunate friends and many other members of the opposition arrested by the regime of President Daniel Ortega and his weird wife and vice president, Rosario Murillo, beginning in June. But in view of the fate of their friends and colleagues, Ramírez and his wife, Tulita, decided to leave Nicaragua. It was a wise move: in September, Ramírez learned that he stands accused of money laundering and "provocation, proposition, and conspiracy."

Ramírez is seventy-nine, and it is a cruel fate for someone who loves and has served his country as consistently as he has to know that he may never see it again, or his imprisoned friends, or his beloved writing desk and its surrounding walls of books. On the other hand, all experience is fodder to a writer, and Ramírez's rich array of novels and historical essays—sixty years of ceaseless production—is a tribute to the tragic and absurd history of his beautiful homeland. Nicaraguans survive their lot with a trickster's sense of humor, and Ramírez's latest novel, *Tongolele no sabía bailar* ("Tongolele had no rhythm" might be the best translation of a title as clumsy as its protagonist), is a grim, wildly funny, surrealistic account of the grievous events of the spring of 2018, when student protests broke out in Managua and other cities around the country, and the repression served up by Ortega and Murillo left three hundred dead.

Ramírez tells the story through the character of Detective Dolores Morales, who was severely wounded in the fight to overthrow the dictator Anastasio Somoza back in the 1970s and wears a leg prosthesis as a result. The book's other characters, however—all portrayed with swift dialogue and the author's unerring ear for the sweet and extravagant Spanish of Nicaragua, with its sixteenth-century *thees* and *thous* and wild similes, and its joyful use of vulgarity whenever the occasion demands—are the most fascinating. They include Tongolele, a top intelligence officer working in the darkest corners of the government; a mild-mannered and heroic country priest; a startling woman who runs all the itinerant salesmen and -women in the country, with a sideline gathering intelligence for Tongolele; and a mystical spiritual adviser to someone referred to only as *la compañera*. That someone would be Vice President Murillo, and though she is never seen or even named in the novel, Ramírez avails himself of the opportunity to trample merrily all over her shadow.

The novel's account of the events of May 2018 is accurate, but it is when Ramírez's narrative invention runs wildest that his portrayal of Nicaragua under the thumb of the improbable Ortega–Murillo duumvirate is most truthful. Because he was vice president or the equivalent for the first ten years of the Sandinista regime, Ramírez has intimate knowledge of Ortega and his associates in the underworld of power as well as of everyday *Nica* life. Non-Nicaraguans, though, might benefit from a decoder.

Ortega, seventy-six, loves to use the insult *vendepatria*—fatherland seller—but he once agreed to sell the rights to a 278-kilometer-long strip of Nicaragua running from the Atlantic to the Pacific to a shadowy Chinese businessman who intended to build a canal parallel to and competitive with the one in Panama. Murillo, seventy, keeps meticulous track of every offense or snub she has ever suffered and communes with spirits who let her know who her hidden enemies are. Police and army battalions being insufficient to hold all the couple's adversaries at bay, paramilitary groups are now deployed against peaceful demonstrators. Murillo had colorful curlicue metal silhouettes of trees installed all over Managua to channel positive energy from the skies. Strong evidence would indicate that Ortega is a pedophile and a rapist. Together, the doddering couple have created what Monsignor Silvio Báez, the auxiliary bishop of

Managua (currently in exile), has called "a situation of . . . irrationality, violence and evil that surpasses the imagination."

Who are these people? How did they get where they are? And why, after forty-two years of Sandinismo, are they still around?

YOU COULD SAY that Ortega's real life began in prison. He was the son of an itinerant father, a barrio kid who together with his buddies joined the Frente Sandinista de Liberación Nacional (FSLN, Sandinista National Liberation Front)—a tiny organization back then—as a fundraising unit: the group held up stores and banks. He was first briefly jailed and tortured at the age of fifteen, then jailed in Guatemala and subjected to even greater abuse a year later, jailed again in Nicaragua, and then freed under a general amnesty. In 1967, at the age of twenty-two, he was given a fourteen-year sentence for bank robbery that ended seven years early, when his guerrilla comrades rounded up a few hostages at a dinner party and exchanged them for him and thirteen other prisoners. The handful of poems Ortega published long ago mostly center on his prison life, and they are stark. "If you feed me you can fuck me / Three cigarettes gets you a blow job," one begins. In another, he depicts the episodes of torture that prison authorities practiced on him almost recreationally: "Kick him / like that, like that, in the balls, the face / the ribs. / Get the cattleprod, the bullwhip / talk / son of a whore / talk."

In a perceptive and thorough biography, *El Preso 198* (Prisoner 198), the journalist Fabián Medina Sánchez makes the case that Ortega has never really moved out of a prison cell. He quotes a *Playboy* interview from 1987, in which Ortega describes how uncomfortable he was when he was released in 1974 and sent to Cuba, free to go wherever he pleased, and how, during a brief time back in Nicaragua in 1976, he discovered that he was actually much more relaxed in clandestinity, locked up in one room in a safe house, working in his underwear in the steaming Managua heat, meeting with the members of the Sandinista urban network, and coordinating communication with guerrillas in the mountains. Medina tells us that after the Sandinista triumph in 1979 Ortega had a small room built in his new, expansive house, with a small window covered by a curtain and a hammock suspended in it, prison style, where he would spend much of his time. He ordered a similar, though windowless, room constructed for him in the bank building that initially served as the new government's headquarters.

Ramírez, who as Ortega's vice president from 1985 to 1990 essentially administered the country, confirmed this in a conversation and added that whenever he stopped to pick up Ortega on the way to some early event, he was struck by the fact that Ortega would never sit down for breakfast but ate hurriedly while standing, and was never partial to anything other than the typical Nicaraguan rice and beans, tortillas, cheese, and black coffee. Better-quality ingredients than the gunk ladled out in prison, but a meal not unlike the one that would be on the prison menu.

Ortega has a younger brother, Humberto, who is articulate, ambitious, and very smart. Long ago, he mentioned to me in passing—I am paraphrasing, but not by a lot—that every family has a son who is audacious and *destacado* (stands out more), and another who is . . . not so much. Humberto has buckets more personality than his brother, which isn't hard, considering that Daniel is as memorable as your average mop, and there is consensus among knowledgeable former Sandinistas I recently interviewed in Costa Rica that in 1978 the idea of bringing their scant guerrilla forces down from the mountains, where they had been circling for years, and into the cities, where they could spark a political movement against the dictator Somoza, was indeed Humberto's, if you don't count the constant backseat coaching by Fidel Castro.

Why, then, is Daniel president and not Humberto? Because, it is said, the struggle for power among Humberto and the other top two guerrilla leaders would have broken the FSLN, and it was reluctantly agreed to accept Humberto's suggestion to put unthreatening Daniel in the highest position, first as a member of a transitional FSLN-civilian junta, in which Ramírez was the top civilian representative, and then as the triumphant Sandinista presidential candidate in 1984. But we are getting ahead of our story, because we have to describe Daniel's momentous meeting with his future wife and vice president, Rosario.

MUCH LIKE NICARAGUA'S history, which is to a striking degree the history of the same six or so last names, family traumas tend to run in loops. In addition to its account of the life and times of Ortega, Medina's *El Preso 198* provides an informative chapter on his wife. In 1967, he tells us, Murillo, a lively, rebellious sixteen-year-old, gave birth in Managua to a little girl. At the hospital, her mother immediately took the baby away. A firm believer in spiritism, addicted to the Ouija board, she did not let Murillo nurse the child even once, convinced that her milk carried sinister humors. Instead, she turned the young woman out of the house, forcing her to marry the unwilling, clueless, and equally young father. The unhappy couple had one more child before the father died, allegedly of a drug overdose, in 1968.

Meanwhile, the grandmother had baptized the first baby with her own name: Zoilamérica. We can usefully compress some history here by explaining the name. It is pronounced identically to the words "Soy la América" (I am America)—America not in the sense of "United States" but in the sense of Latin America and the hemisphere—and it was a highly political name when it came into fashion a hundred years or so ago, expressing rejection of the US Marines who occupied Nicaragua from 1912 to 1933. It also implied admiration for Augusto César Sandino, who led a guerrilla war against the occupiers and was assassinated by the head of the National Guard, Anastasio Somoza García. Somoza went on to found a family dictatorship in 1937. The guerrillas who overthrew the last Anastasio Somoza in 1979 took the name of the hero Sandino for their movement. Sandino was an uncle of the matriarch Zoilamérica, and so the name was worn with extra pride.

Murillo grew into an adventurous adult. She married a second time; became involved in poetry groups; scandalized her mother by going to parties where marijuana was smoked; recovered her two children, Zoilamérica and Rafael Antonio, after her mother's death; was hired as the secretary to the publisher and principal editor of the venerable opposition newspaper *La Prensa*; joined the underground support structure of the FSLN; got divorced; published a first, slender book of poems (Mexicans sing rancheras, Nicaraguans write poems); married a third time, to a midlevel Sandinista named Carlos Vicente Ibarra; and, while pregnant, fled the country with her new husband at a particularly brutal moment of Somocista repression. Their first stop was Caracas, both of them convinced that they were done with politics and wanted only to study filmmaking in Paris and make movies. Murillo was wandering among the various exhibits and portraits in the house where the hero of Latin American independence, Simón Bolívar, was born, when she bumped into a fellow Nicaraguan with whom she had corresponded while he was in prison, a stolid man in thick square-framed glasses: Daniel Ortega. According to Murillo, she was instantly struck by "his skinniness, his magnetism that was for me electrifying."

For his part, Ortega later said that, as a man of few words, "I'm more about action. There is a communication that is stronger and more profound that is with the eyes." Shortly after locking eyes with Murillo and, presumably, renewing her commitment to Sandinismo, Ortega was appointed the FSLN spokesman abroad, based in Costa Rica. Not long after that, the heavily pregnant Murillo arrived in San José with her husband and children. Ibarra was quickly sent to Cuba to study film, and Ortega and Murillo moved in together, hungry exiles of scarce means and great revolutionary fervor who lived almost in hiding even abroad.

Dramatic events marked the couple's tumultuous life. Murillo's former boss at *La Prensa*, Pedro Joaquín Chamorro, whose ancestors included four presidents of Nicaragua, had participated in armed expeditions against the first Somoza and served time in the second Somoza's monstrous prisons. A highly visible figure, he was assassinated on the third Somoza's orders in January 1978, which sparked a brief, unprecedented popular rebellion.

In August of that year, a second rebellion began, in which the remarkable Dora María Téllez, then twenty-two, was Comandante Dos, or Commander Two. Led by Edén Pastora, Commander Zero, twenty-five guerrillas dressed in army uniforms drove two trucks up to a building popularly known as the Pigsty but more formally as the National Palace, where both the Senate and Chamber of Deputies were housed. "[Our] truck was supposed to be olive green but we couldn't find the right paint, so we painted it parrot green instead," Téllez recalled when I interviewed her a year later. By the time the security forces realized they had not been paying enough attention to the nuances of green, the guerrillas controlled all the strategic posts in the building and had taken some two thousand people hostage.

There was something about Pastora's dashing air, Téllez's youth, and the nose- thumbing chutzpah of the takeover that instantly brought the Sandinistas worldwide attention and earned them a passionate international following. The guerrillas kept a couple dozen hostages to bargain with and designated Téllez—currently being held in one of Ortega's prisons—their chief negotiator: two days later, Somoza agreed to the ransom amount and released fifty-nine Sandinista prisoners. Guerrillas, freed prisoners, and a handful of hostages traveled in a sunny yellow school bus to the airport, where they boarded a plane to Cuba. But along the way, both Somoza and his challengers got a big surprise: the road was lined with thousands of cheering Managuans, most of them visibly poor, all of them experiencing a brand-new kind of laughter: *los muchachos*—the kids—had played such a great trick on that old Somoza bastard! Sandinista recruitment climbed to near-unmanageable levels in the following months as the insurrection spread throughout Nicaragua.

In July 1979, Somoza fled the country. The Sandinista leadership converged in Managua, shocked at the speed of their triumph. They were, for the most part, terribly young, barely educated—like Ortega, many of them had cut their studies short in order to take up arms against Somoza—and dependent on Castro for counsel on every issue. They failed to realize a crucial law of politics: you can voluntarily cede power, but there's no asking for it back. And so Daniel Ortega was appointed to a civilian-Sandinista transitional junta and set on his way to becoming the most powerful man in the land. With Murillo and her three children, whom he eventually adopted, he moved into a luxurious house confiscated from one of the wealthiest men in Nicaragua. Throughout Managua there was a hunt by guerrillas looking for houses to confiscate and move into, the fancier the better. Where else, they may well have thought, were winners supposed to live? Conceivably not in the fleeing oligarchy's houses.

IT'S HARD TO know if by the time she set up housekeeping in her new domain, Murillo was already aware that her husband had made a habit of sneaking into the room where her oldest daughter, Zoilamérica, then eleven, was sleeping. It took years of abuse—variously condoned or ignored by her mother, she told me in an interview—before she felt strong enough to denounce her abuser in public. At last, on March 2, 1998, Zoilamérica, a tall, slender, visibly nervous thirty-year-old with a degree in sociology, sat down in front of a crowd of reporters and announced that the president of Nicaragua, Daniel Ortega, her stepfather, was a rapist:

> From the age of eleven I was sexually abused . . . [by the president] repeatedly and for many years. . . . Recovering from the effects of this long aggression, with the accompanying sexual assault, threats, harassment, blackmail, has not been easy.

In a painfully detailed forty-page court deposition, given ten weeks after the press conference, Zoilamérica related, among other things, that in Costa Rica, when she was small, Ortega would creep into the room she shared with her little brother and grope her while she lay frozen, pretending in shame and horror to be asleep. Later, in Managua, Ortega's sexual predation continued in the privacy made possible by their new house's many rooms. Zoilamérica was given her own room, where he could fondle her in relative isolation. She was forced to spend many hours in the windowless room in his office. He spied on her through the keyhole when she was in the bathroom, then took to walking straight in. Eventually, she wrote, Ortega "no longer simply watched me as I bathed; he would . . . masturbate. It was horrible at that age to see a man leaning against a wall for balance and shaking his sex as if lost, unconscious even of himself."

In time, Zoilamérica reached puberty. Ortega walked into her room one night, examined her, said, "Ya estás lista" (You're ready), and raped her.

In the first of Sergio Ramírez's Detective Morales novels, there is a hidden detail. It's tiny, but Nicaraguan readers knew why it was there: Morales spots a truck driven by an older man who is enthusiastically telling a story to a little girl in the passenger seat. She listens with her eyes fixed solemnly on the road. A grandfather and his grandchild, Morales thinks in a rare sentimental moment. Then he sees the truck drive into a sex motel. The second Morales novel hinges on the story of a young woman who since childhood has been raped by her stepfather, a powerful businessman.

Zoilamérica's case against Ortega went nowhere: one of the many judges with whom he had filled the judicial system ruled that the statute of limitations on his alleged crimes had run out. The Inter-American Commission on Human Rights ended up recommending that the dispute be resolved between the parties involved. Public reaction would have been different if Murillo had come out in defense of her daughter, but instead, Zoilamérica says, her mother had fits of jealousy, accused her of seducing her stepfather, ran her out of the house just as her own mother had thrown her out, and then, when the scandal finally broke, stood weeping and sniffling beside Ortega while he told a crowd, "Rosario said to me that she wants to apologize to the pueblo for having given birth to a daughter who betrayed the principles of Sandinismo."

Afterward the couple's physical transformation began. Murillo used to dress normally but with a certain snap, an occasional extravagance. Today we have the Murillo of the crazy makeup, the pink or turquoise Indian-style dress, and the dozens of good-vibration-channeling rings, bracelets, necklaces, and earrings she arms herself with every day. She consults the spirit of Augusto César Sandino's brother on a regular basis (why, one wonders, is she not allowed to commune with the great hero himself?) and paces about lighting incense sticks in a house filled with plaster cherubim and images of the Buddha. In her fluty voice, she swerves from preaching peace and love, as the spirit of Sai Baba, her Indian spiritual master, demands, to denouncing

> those diminished brains that work . . . receiving messages . . . from other galaxies, really, from other planets, that supposedly come to elevate their fatherland-lacking condition. . . . the abject condition of people who do not know love for the fatherland and are waiting for the spaceships to activate their diminished brains.

THE SCANDAL OF Ortega's systematic rape of his stepdaughter subsided, but its poison continues to seep through Nicaragua's history because it forced Sandinistas at every level to believe yet more lies from their leaders: they did not engage in small or large acts of corruption; they were really democrats at heart, or they were really socialists at heart; the majority of the population really loved them; and of course Zoilamérica was lying. (Even though, as a canny Nicaraguan journalist observed, in the anything-goes promiscuity that followed the Sandinistas' victory, it was generally assumed among his inner circle that Ortega's good-looking stepdaughter, all grown up, was in fact his mistress: "What shocked everyone was her revelation that he was also a pedophile.")

Throughout the long years of Zoilamérica's abuse (she was divorced with two children by the time she went public with her accusation, in an attempt to stop Ortega's unremitting pursuit), Nicaraguan politics unfolded in their circular way. In 1990, Ortega was defeated at the polls by the fifth Chamorro to become president: Violeta Chamorro, a straight-backed, pious homemaker and widow of the assassinated editor Pedro Joaquín Chamorro. Jimmy Carter, among others, persuaded Ortega and the Sandinista party leadership to recognize Doña Violeta's victory. Five years later, Sergio Ramírez, Ortega's former vice president, resigned from the party and founded an opposition movement with other dissident Sandinistas, while Ortega spent the next seventeen years attempting to get the presidency back.

Fabián Medina reminds us that Ortega succeeded thanks to some skillful constitutional meddling that allowed candidates to win with as little as 35 percent of the vote. With further wrangling, Ortega returned to power in 2007 with 38.07 percent of the vote and has been president ever since. His corrupt and dictatorial brand of Sandinismo has destroyed the movement's proudest achievements. The stubborn journalist Carlos Fernando Chamorro—a former Sandinista, son of Doña Violeta and Pedro Joaquín, and founder and editor of the invaluable online magazine *Confidencial*—put it succinctly:

> Ortega reestablished electoral fraud as a practice, outlawed and repressed the opposition, and established a monopoly over the estates— the Supreme Court, the electoral authority, and the Office of the Comptroller—transferring the one-time jewels of the democratic transition, the Armed Forces and the Police, to the political control . . . of the presidential couple.

There is no way of knowing whether Carlos Fernando Chamorro's older sister Cristiana, one of Ortega's potential opponents, would have been elected president on November 7 if she had not been under house arrest since June. But the ruling couple, with a network of spying "people's associations" and top-notch private pollsters at their command, must have thought in panic that

Chamorro's victory was indeed likely, or they would not have risked the international opprobrium and renewed sanctions that inevitably followed the move against her—the might-have-been sixth Chamorro family president of Nicaragua—and the equally outrageous imprisonment of six other candidates who might have run against Ortega and honorary co-president Rosario Murillo. (Ortega promoted her from her previous position as vice president just before the election.)

However that may be, elections in Nicaragua came and went, and nothing happened that was not foreseen: Ortega and Murillo remain in power despite an estimated 40 to 80 percent abstention rate, depending on who's counting. With the help of judges who do the couple's bidding, their victory was certified as fair, even though the seven arrested would-be candidates have not been freed, nor have the dozens of other activists, opposition leaders, lawyers, journalists, and ordinary citizens rounded up since June. Most of the prisoners are elderly, and several are being held under appalling conditions of hunger and psychological torture.

But the so-called elections are an unimportant chapter in this dispiriting telenovela. What matters is what happens next. Can renewed or stiffer international sanctions accomplish anything more than increasing the privations of the impoverished citizenry? Has the terrible Ortega–Murillo assassination spree against students and campesino leaders in 2018 permanently terrified the population into despair or indifference? Will the plump and satisfied business sector—so recently the regime's greatest ally—rebel now that police have jailed two of its most important representatives? Nicaraguans at home and in exile are anxiously waiting to find out. Perhaps nothing will happen. Perhaps, in history's unpredictable way of jostling itself awake and taking off at a canter, some enormous change will come to ease the suffering of that troubled land.

POSTSCRIPT. In February 2023, following an intense negotiation with the Joe Biden administration, the Ortega–Murillo duumvirate ordered the release of 222 political prisoners, who, without knowing where they were going or why, were put on a plane that landed in Washington, DC. They included Dora María Téllez. The Catholic bishop of Matagalpa, Rolando Álvarez, who chose to remain in jail in solidarity with the remaining prisoners, was promptly sentenced to twenty-six years and deprived of his "citizens' rights for all time." In January 2024, he was released and exiled to the Vatican City. Some prisoners' relatives, who had earlier had their passports confiscated by the government—some are mortally ill—have not been able to leave the country to seek treatment or see their loved ones now in exile. Shortly after the prisoners' release, a government decree canceled their citizenship and that of many others who had been forced to flee their country to avoid imprisonment. Subsequently, the houses and other property of the opposition have been confiscated. Sergio Ramírez, the esteemed novelist and former vice president of Nicaragua, had his citizenship canceled along with his pension. His house, too, was confiscated. A few days later, a communiqué announced that his law degree was "annulled," whatever that term means or implies. Traditional Catholic processions and festivities are now forbidden.

Perhaps no event has been as shocking as the death of Humberto Ortega, brother to Daniel and the real commander in charge of the insurrection that overthrew the dictator Anastasio Somoza. He died on September 30, 2024, after three months as a prisoner of the Nicaraguan state. Four months earlier, he had given a rare interview to the Argentine news site *Infobae*, doubtless trusting that his relationship to his brother would protect him from his loathed sister-in-law. Boldly, he declared that Daniel would have no natural successor; in other words, neither Rosario Murillo nor his nephews and nieces were qualified to take Daniel's place. Police surrounded his home soon after the interview went online and kept him under house arrest, despite a serious heart condition. He is believed to have suffered a massive stroke on June 12, and was rushed to a military hospital, where he died a prisoner of the regime he had helped bring about.

NOTE

First published in the *New York Review of Books*, December 16, 2021.

Works referenced: Fabián Medina Sánchez, *El Preso 198: Un perfil de Daniel Ortega* ([Nicaragua]: La Prensa 2018); Sergio Ramírez, *Tongolele no sabía bailar* (Barcelona: Alfaguara, 2021).

Death Comes for the Archbishop

MAY 27, 2010

I was in Managua, Nicaragua, thirty years ago, recovering from dengue fever, when my editor at the *Guardian* called from London to say that I should get on the next plane to San Salvador: the archbishop of El Salvador had been gunned down while saying Mass. I remember laughing at the impossibility of this too literary story—murder in the cathedral; of course it wasn't true!—and then feeling sick. Óscar Arnulfo Romero, a self-effacing, not particularly articulate, stubborn man, who insisted every day on decrying the violence and terror that ruled his country, was, after all, the hierarch of the Catholic Church in El Salvador. Did he not have all the weight of the Vatican behind him and the natural respect of even the most right-wing zealot for such a holy office? And then there was the act itself: murder at the most sacred moment of the Catholic Mass. Who, in such a Catholic country, would dare to violate the transubstantiation of Christ's body?

But of course the story was true. Around 6:30 p.m. on Monday, March 24, 1980, a red Volkswagen Passat drove up to the small, graceful chapel of the Divina Providencia Hospital, a center run by Carmelite nuns where Romero lived. It was, as it almost always is in San Salvador, a hot day, and the wing-shaped chapel's doors were open. As Romero stood at the altar just after the homily, a tall, thin bearded man in the back seat of the Volkswagen raised an assault rifle and fired a single .22 bullet into the archbishop's heart. Then, in no particular hurry, the car drove away. A grainy black-and-white photograph from that day shows the victim on the floor. As Romero's heart pumps out the last of its blood, the white-coiffed nuns gather around him like the points of a star, or like the figures at the feet of Christ in Renaissance murals, which were intended simultaneously as representations and as prayers.

Historical turning points are so often the result of stupidity. The Sandinista Revolution, which had triumphed in Nicaragua barely eight months before, had set the dream of revolution flaring across Central America. But Romero's murder and the mayhem and bloodshed set off by a sharpshooter at his funeral the following Saturday were perhaps the immediate sparks for the bloody twelve-year civil war that started in El Salvador just months later and killed some seventy thousand Salvadorans, with the United States providing financial and military backing to the government side. It is hard to overstate how fervently the campesinos of El Salvador believed in Romero and what became known as the Liberation Church. When he was gone, entire villages placed themselves at the disposal of the guerrilla factions, which came together as a united front, the Frente Farabundo Martí para la Liberación Nacional (FMLN, Farabundo Martí National Liberation Front), a few months later.

THE ARCHBISHOP MADE a long journey to arrive at his death. During the 1960s and 1970s, an assortment of guerrilla groups had attempted to stir poor Salvadorans to revolution, managing only to recruit university students and a smattering of the impoverished working class. Around that same time, a great many Catholic nuns and priests, including foreign missionaries, became increasingly radicalized and sympathetic, or even linked to, the guerrilla organizations. By all accounts, the studious Romero was not among them. He was not even attracted to the tenets of what became known as Liberation Theology, the "preferential option for the poor."

Hardworking and conscientious, he rose through the ranks and eventually became bishop of the rural province of San Miguel, maintaining all the while a strict distance from what he called the left's "mystique of violence." By then, however, the insistent defense of human rights by the new generation of radicalized priests and nuns, and the murderous government's determination to violate those rights, particularly in the case of the landless peasantry, had created a small army of conscripts for the guerrilla organizations, which promised an equal and just world order born of socialist revolution.

During the presidency of General Arturo Molina (1972–77), the army and security forces were essentially transformed into death squads: Romero watched in horror as campesinos in his parish were displaced, threatened, terrorized, and increasingly shot, stabbed, or hacked to death by underfed, underage soldiers wielding machetes against their own kind. He began speaking out against these atrocities and received his first death threat (from General Molina himself, who wagged a finger at him and warned that cassocks were not bulletproof). And then, in 1977, just weeks after Romero had been ordained archbishop, the Jesuit priest Rutilio Grande, a close friend of Romero's who had been organizing landless peasants, was shot down on a country road along with two of his parishioners.

All Romero's contradictory feelings about church and duty, repression and human dignity, his native distrust of radicalism and politics, his caution and, no doubt, his fear appear to have resolved themselves at that moment. With the same methodical determination that seems to have characterized his rise to the archbishopric, he spent the next three years organizing human rights watchdog groups, asking President Jimmy Carter to suspend military aid to the murderous junta, and speaking out—plainly, but never unreasonably— against the government. "It is sad to read that in El Salvador the two main causes of death are first diarrhea, and second murder," he would say. "Therefore, right after the result of malnourishment, diarrhea, we have the result of crime, murder. These are the two epidemics that are killing off our people."

Those were the days before the internet or even faxes, and the lone opposition newspapers, *El Independiente* and *La Cronica del Pueblo*, were more or less gagged. (The publisher and editor of *El Independiente*, Jorge Pinto, survived three assassination attempts before going into exile.) The murders and disappearances carried out by death squads, army officers, and a notorious security force called, for inexplicable reasons, the Treasury Police were unreported, but Romero took to reading detailed accounts of the week's brutalities—the dozens of cases of torture and murder of peasants that were by then taking place every day— during his Sunday homilies. The sermons were broadcast by the Catholic radio station, and campesinos all over the country gathered around radios to listen to them. So did the military.

The once conservative archbishop, who had been trained and nurtured not in his homeland but in Rome, became the government's most visible opponent. Later he would say that when he saw the corpse of Father Rutilio Grande a few hours after his murder, he thought, "If they have killed him for doing what he did, then I too have to walk the same path."

I HAD A FIRST understanding of the Catholic Church's relationship with poor Salvadorans one Sunday in 1978. César Jerez, who was then the superior of the Jesuit Order in Central America, suggested that I travel over back roads to a village deep in the craggy hills of Cabañas province. The Church had been organizing there for years, creating "Christian Base Communities" in which villagers learned to read, studied the Bible, and gradually became aware of their rights. But this was not all; the priests—and, on a smaller scale, the female religious—organized schools, soccer teams, and infirmaries. They set up scholarships in the cities for talented students. They heard everyone's confession. And they taught, according to the tenets of Liberation Theology, that poor peasants like themselves deserved to inherit God's kingdom right here on this earth. In response to this wave of radical activism, the government and the ruling families of El Salvador set up a peasant paramilitary force called Organización Democrática Nacionalista (ORDEN, National Democratic Organization), which worked hand in hand with the Treasury Police.

On my first trip to Cabañas, Father Jerez had provided me with a guide—a young Christian activist—and with him I listened and asked questions in whispers as the villagers snuck into a mud-wattle house where we were hiding. The ORDEN snitches, who were members of their own communities, were all around us, they warned, and they were risking their lives by talking to us. One by one, the victims told the stories of how the killers had taken away one woman's son and slit his throat, and of how another woman had found her husband in a ditch, "chopped into little bits" by the machetes of the killers, so that she could not even bury his body whole. Finally, they produced statements—this was the Jesuit influence at its most distinctive—meticulously written out in pencil, in which they detailed the date and time of each attack and listed the treasures that "los ORDEN" had pillaged from them. "I was robbed," a typical statement would say, "of a dozen oranges and four candles. And they cut up the ropes of my cot, so that I have no bed."

I made many trips to the countryside after this one (I remember seeing men tie themselves to trees, so that they could farm the miserable patch of land they had inherited without tumbling down a mountainside's steep incline). But it was only two years later, after Romero's funeral had dissolved into grim chaos, that I had my first real understanding of the feudal ignorance in which Salvadoran campesinos were kept. As red-robed cardinals from abroad milled around the vast unfinished cathedral together with humble worshipers who had lost their shoes, their false teeth, their satchels, or their eyeglasses in the stampede to escape from a sniper's bullets, everyone trying to understand what had happened and why, a tiny, trembling man approached my friend the photographer Pedro Valtierra. "Please, my daughter's lost," he said, and then he repeated several times, until we understood: "Please use your loudspeaker to call out her name." He was pointing to Valtierra's camera.

THANKS TO AN EXTRAORDINARY piece of reportage posted last month on the Salvadoran online newspaper *El Faro*, we know that the tall, skinny shooter who killed Romero was contracted by General Arturo Molina's son, while the weapon and the getaway car were provided by the drinking buddies and death squad associates of a former army major called Roberto D'Aubuisson. Not that anyone doubted from the moment it happened that the murder was D'Aubuisson's work. He died of cancer of the esophagus at the age of forty-seven in 1992, but while he lived, this slender, charismatic psychopath was king. Although he was briefly arrested, he was never tried for murder and soon rose to become the head of the Constituent Assembly; he was defeated only narrowly when he ran for president in 1984. Until last year, the party he founded, which had its origins in the death squad he also put together, governed El Salvador. (Only this year, after Mauricio Funes, the candidate of the party founded by the guerrillas, the FMLN, won the presidential elections, was there for the first time an official commemoration of Archbishop Romero's death.)

Over a two-year period, *El Faro*'s director, Carlos Dada, hunted down and twice interviewed one of the surviving participants in D'Aubuisson's conspiracy against the archbishop, a former air force pilot by the name of Álvaro Saravia. Four other alleged coconspirators named by Saravia have been killed; another committed suicide. Some, like Mario Molina, General Molina's son, are enjoying the good life, but Saravia, pursued by his own demons, is living in abject poverty in another Latin American country that is not disclosed in the newspaper's report. Perhaps out of sheer loneliness, he told his story to *El Faro*.

Saravia recounts the details about the hit man and Mario Molina's role in hiring him. He also reveals that an announcement placed in *La Prensa Gráfica* by Jorge Pinto, the owner of the independent newspaper *El Independiente*, inadvertently sealed Romero's fate. Published on the morning of March 24, it informed readers that the archbishop would celebrate a Mass in memory of Pinto's mother at 6 p.m. that day, in the Divina Providencia chapel. Hungover after a party with other members of D'Aubuisson's group, Saravia woke to the news that the boss had ordered Romero's murder at this conveniently secluded location.

Óscar Romero is one of the four contemporary Christian martyrs depicted above the west door of Westminster Abbey (the others being Mother Elizabeth of Russia, Martin Luther King Jr., and Dietrich Bonhoeffer), and it says something that the admiration of the Anglican Church has been more spontaneous than that of the Vatican. Karol Wojtyla had been anointed pope in late 1978, and with the assistance of then-cardinal Joseph Ratzinger he was busy dismantling the progressive church of Latin America, replacing Liberation Theology bishops with conservative ones, and transferring priests. Pope John Paul II's response to the crime—he called it "a tragedy"—was hardly as emphatic as his attacks on the pro-Sandinista clergy when he visited Nicaragua four years later. A spontaneous movement in favor of Romero's canonization has been stalled for years now in Rome.

BUT FOR THE CHURCH rank and file, Romero has become an extraordinarily meaningful figure, as a quick internet search of his name can attest. We can find evidence of this in yet another work intended to commemorate the thirtieth anniversary of his death: a documentary film, *Monseñor: The Last Journey of Óscar Romero*, directed by Ana Carrigan and Juliet Weber and produced by Latin American/North American Church Concerns. The film is, unintentionally perhaps, or at least effortlessly, a hagiography, a record of a saintly life. It is an astonishing compilation of footage from the last three years of Romero's life, not only of the archbishop himself but of army patrols and mothers of the disappeared and guerrillas on the move—and above all of those unforgettable Masses in which the small, unprepossessing archbishop read out loud the record of the government's atrocities while hundreds of ragged, persecuted campesinos listened in gratitude, their existence and suffering recognized at last.

I interviewed Romero two or three times before he died, and although I cannot locate any of my notebooks from those dreadful years, I have the distinct recollection that he did not say anything particularly scintillating or inspirational or visionary: he was deeply distrustful of rhetoric and purposefully self-effacing. Instead of words, I have the memory of a peculiar ducking gesture he used to make with his head when, after Sunday Mass, he stood outside the cathedral doors shaking hands with the knobby-jointed, malnourished campesinos who came from miles away to hear him, a few coins knotted into their handkerchiefs for the journey back. They would clasp his hand and stare into his face and try to say something about what he meant to them, and he would duck his head and look away: *not me, not me.*

The day before his murder, on Sunday, March 23, after a crop duster had sprayed insecticide on a protest demonstration, and we reporters had gone nearly mad from the obligation to hunt every morning for the mutilated corpses that D'Aubuisson's people had left at street corners the night before, and distraught mothers lined up every day outside the archbishopric's legal aid office asking for help in finding their disappeared children, and the waking nightmare of El Salvador clamored to the very heavens for justice, Óscar Arnulfo Romero for the first time spoke in exclamation points in his Sunday homily:

> I want to make a special request to the men in the armed forces: brothers, we are from the same country, yet you continually kill your peasant brothers. Before any order given by a man, the law of God must prevail: "You shall not kill!." . . In the name of God I pray you, I beseech you, I order you! Let this repression cease!

The next day he was shot.

POSTSCRIPT. Óscar Romero was canonized in a ceremony presided by Pope Francis on October 4, 2018. His feast day is March 24, the anniversary of his assassination.

NOTE

First published in the *New York Review of Books*, May 27, 2010. Reviewed: Carlos Dada, "Así matamos a monseñor Romero" (How we killed Archbishop Romero), *El Faro* (San Salvador), March 22, 2010, https://www.elfaro.net/es/201003/noticias/1416; Ana Carrigan and Juliet Weber, dirs., *Monseñor: The Last Journey of Óscar Romero*, produced by Latin American/North American Church Concerns, Kellogg Institute for International Studies, University of Notre Dame, 2010.

In the New Gangland of El Salvador

NOVEMBER 10, 2011

I'm back in El Salvador for the first time in thirty years, and I don't recognize a thing. There are smooth highways from the airport up to San Salvador, the capital, and even at this late hour, along the stretch of dunes dividing the road from the Pacific Ocean, there are cheerful stands at which customers have parked to buy coconuts and *típico* foods. But I remember a pitted two-lane road, a merciless sun that picked out every detail on the taut skin of corpses, a hole in the sandy ground, the glaring news that four women from the United States, three of them nuns, had just been unearthed from that shallow pit.

"Is there a monument or a sign marking where the four *Americanas* were killed during the war?" I ask the driver of the hotel van.

"Yes, up in the university, the UCA, where they died."

"No, those were the six Jesuit priests, years later, in San Salvador. I mean the nuns, in 1980, here."

"Oh," he replies. "I don't remember."

That event, the rape and murder of four religious workers on their way from the airport up to the city, was no doubt memorable to people like Robert

White, the US ambassador in El Salvador during the last year of the Carter administration. He stood grimly at the funeral the next day, looking like another potential target of a putschist right-wing junta that had gone rogue. Already that year, Óscar Arnulfo Romero, the fearless archbishop of San Salvador, had been assassinated—to loud rejoicing by a ruling class that used to call him "Beelzebub." Weeks after his murder, orchestrated in the darkest back channels of the regime by the notorious ideologue Roberto D'Aubuisson, the Ronald Reagan administration cranked up its military involvement in El Salvador and dedicated billions of dollars to the junta's fight against an insurgent coalition of guerrillas—Marxist radicals grouped under the umbrella name Frente Farabundo Martí para la Liberación Nacional (FMLN).

The twelve-year-long war would leave as many as seventy thousand people dead by its end, but it started before more than half of all Salvadorans alive today were even born, and ended nearly twenty years ago. Why should a young van driver remember? And yet the El Salvador of today, riddled by worse violence than at any point since the early years of the war, linked inseparably to the United States by an immigrant stream that started during the conflict, haunted always by the memory of the assassin Roberto D'Aubuisson, who went on to found the party that ruled his country uninterruptedly until the most recent election in 2009, is inconceivable without the years of bloodshed.

SALVADORANS LIKE TO SAY that if someone bothered to iron their country it would actually be large. But it is tiny, and wrinkled, the lava of long-exhausted volcanoes furrowing and bending the landscape this way and that. San Salvador sits in a valley at the foot of a volcano, and guessing wildly one could say that it now has as many shopping malls as, say, Fort Lauderdale, and plazas and traffic roundabouts too, and tranquil neighborhoods with security guards on every block. It is very green, and even the slums creeping up the hills on the outskirts of the city seem lush to those used to more urban kinds of poverty.

On the very flank of the San Salvador volcano sits the town of Mejicanos, famous for its combativeness during the war. A long narrow street climbs up from it and then winds down and around the sides of a narrow canyon. Following it as it plunges along, one can see that the leafy shadows are dotted thickly with makeshift houses and shacks. Here and there, a knot of skinny men huddle around what looks like a crack pipe, but otherwise the street is silent and empty.

The neighborhood and the road are both called Montreal, and they are notorious. Last year a Montreal public transport bus making the trip to the center of Mejicanos was set on fire as it reached the Mejicanos market. Seventeen people burned to death. The toll included an eighteen-month-old child, but at least a few of the dead are said to have been members of one of the warring *maras*, ferocious gangs that are El Salvador's own contribution to the drug trade and the world of transnational crime in which it takes place. Children of the war and the United States in more ways than one, they are responsible for most of the harrowing violence of today. They first began to attract public notice some twenty years ago, when what used to be a furious open conflict gave way to an ever- growing, pervasive sense of menace.

Around that time, Marisa D'Aubuisson de Martínez, sister of Roberto D'Aubuisson, decided to create a project for market women and their youngest children in a neighborhood like Mejicanos. Marisa's forceful personality and easy laugh are in contrast to the will-o'-the-wisp, mesmerizing quality of her brother, as are her politics: she is a lifelong Catholic activist, a follower of the fearless archbishop her brother murdered. Roberto, who was to die of throat cancer in 1992, moved into electoral politics in the 1980s. As the war wrapped up, Marisa, too, changed, moving away from world-changing utopian dreams in order to focus on more attainable projects. I talked to her one day in the sunny, plain office where she works.

"At that time international aid went largely to macroprojects, but I started to write up something very small," Marisa said. With international money, she founded an organization called Centros Infantiles de Desarrollo (CINDE) to provide day care for babies and toddlers, primarily for the children of women who make their living selling in the marketplace. Now there are three such centers, including one in Mejicanos, to which preschool and kindergarten facilities were eventually added. A few years ago, CINDE created a program known as "school reinforcement," in which older children can do their homework in safe surroundings and with adult guidance. One of them is in Montreal, and it is one of the few places in that neighborhood where outsiders can feel welcome and safe from the *maras*.

The after-school center is just an open-air hangar attached to two makeshift rooms that are rarely used because they get oven-hot. On the breezy afternoon when I arrived, the children were outside, enjoying an uproarious play break, but when the teacher in charge blew a whistle they returned at once to the open-air work tables and applied themselves to their homework almost voraciously. Everyone there, from the teachers to the volunteer monitors, seemed nearly feverish in their involvement. I interrupted the schoolwork of the older girls—who had ambitious English names like Jennifer and Natalie—to ask one if she came here to learn or to have fun, and she replied instantly and seriously, "I learn and I have fun." Her grades had improved, up from Cs and Ds the previous year to a steady B average, but she was struggling, she said, with her least favorite subject, math.

Perhaps the general enthusiasm was due to the last-chance quality of the center itself. During a play break I watched a beautiful young girl kick a soccer ball around with her playmates as if she were still a child, but she was tall for her age and already nubile, and I felt almost sick with fear for her, having heard over and over that *mareros*—gang members—routinely force young girls in their territory into sexual service, a duty that often begins with collective rape. Or, on *visita íntima* day, which throughout Latin America is nominally the day when wives are allowed privacy with their jailed husbands or established partners, older girls may be sent as "wives" to the prisons where gang members are serving sentences. No one knows exactly how often the *visita íntima* may take place in Salvadoran prisons. As one friend pointed out, anyone who is admitted to some of the more notorious jails has access to the *visita íntima* rooms. Parents desperate to keep their daughters away from any sort of contact with the *maras* send them to the countryside to be raised by relatives, but not everyone has rural cousins or parents, and the barrio of Montreal and its dangers were this girl's unavoidable circumstance.

As it is for the boys. "We have a boy who comes here all the time who is incredibly bright, really special," one of the teachers told me in a low voice. "But he's just a step away from joining the *maras*. He's so little! Just a *muchachito*. We've talked to him about it, we try not to gloss over reality here, but he's ready to go. We won't be able to keep him away."

I discovered some of the more immediate rewards available to boys who join the *maras* in the Mejicanos market, downhill again from Montreal. There, the market women, who have no problem at all with math, explained their lives to me in numbers: they pay the municipality thirty-five cents daily rent per each 1.5 linear meters their stands occupy. They spend fifty cents in bus fare to get to and from home, multiplied by the number of school-age children. Four dollars' worth of produce purchased wholesale plus three dollars to ferry the merchandise back to their stands. The day's earnings minus four dollars for the next day's purchases, minus bus fares and taxis, leaves three, on a good day four, dollars to buy food for the family.

Then there is *la renta*, the daily extortion fee charged by *mareros*, but no one would do that math for me. Whether the *renta* around the market is charged by members of the Mara Salvatrucha—also known as the MS-13—gang or by the increasingly powerful rival group, the Barrio 18, was also left unclear. Several minors who belonged to the Barrio 18 were tried and sentenced for setting fire to the bus, but still no one I met, not even the teachers at the CINDE preschool center, was willing to talk about the incident.

I was chatting one afternoon with a particularly lively woman—let's call her María—who started to tell me how CINDE and the microloan program it manages had changed her life because she now had a cart in which to trundle her wares back and forth, when two boys who looked to be around fifteen years old arrived at her stand. She cut the conversation short as the kids selected some of her wares and left without any money changing hands. Maria's eyes flickered with terror when I asked her if she was being *renteada*, or extorted, by the *mareros*. "Not really, not really," she whispered, looking at me pleadingly. "They don't ask me for money. Not yet. Just . . . little gifts."

"WE DON'T *RENTEAR*," José Cruz declaimed loudly, as if for the world. "That is an invention of the press." He has a great speaking voice, Chinese eyes above high cheekbones, none of the *mareros*' trademark face tattoos, a lithe body, and a fantastically authoritative manner. "How are you doing?" he boomed as he walked into the prison visitors' room, extending a wrist-cuffed hand, and never stopped lecturing from that point on. After our conversation, a prison guard came up and, while one of his mates looked on, whispered that as a leader of the Barrio 18 gang Cruz was the de facto head of the penitentiary. It was Cruz, the guard said, who decided who gives press interviews (he did); which prison guards are allowed into the cell area where forty-five to fifty prisoners are confined every night in cells six by six meters large; and who gets punished.

He was very focused: at age twenty-nine he had already served seven years of his homicide sentence and had fifteen left to go, and he wanted to get out on time and alive. "I am a rehabilitable prisoner," he informed me. He keeps his temper. At night, I heard, he retired early (I assumed he had larger headquarters than most) and slept soundly. After our conversation, I was told that under the do-rag, or bandana, that imprisoned gang members wear he did, in fact, have tattoos—two eyes on the back of his head that allow him, he was not the only one to believe, to see his enemies at all times. He had been interviewed, he boasted, by French, Dutch, German, American journalists, you name it, and now he was trying to catch me with his rhetoric—we are victims of society, the rich get richer and the poor get poorer—but nothing he had to say was as arresting as his physical presence, or the information whispered by the guard but widely known outside the prison, that beatings and executions by knifing or beating were a fact of life in the penitentiary of Quezaltepeque.

Unlike the market women in Mejicanos, the guard had no particular reason not to talk: everyone knows that the prison system is bankrupt and that it is impossible to control a detention system in which prisoners—nearly half of them accused or convicted killers—are stuffed into cells like industrial livestock. In El Salvador there are 65 homicides per 100,000 inhabitants, which is more than triple the current rate in Mexico and significantly higher than the yearly death toll in the second half of the war. In a total prison population of 25,000, a third have never been sentenced. Overcrowding is so extreme that the prison system this year refused to take in more inmates. New detainees are being kept in police holding pens, but given the crime rate and the number of arrests the pens quickly become just as crowded.

There have been riots and peaceful strikes by prisoners demanding better conditions, but the men are not high on anyone's list of priorities. It's just one of the many catastrophes in El Salvador, where, twenty years after the war that was supposed to save the country—from capitalism or from communism, depending on which side you were on—there are half a million single parents, mostly women, trying to bring up their children safely. The government is bankrupt, the poverty rate is 38 percent, and the economy, which rose slightly from a negative growth rate of -2 percent in 2008 thanks only to an increase in the price of coffee, seems paralyzed.

It would be easy to lay the blame for this social and economic disaster exclusively at the feet of the party founded by Roberto D'Aubuisson—the Alianza Republicana Nacionalista (ARENA, Nationalist Republican Alliance)—which governed the country with evident if not single-minded interest in the well-being of the wealthy for twenty years after the peace accords were signed in 1992. (In 2009, Mauricio Funes, the candidate of the party founded by the former guerrillas, the FMLN, won the presidency.) But there is also the enormous fact of the war itself: the demolished roads and other infrastructure, the collapse of rural society, the rise of urban slums peopled by campesinos fleeing those remote areas of the country that were the war's principal staging ground, the systematic practice of ruthlessness, the drastic increase in single-parent families, the loss of an educated elite, the huge stockpile of leftover weapons no one kept track of. None of this, however, adds up to a complete or satisfactory explanation for the proliferation of the *maras*, currently estimated to number some twenty-five thousand members at large, with another nine thousand in prison.

THE PHENOMENON STARTED in Los Angeles, where the children of immigrants who had fled the war had parents no one looked up to and were bombarded with ads for consumer goods they couldn't have. They grew up in bad neighborhoods and inherited someone else's enemies and turf wars. Among the second-generation Salvadorans in Los Angeles a significant number ended up creating their own groups to confront the Mexican and Afro-American gangs in whose neighborhoods their parents had settled. Of the two groups currently taking over just about every poor neighborhood in El Salvador, the Barrio 18 gang takes its name from the 18th Street gang in Los Angeles, whose members number in the thousands. As for the Mara Salvatrucha, who started it all, the only part of their name everyone agrees on is that "Salva" must stand for Salvadoran.

As US immigration policy has focused on deporting the greatest possible number of undocumented migrants, no matter what their situation, a great many Salvadoran deportees, some of whom grew up in the United States and hardly speak Spanish, have found themselves back in their country of birth. A number of these unwilling returnees are *mareros*, who either join the local branch of their organization or try to flee back home (that is, to the United States), joining a migrant trail across Mexico used by hundreds of thousands of would-be US immigrants every year. Along the way, the *mareros* are often recruited by Mexican drug traffickers, who have developed highly lucrative sidelines in white slavery, child prostitution, and migrant extortion. Assault, robbery, and rape are now an expected part of the migrant journey through Mexico.

The most unlucky travelers are kidnapped in Mexico and held for ransom, usually between $500 and $2,000. If relatives back home cannot come up with the money quickly enough, the kidnap victims are killed. According to Mexico's Comisión Nacional de los Derechos Humanos (CNDH, National Commission on Human Rights), eleven thousand migrants were kidnapped in the first six months of 2010. There are no statistics on the total number of dead, but we know that in August last year seventy-two migrants were kidnapped and killed in a single incident. Six months later, another 195 bodies were unearthed in the same municipal district. *Mareros* were probably among the assassins.

Howard Cotto, subdirector of investigations for the Policia Nacional Civil (PNC, National Civil Police), has been learning about the *maras* for years. He is the trim, articulate product of the peace accords signed between the ARENA wartime government and the FMLN guerrillas, which included a UN-mandated restructuring of the various murderous police corps into a single force that integrated and trained members of both parties to the war.

Another police commander, Jaime Granados, laughingly described the resulting National Civil Police to me as the homely child no one wants, largely due to its efforts at neutrality. "We're good police, very good," he said. "But nobody is on our side." The police are underfinanced and underequipped (there is one forensic expert for the whole country) and corruption is spreading, but they have managed to retain pockets of efficiency and professionalism, and the international diplomas and certificates that line the wall of Howard Cotto's office—one is from the FBI—are signs of the commander's prestige.

Cotto estimates that the gang's support community in the barrios numbers perhaps eighty or ninety thousand, which together with the number of active and imprisoned *mareros* add up to about 1.5 percent of El Salvador's population. Although the *maras* are on the retail end of the illegal drug trade in El Salvador, he does not attribute their growth to the drug-trafficking bonanza in Central America, now that the region has become the principal corridor for moving South American drugs to North America. "The gangs are clearly a part of organized crime, as are the traffickers of drugs and arms and stolen cars and so forth," Cotto told me one morning in his sparsely furnished office. "But traffickers build hierarchical organizations around specific interests—white slavery, smuggling, drugs—and the traders lure people in on the basis of that [business]. The gangs do the opposite: they recruit from the bottom up."

The gangs distribute drugs in the barrio while casting themselves as its defenders, Cotto said.

> But in reality, they don't defend the barrio; they terrorize it. The barrio is the territory where they extort, distribute drugs, kill, and make money. But they don't live with a lot of luxury; they're not narcos. Their origins are in the community, and what they fear more than death itself is losing their authority there, because the moment they do that, they're dead. But it's an excellent way of living comfortably and giving money to a lot of people; their strength lies in not breaking that chain of money distribution. That's how they can say [to their underlings], "fight for me."

Cotto chatted easily under a wintry blast of air-conditioning. "[A *marero's*] life is very short," he continued.

They get sentenced to thirty years in no time. But in this country, as they see it, they have two choices: you can be a loser and keep on studying, and let's see if you can find a job once you've graduated, or you can be a powerful man by the time you're fourteen or seventeen. You can give orders, be in charge of distributing drugs in the neighborhood. You won't have to give your elders any respect, you'll be the one who can say to a neighbor, "You're going to leave this barrio this minute," and then take over his house. You'll be able to say to that girl you like and who doesn't like you, "You know what, whether you like it or not you're going to be mine, or whoever else's I decide."

Cotto has seen a lot of corpses by now: beheaded, dismembered, set on fire. (It is said that the first thing a new *marero* must do, no matter how young, is arbitrarily kill someone. After that, they're ready for reprogramming.) But the most upsetting murder scene he ever arrived at was in a *mara* stronghold, in one of the collective homes the kids call *casa destroyer*. "I was nonplussed," he says. "We walked into the house and all the kids were there, in a circle. And there was the dead person. He'd been dead a few hours already, but they hadn't [disposed of him]. They were just sitting around the corpse, chatting and taking it easy."

ALEXIS RAMÍREZ, who joined the *maras* when he was fifteen, doesn't look like he could kill people thoughtlessly, although he is serving fifty years for homicide and has forty-eight left to go. He has dark skin, full lips that look sculpted, big black eyes, and looks much younger than his twenty-nine years. I asked him if, when he was free, it hadn't been dangerous for him to walk down the street covered in tattoos, and he gave a sideways smile. "If you know how to walk it's not. From corner to corner . . . that's how I've been all over El Salvador." And he made a ducking, aw-shucks movement that made me see how he could, in fact, slip and smile his way around many obstacles.

He came, he said, from a nice family; his father, an evangelical, "was always involved in matters of the church," while his mother "for approximately fifteen years has been persevering in the things of God." His brothers work in a carpentry shop. His father-in-law recently managed to smuggle Alexis's wife out of the country, presumably in order to get her away from Alexis's influence, and the couple lost custody of their two children—now aged five and nine—who are in the care of their grandparents.

He was still in school when he decided to join the *maras*. "I saw the tattoos [of the *mareros* in his neighborhood]. I saw the way they behaved toward each other," he said. "In my neighborhood they didn't steal from people; they took care of them. I liked all that."

He had, I pointed out, a fairly dismal life. Didn't he regret the decision to join?

"When we took the option of being what we are," he answered, "we knew there was no turning back." I tried, unsuccessfully, to figure out if that ducking, swaying thing he did was an authentic remnant of what had once been a whole and gentle person or an ingratiating trick that a thoughtless killer kept stored among his array of weapons.

José Eduardo Villalta, twenty-four, has the word *eighteen*, as in Barrio 18, tattooed in French and English on his arms and fingers and in Latin numerals and various other codes wherever else a tattoo can fit. He has no charm, but in the course of our conversation it came out that he was originally from the countryside and that his mother visits him regularly. I asked him to describe how one sets up a milpa, or corn field, and as he was going through the procedures—cutting down, burning, overturning, hoeing, planting—I had a momentary vision of a youth breathing free air. He has most of a fifty-year sentence still ahead of him, and I asked him if he didn't find that depressing.

"No," he said firmly. "I feel at ease here. This is my home."

POSTSCRIPT. Thirty years after a peace treaty brought an end to a long and bloody conflict, the unspeakable violence that had come to dominate life for many of El Salvador's poor came to a sudden end, courtesy of President Nayib Bukele, forty-one, who likes to refer to himself as "el dictador más cool." At this writing he may not have checked all the boxes in the dictator requirement, but he has packed the courts, whose members altered the constitution to allow multiple reelections, as an important first step. And he has achieved enormous popularity, in his native country and abroad, through the use of dictatorial methods to destroy the Mara Salvatrucha transnational gang and all its rivals. "Cool" perhaps not, but slick for sure; in March 2023 the Bukele administration released a series of short, exquisitely filmed videos featuring hundreds of men clothed in identical spotless, long, white boxers, their torsos bare and their heads shaved right down to the skull, all bowed down so low that one can never see their faces, some men handcuffed to each other. In carefully rehearsed sequences, the prisoners run in step, kneel in step, crouch together, and slide against each other to form a human canoe, while men in black uniforms holding sticks herd them around an enormous new high-security prison—the continent's largest, allegedly. In violence-riddled countries, these videos are a hit.

The men performing running exercises in a crouch are identified as members of the Mara Salvatrucha and rival gangs, but in reality, they could be just anyone. According to Amnesty International, under the state of exception declared by Bukele and still in force, "procedural safeguards, such as the presumption of innocence and the right to a defense, have been suspended, which has allowed the arbitrary detention and imprisonment of more than 66,000 people in record time." According to official figures, El Salvador now has a prison population of more than 100,000, involving mostly young men, making it the country with the highest incarceration rate in the world, with more than 1.5 percent of its population in prison. One can imagine, beyond the videos, the real condition the prisoners live in.[1]

NOTES

First published in the *New York Review of Books*, November 10, 2011. Research support was provided by the Investigative Fund at the Nation Institute.

1   See "La megacárcel que Bukele inauguró en El Salvador, el país con la mayor tasa de población penitenciaria del mundo," BBC *News Mundo*, February 1, 2023, https://www.bbc.com/mundo/noticias-america-latina-64491586.

Part III

———

Mexico

"The Morning Quickie"

AUGUST 12, 2004

1.

Four years into Mexico's newly minted electoral democracy, all is not as it should be with the body politic. One indication is that the host of the most influential news show in the capital is a clown. Another is that the clear front-runner in the unacknowledged race for the next presidential elections in 2006, Andrés Manuel López Obrador, the mayor of Mexico City, is currently embroiled in a scandal that first saw light with a secretly filmed video released in March. It showed the mayor's all-purpose political operator, René Bejarano, who has served as his campaign chief and government minister for the city and was at the time the majority leader of the capital's Legislative Assembly, receiving enormous amounts of cash from a notorious *empresario*, or rich businessman, whose face was blacked out on the film. The video was first broadcast in March on the clown's television show.

Watching the video of René Bejarano on the take is a fascinating and nasty experience—as if Mexicans had not already enjoyed opportunity enough to exercise their voyeurism on a multiplying number of sex-talk programs, sex tour-o-ramas (E! Entertainment *en español*), and local franchises of *Big Brother* in which sexual congress supposedly takes place before our very eyes. Brozo the Clown, who has made a career out of mocking, and exploiting, the prurient interests of a society only recently still in the grip of extreme modesty and repressive sexual codes, seems in this light just the right presenter for the corruption tape, which was exhibited at 7:26 a.m. on the fateful morning of March 3 on Brozo's daily news program. The cameras in Brozo's studio closed in on a grainy black-and-white video with terrible audio quality, in which the glum, balding Bejarano, wearing a dark suit, opens a briefcase, lays it flat, and proceeds to stuff it with wads of US and Mexican currency. Weeks later, the bit that was still getting replayed was the sequence in which, having tried and failed to close the case, Bejarano hurriedly stuffs his pockets with more cash.

IT'S NOT AS if Mexicans were new to corruption, which by long political inheritance is practically taken for granted. But it's not every day that the act itself is shown on screen. And then there is what Bejarano himself had to say about what he was doing in this and in another video that was released that evening on the major evening newscast. In that second tape, Bejarano is not actually shown with money in hand, but he talks more. Bejarano's interlocutor, annoyed and threatening, possibly a little drunk, sits off camera in an office that people who have done business with the man instantly recognized. He wants, he says, to get paid for the construction work he has done under contract with the city—contracts obtained in exchange for the kickback money he previously delivered to Bejarano—but Bejarano explains that there's no money in the city's coffers.

"You're fucking with me, I'll fuck you over," the *empresario* says.

Bejarano, conciliatory, tries to make clear his own risks: "I've done a lot of things for Andrés [i.e., the mayor] that not many people would do—a lot, you can't imagine. And if I'm ever caught . . . I prefer not to tell him about a lot of things, although he supposes that I do those things, but he doesn't know, and he doesn't ask, how I managed to finance . . ." He leaves the sentence unfinished. "But of course, he knows perfectly well, because it's implicit, because I was his operator, that if they catch us one day, it was me, not him. He'll take a beating of course, but they'll hit me harder."

If this second, more damning video is less memorable than the first, it is mostly because of the way Brozo presented the first tape on his program. By a most unusual coincidence, René Bejarano himself was being interviewed that morning, in his role as Legislative Assembly leader, in the Televisa studio next to Brozo's. Bejarano was asked to step over to Brozo's set, and then in some perplexity sat down to watch what the clown warned him would be "a missile." The tape was then played all over again.

A small picture inset on the screen allowed us to peep in real time at Bejarano, poker-faced, realizing that he had been set up, first by the man who was being shown handing him money and now by Brozo. We saw him watching himself stuffing money into his pockets, watching his career, his life, his reputation, go up in flames. "What is this, René, what is this?" Brozo roared at Bejarano, his wig waggling, a finger aloft. Live, Bejarano identified the man with the blacked-out face as the businessman Carlos Ahumada Kurtz—a darkly handsome Argentine-born businessman, we would find out later. He declared that the money was not a personal bribe but a campaign contribution offered by Ahumada. "Don't make an asshole out of me, René, please!" an angry Brozo interrupted. Bejarano mumbled a few other wobbly explanations, offered several times over to renounce his right to congressional immunity, and then we went to the station break.

BROZO THE CLOWN, grease-stained, foul-mouthed, and leering, presides over the morning news show called *El Mañanero*, slang for "The Morning Quickie," which lasts from 6 to 10 a.m. every weekday morning. Never mind that the length of the program contradicts its title; lacking attention to the finer details, it often feels spur-of-the-moment and displays a roaring devotion to all things having to do with reproductive organs and their exercise. In a green wig, rubber-ball nose, threadbare tailcoat worn over sagging pants, with a menacing scowl and a whiskey voice, Brozo—the creation of the comedian Víctor Trujillo—has been a well-known television personality for some years. Wearing a sweatsuit, he used to cohost a late-night talk show with another Trujillo creation, La Beba Galván, who was a rather less respectable version of Dame Edna Everage and proved to have a surprising talent for conducting interviews.

Because Trujillo's Brozo character took an active interest in politics long before becoming part of the political scene himself, he and his sponsors on an independent Mexico City television channel eventually figured out that having him read the news was not as stupid an idea as it sounds. Most citizens in greater Mexico City are poor, have less than ten years' formal schooling, and share, by and large, a bitter disrespect for the solemn fashion in which news and politics are treated by the characters in power.

In costume, Brozo is also part of a long tradition of cultural heroes in masks who are dear to the Mexican heart. There is, for example, El Santo, star of action movies for several decades, who was never to be seen—onscreen or off—without his silver wrestler's mask. And Marco Rascón, the leftist congressman who always attended presidential state of the union reports wearing a pig face. There is Subcomandante Marcos, the most famous masked hero of them all. For intellectuals, Brozo has the charm of the *popular*, a word that in Spanish is used to describe what is close to *el pueblo*. On the initial *El Mañanero* show, Brozo talked in slang and presented current events in his own subversive manner. Somewhere between the wisecracks and the leering asides the news actually got read and put in some sort of context, and guests were interviewed. Three years later he was hired by Televisa, Mexico's once-staid media conglomerate, to bring the formula to their studios. They wanted his credibility.

Out of costume, Trujillo is thoughtful, self-effacing, mild-mannered; when I first interviewed him ten years ago, I thought he could have passed for an academic, but it was his father who was an economist. In Brozo's restless youth, he spent some time in the theater, and gradually was drawn to comic satire because *la carpa*—a cheerful combination of vaudeville and circus that in Mexico has always had strong political overtones—struck him as "Mexico's only indigenous theatrical form." (The great comedian Cantinflas, too, came out of the *carpa* tradition.)

"My intention has never been to say dirty words," he said in an interview recently, in his office at Televisa. "My intention has been to talk the way people do. People come out on television looking pretty and acting refined, but that's not the way we are. How could we act blond if we're not blond, pretty if we're not pretty, solemn if that's not us?" He wondered aloud about his decision to screen the Bejarano tape. "I was very happy to have such strong material on the program," he said. "But on the other hand it was very sad to confirm that all the politicians were part of the same underworld." This kind of scandal, he said, "makes people, in their depression, turn dangerously away from the voting booth. But we couldn't just make believe that nothing was going on!"

FOR THE 2001 presidential elections, Brozo announced the creation of a farcical "party," the PRAU—*Prau!* being a nonsense word he had invented to accompany the rude two-handed gesture that is common in Mexico. The Federal Electoral Institute did not make public the itemized results of the write-in votes, but people familiar with the final vote count, Trujillo says, told him that the PRAU did rather well.

Trujillo tries to sidestep the fact that he may well have become Mexican politics' most important arbiter; his own credibility is increasingly at risk the more successful he becomes. Perhaps not even he quite understood this before the López Obrador–Bejarano video episode, which has come to seem inseparable from its existence as part of the Brozo show. It was also the moment in which Trujillo stepped out of character. Appealingly, the clown had always managed to come across as sleazier than any of his guests, but that morning he was, in some sense, as trapped as Bejarano. If he was important enough to receive and air a video that could alter the results of the next presidential elections, how could he be a clown? And if he is a clown, what does that make us, his viewers? In accepting a tape that came from a ruling party congressman who is a known political enemy of the mayor's, Trujillo lost his bearings and turned into an inquisitor.

The uncharismatic Bejarano, who was known as an important fixer only to political insiders, is not, of course, the real star of the video. Nor is Carlos Ahumada Kurtz, the magnate who has major contracts with the city and who, until the scandal broke, was the owner of two soccer teams and a one-year-old newspaper that employed some of the most respected reporters in the country. The *videoescándalo* would not have truly been a scandal if it had not implicated Andrés Manuel López Obrador directly and set up a considerable obstacle to what only recently looked like the mayor's unbeatable ambition to run for the presidency in the 2006 elections. *Complot!*—a conspiracy—was the cry from his supporters from the moment the video came on the air. In Mexico, where conspiracy theory is a popular art form, the *complot* explanation for the tapes was guaranteed instant popularity.

Within hours, López Obrador himself endorsed it. The conspirators against him included, the mayor said in various interviews and press conferences, the government intelligence agency, a prominent right-wing senator, the president's wife, and Carlos Salinas de Gortari, the former president who since his fall from dizzying popularity has become the country's all-purpose evil genius. Rather than call for an immediate investigation of the city's finances and of his closest associate's methods of fundraising, López Obrador invited his supporters to rally in the Zócalo—the city's monumental central square. On the appointed day, the square was packed.

2.

Andrés Manuel López Obrador was born forty-nine years ago in the torrid southern state of Tabasco, to a family of tradesmen. Like many Mexicans who went to college during the 1970s and took an interest in politics, he graduated from the National University's school of political science. Back in Tabasco, he joined the long-ruling Partido Revolucionario Institucional (PRI, Institutional

Revolutionary Party) and built a career within the government. In 1987, a group of dissidents broke away from the PRI to support the candidacy of Cuauhtémoc Cárdenas in the following year's elections, and López Obrador joined them. Those elections were won—or stolen, as many people believe—by the PRI leader, Carlos Salinas de Gortari. The dissidents went on to form the Partido de la Revolución Democrática (PRD, Party of the Democratic Revolution), in alliance with the principal old left parties and a number of student activists and survivors of the 1968 student movement. Their platform has much in common with the program advanced by Cuauhtémoc Cárdenas's father, Lázaro, who as president in the 1930s nationalized the oil industry and created a large part of the social welfare system that is still in place today.

Once the new party was established, López Obrador rose fast, becoming, in 1994, one of the PRD's first politicians to be elected governor of a state. (He did not, however, become governor: the office was literally taken over from him, with the help of armed thugs, by the PRI candidate, who remained there for a full six-year term.) In the tense relationship between the former PRI party members and the former radical left-wing militants who form the main branches of the PRD, the ex-PRI-istas generally act the part of elder statesmen and campaign to be governors of states, while the former student leaders and activists stage demonstrations in favor of revolutionary causes and run for municipal office. López Obrador has chosen a different approach, leading thousands of Chontal Indian farmers who in 1996 took over hundreds of oil wells along the Gulf Coast. Two years later, he marched at the head of thousands of residents of the state of Tabasco all the way to the Zócalo, dumping in the square truckloads of documents that allegedly contained proof of official corruption. The boxes may or may not have contained proof, but it seems that no one ever went through them.

AS MAYOR, LÓPEZ Obrador has been controversial and highly unpopular with the city's upper classes, but in the outlying *delegaciones*, or boroughs, where most of the city's inhabitants live and where nearly everyone is poor, he has wide support. When, in 2002, he held a curious referendum against daylight savings time, the outer boroughs backed him. When he calls for a meeting in the Zócalo, people from these boroughs fill it. It is said that the city's bureaucrats are told to show up for the demonstrations, in the best old-PRI style; but the mayor also has sincere, and unswervingly loyal, supporters. From the first, his administration has moved to improve public services in the larger outer boroughs and devoted large amounts of money to the welfare payments called *subsidios populares*. More than half of the available *subsidio* funds, or nearly $300 million, are earmarked for monthly payments of around $60 to any city resident over seventy years of age who is willing to fill out the appropriate form. Much else goes to handouts to the unemployed and the handicapped.

At $7.3 billion, López Obrador's yearly budget is much bigger than that of every government ministry except the Education Ministry, but the city may be bankrupt. As Bejarano tells Ahumada in the video, the city government is having a hard time meeting its payroll; it has nearly doubled the debt accumulated by his two immediate predecessors as mayor—the PRD icon Cuauhtémoc Cárdenas and the energetic Rosario Robles. She left office with a surprisingly favorable image among all parts of the city's population and was considered a strong contender for the presidency. It's unfortunate that Robles—a bitter enemy of López Obrador within the PRD—turned out to be having an affair with the very same Carlos Ahumada Kurtz who is seen in the videos handing over money.

In the wild hours that followed the episode of the video-on-the-clown-show, astonished viewers suddenly heard much gossip about the Robles–Ahumada affair: how her own passion explained her transformation from a businesslike, if slightly frumpy, Mexican woman wearing glasses to a svelter self in chic suits, contact lenses, eye makeup, and an expensive haircut. She had moved to a house in the beautiful neighborhood of Coyoacán, rented to her by Ahumada's wife. (Where, one wondered in the midst of all this gossip-magazine rapture, did his money come from?) She was besotted, rumor goes. So, she appears to have believed, was he. According to another member of the city government who was also filmed with Ahumada, she pushed her colleagues in city government to do business with him.

By the time the video scandal broke, however, Ahumada was hiding in Cuba and Robles's reputation was in ruins. According to flight records retrieved by the newsweekly *Proceso*, Robles flew to Cuba twice in Ahumada's private jet during that scandalous week. She was taking him a supply of his favorite Tabasco sauce, among other items. It seems he intended to lie low for some time in Cuba, but on April 5, Cuban authorities held him for questioning. Two weeks later, they deported him to Mexico, without waiting for Mexico to complete extradition proceedings. The consequences of that decision are still reverberating throughout the Mexican political scene. Mexico recalled its ambassador, and the Cuban foreign minister called a press conference to denounce Mexico's treatment of the scandal and of Cuba in general (notably,

President Vicente Fox's decision to vote against Castro's regime in the yearly UN Security Council Resolution on Human Rights).

3.

Democracy, or, at least, free and fair elections, arrived in Mexico nearly a century after a devastating revolution was fought for that goal. ("Effective suffrage, no reelection" was the slogan that brought down dictator Porfirio Díaz in 1911.) The victor in the 2001 elections was Vicente Fox, but it says something about his failure to establish a strong political presence that among those the mayor accused of conspiring against him, he initially mentioned the president's wife, Marta Sahagún de Fox, and not Fox himself. The president looks not so much tired as beaten, his deep voice hollow, much like his speeches, which carry no conviction.

An informal poll of four leading columnists of contrasting political leanings left them all searching for significant accomplishments in Fox's first four years. One praised him for having fired the imagination of a good many Mexicans back in 1994, "enough to believe that the PRI could be overthrown in the voting booth." Two agreed that the anti-poverty program Fox inherited from Presidents Ernesto Zedillo and Salinas de Gortari seems to be efficiently run and is producing results. Another pointed to a new freedom of information law. He observed that since Fox has no majority in Congress and most of the state governors also belong to rival political parties, the president has little scope for action. "But [despite this] he's never tried to subvert the legal order, which is important," he concluded. It could be added that, given the near-zero growth of the economy, salaries for those lucky enough to have employment (about 60 percent of the work force) have remained more or less constant.

But this is not what was expected of Vicente Fox, the big, impetuous former Coca-Cola executive in cowboy boots. Having promised an urgently needed immigration accord with the United States, he was expected to deliver it and instead obtained nothing more than Bush's half-baked proposal for temporary residence. With respect to human rights, it was hoped that the country's first truly democratically elected president would, at a minimum, voice his concerns regarding the scandalous and ongoing case of the assassinations of women in the border town of Juárez, so that at least due process might be followed in investigating the crimes. He was expected to turn his party, the Partido Acción Nacional (PAN, National Action Party)—a small, mild-mannered, and deeply conservative party—into an effective force in the legislature. He was also supposed to know how to make a fractious Congress accept major changes in the economy. In short, he was supposed to govern.

MEXICO'S LONG PROGRESS from a dreadful civil war, through seven decades of authoritarian rule, to genuine elections is often compared to Spain's history: the civil war, Francisco Franco, democracy. But Fox seems to think that he was elected to play the benevolent overseer role of King Juan Carlos rather than undertake the deal-making, lobbying, governing activities of President Adolfo Suárez, the shrewd Spanish conservative. "Yo ya cumpli," Fox has said. I did my part.

Last month, Fox publicly scolded his energy minister for attending a PAN political rally in support of the minister's presidential ambitions. But he never reprimanded his wife, Marta Sahagún, for talking openly about her own possible future candidacy. The energy minister, who was an active militant long before Fox even joined the PAN, quit his post in fury, and Fox was left to ignore a wave of rebellion within his own party. "We don't take instructions from anyone," a PAN congressional leader said. One month later, the president's spokesman resigned, after distributing copies of a twenty-page letter in which he decried, particularly, "the incursion of the First Lady into the list of possible presidential candidates."

In Mexico City, the first lady is often portrayed as both predatory and simpering, a terrifying combination. But in the *provincia*, which she tirelessly visits, Sahagún may be the most effective politician in Mexico today. She was Fox's spokesperson during the campaign, and she learned a great deal then about gaining power for herself and her candidate even without party backing. Her charity fund, Vamos México (Let's Go, Mexico), now has a nationwide organization (even if recent articles in the *Financial Times* exposed its extreme inefficiency and, at best, murky fundraising methods). She is sometimes irritatingly moved to tears by her own words (as when she compares herself to Mother Teresa). But she appears to be fearless, as her husband also seemed but was not.

Nevertheless, as her own party's unhappiness with her ambitions escalated, and the threat of nepotism in the succession generated a national scandal, Marta Sahagún's husband called a halt. The future of the presidential couple was not in politics, he declared on July 6. It took a week for her to agree with him in public. In a press conference held on July 12 at Los Pinos, the presidential residence, she professed her loyalty to the president and renounced all presidential ambitions for the 2006 elections. She would not, however, give up her commitment to the unprotected, she said, and she would "continue her struggle in favor of women." One had the feeling that the curtain had not come down; she could, at the least, and more sensibly, decide later on to run for office in Mexico City or in the state of Guanajuato, the Foxes' official residence.

As for the PRI, during its seventy-plus years in power it set up and dominated the modern Mexican political system. The PRI has a machine, experienced workers, political know-how, and the support of many former and current bureaucrats. Widespread disillusionment with the recent performance of electoral democracy might lead to a PRI comeback in 2006, if candidates can be found who are not engaged in slitting each other's throats. Also, with the loss of omnipotence, the PRI's tradition of arbitrary rule is coming into view, like the murky bottom of a lake going dry. José Murat, governor of the state of Oaxaca, was accused in June by the attorney general's office of staging an attempt to assassinate himself in March—either to glorify himself or to cover up a squabble among his bodyguards that left one policeman dead. In Chihuahua, a ten-year-old string of murders of young women and girls, committed with what can only be the connivance of law enforcement officials, has long been a scandal; but this month it was temporarily overshadowed when two members of the feared Policía Judicial were found to have three kidnap victims in a station wagon they had left parked in Judicial headquarters in the state capital. The *judiciales*, who have been released having been charged merely with extortion, were part of PRI governor Patricio Martínez's security detail.

BY COMPARISON WITH the PRI, the corruption scandals within the PRD seem positively benign, which helps explain why, his current troubles notwithstanding, Andrés Manuel López Obrador remains the country's most popular politician. But he has been chopping down many branches of his fractious party, without, perhaps, realizing the damage he is doing to himself. Witness his reaction to what was very probably the largest protest march in Mexico's history. As in the historic marches of the 1968 university student movement, the hundreds of thousands of orderly protesters who walked down the Reforma to the Zócalo on June 27 were largely self-organized, if at all, and predominantly middle class. The marchers wanted the local and federal governments to do something—anything—about the frightening rate of violent crime (Mexico now holds second place after Colombia in the number of kidnappings, for example). The march was first proposed and coordinated by López Obrador's right-wing Catholic enemies (and eagerly promoted by the principal newspapers and television stations). But it's also unquestionable that the capital city is at the moment a frequently scary place to live for everyone and that, after a brief lull, the crime rate seems to be climbing sharply again.

The day after the march the mayor repeated his earlier conviction that the protest had been the result of a conspiracy and cited, as evidence, "one, the manipulation by the right; two, the federal government's opportunism . . . and also, the yellow journalism in some of the media." The day after that, the leading newspaper, *Reforma*, ran an oversized headline calling for his resignation. Clearly, there was a political struggle behind the march, but López Obrador, characteristically willing to decide that all the marchers were his enemies too, staged a confrontation and in the process alienated many leaders in the PRD, who in some embarrassment publicly suggested that he rethink his position.

López Obrador is the kind of man who collects enemies: he seems to fear Salinas and Marta Sahagún, but within his own party he is hated by several factions, including the one led by Cuauhtémoc Cárdenas, the PRD's *líder moral*, who resigned last March from the party's governing council in protest against López Obrador's failure to deal with the video scandal. Is there, in fact, in view of these hatreds, a *videocomplot* against the mayor? In the fragment of the declarations made in Cuba by Ahumada that the Cuban foreign minister presented on May 5 to foreign correspondents, a seemingly relaxed Ahumada tells an unknown interlocutor that he gave "them" the videos because it was his way of "proving what they were asking me about." He didn't at first intend to have the tapes shown on television, he said, but "then later they told me that it was important to have them publicized on television."

But who are "they"? Behind this answer lies the mystery of the *complot*. Ahumada is clearly both untrustworthy and inventive: "they" could be whoever he feels might be useful to name at any given moment, including López Obrador and Bejarano, or López Obrador's many enemies within or outside the PRD. It strains belief to imagine that the unlikely Gang of Four named by the mayor as the *complot* authors were collaborating on anything, but it is equally difficult to believe that René Bejarano just happened to be sitting for an interview in the studio program next door to Brozo's the day the tape was aired.

In fact, two days earlier, another tape had been released on the evening news, showing the city's highest finance official gambling for huge sums in Las Vegas. In June, when the *videoescándalo* seemed to be getting nowhere, the Mexican attorney general presented López Obrador with a summons for criminal violations involving the city government's expropriation and use of a valuable piece of land (expropriated, in fact, during the term of his predecessor, Rosario Robles). López Obrador risks being caught in a trap. If he resigns six months before his term of office ends in December 2006, he loses his mayoral immunity and can be prosecuted, disqualifying him as a candidate. If, on the other hand, López Obrador serves out his full term of office, he cannot run for president. There does indeed seem to be a clear effort to get the front-runner out of the race before it has even begun. In response, the Mexico City government has begun distribution of two million copies of a comic book titled "The Dark Forces against Andrés Manuel López Obrador," which shows a salivating shark threatening a nice middle-class family on the cover and goes on to explain the blows, or coups, against the mayor. "If we let him, this Tabasqueño will win the presidency," a business-suited Dark Force explains to his hand puppet.

HAND PUPPET: Can't we buy him, like the other one?
DARK FORCE: He's not interested in money, and he has principles.
HAND PUPPET: That evil one! He must be stopped at any cost.

WITH LEADING POLITICIANS thus disporting themselves, what is undeniable is that the people at Televisa are making sure that the Mexican viewing public gets maximum entertainment value out of its elected officials (including a congressman who was a cast member, and a finalist, on the latest *Big Brother* retread). Spicy infotainment sells, Televisa discovered some years ago, and the rest of the media have been happy to bring politics into the same sphere: *Bang!* goes the tape, and Bejarano bites the dust. *Sob!* weeps the heartbroken girlfriend/party chairman/former mayor. "They accuse me, and accuse me, and I don't understand why." *Wham!* goes the Clown Inquisitor, and morality gets reestablished.

Meanwhile, Brozo announced in June that he would be taking a leave of absence from Televisa following the death of Carolina Padilla, his wife and inseparable partner. One had only to watch the final broadcasts of *El Mañanero* to realize how great is the influence he wields. Manuel Bartlett, the senator from Puebla who in 1988 oversaw the manipulation of the presidential election vote count, called in to send his best wishes. So did President Fox and the attorney general. So did Salinas de Gortari, the old devil himself, sending *saludos* during a live radio interview.

Even López Obrador, during his daily predawn press conference, congratulated Brozo as "a very intelligent social communicator." Then, unable to resist a populist opportunity, he expressed his hope that the program's workers would not be fired but "be given a vacation of a week, fifteen days, before being allowed to return on a full salary." At the studio, cameras showed Brozo's team mockingly cheering the mayor. Brozo was temporarily off the screen, but he will most certainly be back. As for López Obrador, for all the efforts to get rid of him, he may well be around for a very long time.

POSTSCRIPT. Nearly two decades after he vacated his office in the Mexico City mayoralty, right on the imposing Zócalo plaza, and after years of virtually uninterrupted campaigning, Andrés Manuel López Obrador finally won the presidency in 2018. It took three tries, but he believes, and there are many who would agree, that he actually was the victor in at least one of the previous two races as well. Back on the Zócalo, in the grand old Palacio Nacional, he has brought several old habits to his new residence: his daily early-morning press conference, his willingness to ignore scandal, and his practice of collecting enemies. Near the end of his six-year term, awaiting the swearing in of president-elect Claudia Sheinbaum in October 2024, he remains overwhelmingly popular. René Bejarano severed his ties with López Obrador years ago. Brozo is still presenting the news.

NOTE

First published in the *New York Review of Books*, August 12, 2004.

12

The Mission of Father Maciel

JUNE 24, 2010

Of all the terrible sexual scandals the hierarchs in the Vatican find themselves tangled in, none is likely to do more institutional damage than the astounding and still unfolding story of the Mexican priest Marcial Maciel. The crimes committed against children by other priests and bishops may provoke rage, but they also make one want to look away. With Father Maciel, on the other hand, one can hardly tear oneself from the ghastly drama as it unfolds, page by page, revelation by revelation, in the Mexican press.

Father Maciel, who was born in Mexico and died in 2008 at the age of eighty-seven, was known around the Catholic world. Against ordinarily insurmountable obstacles, he founded what was to become one of the most dynamic, profitable, and conservative religious orders of the twentieth century, which today has almost eight hundred priests and approximately seventy thousand men and women around the world who participate in the lay movement Regnum Christi. The Legion of Christ, nearly seventy years old as an order, is comparatively small, but it is influential: it operates fifteen universities, and some 140,000 students are enrolled in its schools (in New York, its members teach in eleven parish schools). And its leadership has long enjoyed remarkable access to the Vatican hierarchy.

A great achiever and close associate of Pope John Paul II, Maciel was also a bigamist, pederast, dope fiend, and plagiarist. He came from the fervently religious state of Michoacán in the southwest of Mexico and grew up during the years of the Cristero War (1926–29), a savage conflict that pitched traditional Catholics (Cristeros) in provincial Mexico against the anticlerical government in the capital. One of his uncles was the commanding general of the Cristeros. Another four uncles were bishops. One of them, Rafael Guízar Valencia, brought him into a clandestine seminary in Mexico City. As a twenty-year-old who had not even taken his vows, Maciel created a new religious order with the help of another uncle.

The new order was intended to be both cosmopolitan and strict, but given its founder's young age and general lack of education, it is not surprising that the Legion of Christ's aims were poorly defined (although in a fascinating study of Maciel by the historian and psychoanalyst Fernando M. González we learn that one of the order's statutes specified that priests should be *decenti sint conspectu, attractione corripiant*, or graceful and attractive). At the age of twenty-seven, the young Father Maciel had an audience with Pope Pius XII, who, according to the Legionaries' official history, urged him to use the order "to form and to win for Christ the leaders of Latin America and the world." This has been the order's unwavering mission for six decades, and with remarkable speed it emerged as a conservative force to rival even Opus Dei.

"Maciel's discourse was very much within the anti-Communist discourse of Francisco Franco," says Roberta Garza Medina, who is the editor of the weekly magazine *Milenio* and the sister of the vicar general of the Legionaries. The Legionaries' conservatism, she adds,

> above all was expressed in their posture regarding gender roles. Women had to assume a passive stance. It was motherhood or participation in the [unmarried] consecrated movement. . . . Maciel wasn't terribly interested in politics as such: he was interested in hooking the people with power into the movement and milking them.

But for the conservative movement within the Church, a former priest adds, "Maciel was someone who could supply faithful, priests, and money."

Maciel was evidently a man of some magnetism. Dozens of wealthy women contributed generous amounts for the Legionaries' good works, and the Mexican magazine *Quién*, normally known for its society pages and not for its investigative reporting, recently had a story about one of Mexico's wealthiest widows, Flora Barragán de Garza, who donated upward of $50 million during the years of Maciel's glory. "She gave him practically all our father's fortune," Barragán's daughter told the *Quién* interviewer, adding that the family finally had to intervene so that the by then elderly woman would not be left destitute. Her generosity allowed Maciel to travel first class throughout his peripatetic life, but it also provided the seed money for the network of private schools to which wealthy Mexican conservatives dispatched their children.

IN 1997, BLANCA ESTELA LARA GUTIÉRREZ, a Mexican woman who was living in Cuernavaca, looked at the cover of the magazine *Contenido*—a *Reader's Digest* sort of publication—and saw on it the face of her common-law husband. She had been his partner for twenty-one years and borne him two children, and she knew him as a private detective or "CIA agent" who, for understandable work-related reasons, put in only occasional appearances at home. Now she learned that he was a priest and that his real name was Marcial Maciel. He was, the magazine said, the head of an order whose strictness and extreme conservatism appeared to hide some vile secrets: the article, picking up information first brought to light by Gerald Renner and Jason Berry in the *Hartford Courant*, revealed that nine men—two of whom helped establish the Legionaries in the United States and another still an active member, and the rest all former members of the order—had informed their superiors in Rome that Maciel had abused them sexually when they were pubescent seminarians under his care.

The accusations were not new, nor would they be the last. In 1938, Maciel was expelled from his uncle Guízar's seminary and shortly afterward from a seminary in the United States. According to witnesses, Maciel and his uncle had a gigantic row behind closed doors, and one witness, a Legionary who had known Maciel since childhood, told the psychoanalyst Fernando González that the bishop's rage had to do with the fact that Maciel was locking himself up in the boardinghouse where he was staying with some of the younger boys at his uncle's seminary. Bishop Guízar died of a massive heart attack the following day.

Later, it would become known that Maciel had his students and seminarians procure Dolantin (morphine) for him. This led to Maciel's suspension as head of the order in 1956. Inexplicably, he was reinstated after two years. Much later still, someone realized that his book, *The Psalter of My Days*, which was more or less required reading in Legionary institutions and was a sort of Book of Hours, or prayer guide, was lifted virtually in its entirety from *The Psalter of My Hours*, an account written by a Spaniard who was sentenced to life in prison after the Spanish civil war.

Uneducated and mendacious, Maciel nevertheless had a genius for politics and for personal relations. But there was more: in a series of articles for the *National Catholic Reporter*, the tireless Jason Berry has detailed the various mechanisms by which Maciel received money and then channeled it to the Vatican. Maciel's envoys would regularly deliver envelopes with thousands of dollars in cash to key Church hierarchs. Private audiences with the pope commanded as much as $50,000 dollars per visit, money that was channeled through Stanisław Dziwisz, the Polish priest who was the pope's private secretary from 1966 until John Paul's death.

According to a former Jesuit with good knowledge of the story, one of the very first sizable donations that the Polish Solidarity movement received came from Maciel, who raised the money among the conservative Mexican elite he had so steadfastly cultivated. No doubt the Polish Karol Wojtyła, by then John Paul II, heard about this act of generosity and appreciated Maciel's ideological stance. Maciel was at John Paul's side throughout the first three of the pope's five visits to Mexico: Legionary money, its priests, and its very active laypersons' movement, the Regnum Christi, strengthened the pope's campaign to remove socially radical or liberal priests from positions of power and give ascendancy to his conservative Catholicism.

IT IS HARD not to think that these are the reasons the Vatican ignored the detailed and heart-wrenching letter sent in 1998 by eight of Maciel's accusers (the ninth member of the group having died). Even as the public first became aware of the accusations through the *Hartford Courant* and the Mexican press, which picked up the story immediately, the Vatican refused to act. Instead, Pope John Paul II put forward the beatification of Maciel's mother and of his uncle, Bishop Guízar. (The bishop is now Saint Guízar; Maciel's mother is still going through the beatification process.) It was only in 2006, after John Paul's death, that a Vatican communiqué announced that Maciel had been "invited to lead a reserved life of prayer and penitence." He lived out his final years quietly and died in the United States. The Legionaries, however, have continued to grow in numbers and in wealth.

It's risky for a nonbeliever to try to evaluate how the Maciel narrative will affect the Church's standing as a whole because an outsider can understand so little of how a faith is lived among its rank and file. Some days ago, the workmen who are building a kitchen for me prepared the altar they set up every May 3 at whatever construction site they happen to be. The date commemorates the mystical occasion on which the cross on which Christ died was found three centuries later, but it also coincides with the festivities that inaugurated the rainy season in pre-Hispanic times. The workmen lovingly carved and shellacked a small wooden cross, inscribed the year on it, dressed it in a sort of white robe, decorated the robe with blue ribbons, surrounded it with flowers in soda-pop vases, lit a candle, and stood around drinking in its company for a while.

No doubt these men know or have heard of a parish priest who had a "housekeeper" and perhaps a "niece" living with him because these things have never been uncommon here—or elsewhere, probably, although the effort to hide them may be greater. But Paraguayans have not abandoned their cheerful president, former priest Fernando Lugo, despite the fact that he is known to have fathered at least three children (he seems to think there may be more) while he was still a bishop.

Homosexuality has also been tolerated and to some degree almost expected of skirt-wearing priests in this macho part of the world. It is possible, perhaps, that for many Catholics, baptism, confession, and weekly Mass are almost bureaucratic procedures, like voting or getting a driver's license, and that true faith is something that happens at homemade altars and through the magical pathways of much older rituals, leaving priests to live their own lives as long as they do a creditable job with the sermons and the burials. The sexual abuse of children and its cover-up are a different matter entirely, one suspects.

As it turns out, Maciel's common-law marriage to Lara Gutiérrez was not exclusive. Some ten years after he met her, he began a long-lasting relationship with a nineteen-year-old waitress from Acapulco, to whom he introduced himself as an "oil broker." He had a daughter with her, and, according to a recent article in the Spanish newspaper El Mundo, several more children with other partners.

After she found out that her husband was not a CIA agent but a child-molesting priest, Lara Gutiérrez did not come forth with the news that she was married to him. Perhaps she was terrified of the man she had believed "was her God," as she would say a decade later. Perhaps she was simply ashamed. At any rate, she kept silent while some of Maciel's victims and a few journalists—notably the late Gerald Renner and Jason Berry, now of the National Catholic Reporter— kept producing more evidence. And then, last March, two years after Maciel's death, Lara Gutiérrez appeared with her three sons on one of Mexico's most well-regarded talk shows and listened quietly while two of her children testified that their father, Marcial Maciel, had made them masturbate him and had first attempted to rape them, the older one said, when he was seven years old.

WE HAVE A double vision of Maciel: we see the saintly figure known to his followers—one long, elegant hand placed on his chest, the other raised in benediction—and, as if through a keyhole, the other, nightmarish, Maciel, demanding that young boys masturbate him and then assuring the shocked, traumatized children that he was authorized by the Vatican to obtain "relief" by this means from dreadful physical pain. But we know, through Fernando González's investigations, that Maciel was the product of terrible abuse himself. On his deathbed, a boy who grew up with Maciel at last went public with what he knew. The boy came from a poor family in the small, pious town of Cotija, and Maciel was the son of a prosperous merchant there. But he was delicate in his ways, and thus a living offense to his macho father. "One day," González writes, Maciel's father said, "there will be no faggots in my house: I'm going to send you six months with the mule drivers so that you'll learn to be a man."

Maciel was sent to join a mule train together with the boy who would, as an old man, confess what he knew. The mule drivers raped them both. "My father will think I provoked this," the eleven-year-old Maciel told the other boy. "I'd like to hang myself." We also know from several sources that Maciel was regularly whipped by his older siblings until he left for his uncle's seminary at age sixteen. It is possible to read his external life as a fantastic effort to achieve the kind of glory that could compensate for the most abject humiliation.

The Legionaries—that is, Maciel—financed the construction of the church of Our Lady of Guadalupe and St. Philip Martyr in Rome, which Maciel intended for his mausoleum. But strikingly, Maciel the priest nearly always staged his pederastic dramas in the infirmary, or sick room (*enfermería*), of whatever Legionary seminary he happened to be at, as if this were a place where he could be cured. The masturbatory acts were explained to his victims as a remedy for his pain, but perhaps he truly hoped for healing of some sort in the infirmary. He knew, in any event, how sick he was: he left instructions with his delegates not to start the process of his canonization until thirty years after his death—in the hope, one can guess, that the memory of his sins would be erased by then.

Quite apart from the damage to Maciel's victims, there is the pressing question of why the Catholic Church, as an institution, did not condemn him when he was ordained as a priest, or when he founded the Legionaries, or when the story of his pederasty made the covers of magazines, or when enough evidence was found for Pope Benedict XVI to conclude that Maciel should live out the rest of his life in seclusion, or even when the rumors grew strong enough to warrant a Vatican investigation of the order as a whole. The answer surprises no one: at a time in which churches are emptying, the Legionaries have been a rich source of conscripts, money, and influence. In Mexico, everyone from Carlos Slim to Marta Sahagún, the wife of former president Vicente Fox, gave money to or asked favors from Maciel.

It was not until last year that Karol Wojtyła's successor, Pope Benedict XVI, at last authorized a visitation—church-speak for investigation—of the entire order of the Legion of Christ. As usual, the press and some disaffected religious have been way ahead of the Vatican. Now we learn from the press that the order kept some nine hundred women under nonbinding vows as *consagradas*, or quasi nuns, in conditions of severe emotional privation. According to a recent report in *Milenio*, the women, members of the Regnum Christi, live communally although they are not ordained. They are allowed to see their parents once a year and spend two weeks with the rest of their family every seven years. They are expected to donate half their material worth after fifteen years of consecration and donate the full amount after twenty-five. Twice a month they are obligated to have a confession-like conversation with their female superiors, who in turn report on the content of these talks to their own superiors within the Legionaries. The Vatican visitators who conducted the recent investigation of Maciel were allegedly surprised to discover the existence of the *consagradas* and to find these and other violations of canonical law in their statutes.

IN THE END, the scandal of Marcial Maciel, gruesome and grotesque as it is, may turn out to be a scandal of the Catholic Church. There is the distressing question of the Church's last pope, the popular John Paul II, and his relations with the demonic priest. There is the not unimportant fact that the Legionaries—along with Benedict XVI and indeed John Paul II—represent the most morally conservative part of the Church and that they now appear enmeshed in squalid moral scandals. There is, above all, the fact that an entire large, wealthy, international institution is now under suspicion (what did Maciel's fellow Legionaries know, when did they know it, and who was complicit?) and that the greatest institution of all, the Roman Catholic Church, appears to have engaged in a cover-up for decades on its behalf. Catholics who always identified their priests with Bing Crosby films will need some time to adjust to this knowledge.

But there is also the question of the future of the Church and of its priests and nuns as sexual beings. It is not necessarily cheap psychology to speculate that extreme sexual repression of the sort imposed by the Church on its members leads to perversion, an issue that has surfaced importunately from time to time over the centuries. Many priests and nuns, it would seem, opt to "obey" rules but not comply with them, as the Spanish formulation has it (*obedezco, pero no cumplo*). I offer this simply as anecdotal evidence, but in my casual, friendly, and often admiring acquaintance with members of the Catholic orders—all from the social activist branch of the Church, for whatever it's worth—a remarkable number have been involved in some sort of couple relationship. I once attended a major church festivity in a small town at which several of the priests and nuns who arrived to celebrate Mass were openly, and even defiantly, there with their partners, either homosexual or heterosexual. In 1979, at the time of John Paul's first visit to Mexico, I had a conversation with a progressive Spanish priest who lived with his partner, a middle-aged woman, about his split life. Why, I asked, didn't he leave the Church if so many of its norms violated his own convictions and desire for honesty? I remember his saying, in effect, that the possibility of doing good within an institution as enormous and influential as the Church was greater than the chances for doing good outside it. May that equation be changing?

POSTSCRIPT. In 2019, following a Vatican summit on sexual abuse, Pope Francis, leader of the church since 2013, did update canon law, obligating priests and nuns to denounce pederasty and all other forms of sexual abuse to their superiors. Priests convicted of such abuse are to be defrocked. In most civil suits involving accusations of sexual abuse by priests, victims have been willing to settle for an offer by the parish in question of large sums of money, leading not a few churches to declare bankruptcy. The ongoing scandal has also significantly affected enrollment in Catholic schools, but the Legionnaires of Christ still exist and run schools and universities, their numbers undiminished. John Paul II's heartfelt desire to canonize Maciel was thwarted when his protégé outlived him.

NOTE

First published in the *New York Review of Books*, June 24, 2010. Reviewed: Jason Berry, "Money Paved the Way for Maciel's Influence," *National Catholic Reporter*, April 6, 2010; Jason Berry and Gerald Renner, *Vows of Silence: The Abuse of Power in the Papacy of John Paul II* (New York: Free Press, 2010); Fernando M. González, *La iglesia del silencio: De mártires y pederastas* (Mexico City: Tusquets, 2009).

13

Troubled Spirits

MAY 2010

The inmate known as El Niño, or Little Boy, entered the Center for Enforcement of the Legal Consequences of Crime nine and a half years ago. Tall and gangly, with a goofy, childlike smile, he appears never to have grown up, though the memory of his deeds would make another man's hair go white. Abandoned by his father when he was seven years old and raised by his maternal grandparents, he was twenty when he committed the murder that landed him in this prison in the north of Mexico. His buddy Antonio, neatly dressed, alert, quick moving, and round eyed, was shoved into the same holding cell and charged with kidnapping. "We've been friends since then," one says, as the other agrees.

When he will leave prison is anyone's guess, but El Niño has reason to feel hopeful: he relies on a protector who, he believes, prevented jail wardens from discovering a couple of strictly forbidden objects in his possession that could have increased his punishment by decades. "The guards didn't see a thing, even though they were right there," he says. This supernatural being watches over him when his enemies circle around—and she is there, as Antonio says in support of his buddy's faith, after all the friends you thought you had have forgotten your very name, and you're left, as the Mexican saying goes, without even a dog to bark at you. This miracle worker, this guardian of the most defenseless and worst of sinners, is La Santa Muerte, Holy Death.

SHE IS ONLY one among several otherworldly figures Mexicans have been turning to as their country has been overwhelmed by every possible difficulty—drought, an outbreak of swine flu followed closely by the collapse of tourism, the depletion of the reserves of oil that are the main export, an economic meltdown, and, above all, the wretched gift of the drug trade and its highly publicized and gruesome violence. Although the total number of homicides in Mexico has actually decreased steadily over the past two decades, the crimes committed by the drug traders are insistently hideous and have so disrupted the rule of law that ordinary Mexicans regularly wonder aloud whether *las mafias* have already won their war against the Mexican state.

"The emotional pressures, the tensions of living in a time of crisis lead people to look for symbolic figures that can help them face danger," says José Luis González, a professor at Mexico's National School of Anthropology and History who specializes in popular religions. Among the helper figures are Afro-Cuban deities that have recently found their way to new shores and outlaws that have been transformed into miracle workers, like a mythical bandit from northern Mexico called Jesús Malverde. There are even saints from the New Testament repurposed for achieving not salvation but success. In this expanding spiritual universe, the worship of a skeleton dressed in long robes and carrying a scythe—La Santa Muerte—is possibly the fastest growing and, at first glance at least, the most extravagant of the new cults. "If you look at it from the point of view of a country that over the last ten years has become dangerously familiar with death," González says, "you can see that this skeleton is a very concrete and clear symbolic reference to the current situation."

Unknown to most Mexicans until recently, this death figure resembles medieval representations of the grim reaper but is fundamentally different from the playful skeletons displayed on Day of the Dead—the day when Mexicans' departed loved ones return to share with the living a few hours of feasting and remembrance. Her altars can now be found all over Mexico, on street corners and in the homes of the poor. Women and men alike are her followers. In the heart of Mexico City, in a neighborhood that has always been raucous and defiant, Enriqueta Romero leads a prayer session in honor of the skeleton every first of the month.

Simultaneously flinty, foulmouthed, and motherly, Romero was among the first and the most effective propagandizers of a cult that some believe got its start in towns along the Gulf of Mexico but now covers a wide territory up and down the country. In California and Central America as well, young people light candles in La Santa Muerte's honor and tattoo her image on their skin in sizes small to extra-large. A few years ago, the Interior Ministry revoked its registration of La Santa Muerte as a legitimate religion, to no effect. Newsstands sell instructional videos showing how to pray to the saint, and even chic intellectuals are beginning to say that the cult is *muy auténtico*.

IT'S NOT ONLY the crisis but also the types of problems people face these days that have fueled the expansion of the cults. Let's say, for example, that you live in one of the cities along the border taken over by the drug trade and that the crackle of machine-gun fire bursts out every night, filling you with terror of stray bullets. Is it not understandable to pray for protection to someone like the outlaw narco-saint Jesús Malverde, whom drug traffickers revere? Mexicans who retain a strong connection to the Roman Catholic faith might turn instead to St. Jude Thaddeus. At a time when no-win situations abound, he is experiencing a rise in popularity comparable only to that of La Santa Muerte, perhaps because he is known in the Catholic Church as the patron saint of desperate causes.

Fifteen years ago, a sun-weathered man named Daniel Bucio first prayed to St. Jude, and six years ago, he says, the saint answered his prayers and granted his mother release from a long and painful illness. Now Bucio comes every month to a listing colonial church called San Hipólito just behind the main tourist corridor in downtown Mexico City to give thanks to a miraculous statue of St. Jude that was donated to the church some thirty years ago. (Historians of the drug trade might be struck by a coincidence: it was about thirty years ago that traffickers from Medellín, Colombia, who are famously devoted to St. Jude, first established trade relations with their Mexican counterparts.) St. Jude's official feast day is October 28, and thousands of his followers feel inspired to come and pray to him on that day every month. Sixteen Masses are celebrated in the parish from dawn to evening, and worshippers crawl to the statue of the saint on their knees, praying for help, protection, and survival. The crowds are so large that police have to cordon off several traffic lanes outside the church.

Daniel Bucio loves these *romerías*, or religious fiestas, what with the jostling crowds and the street food and the endless parade of statues of St. Jude—some as large as a man can carry, some small but fantastically decorated, like his own, which in obedience to the ancient religious traditions of his hometown is dressed in a glittering ankle-length robe and the feathered headdress of the Aztec emperors. In recent years, though, Bucio's pleasure in the monthly pilgrimage has been spoiled by growing throngs of unsmiling young men and women with tattoos and chains who arrive in groups and push their way through the crowd, often exchanging what look like small, wrapped candies in swift transactions. Bucio thinks he knows what they're up to.

"Unfortunately a lot of these kids have taken to coming here," he says. "They sully the name of Our Lord and St. Jude's too—who have nothing to do with this *narcotráfico* thing. If everyone who came here came with sincere devotion, you wouldn't see this type of crowd."

Father Jesús García, a small, cheerful member of the Claretian Order who officiates at many of these Masses in honor of St. Jude, is aware that certain people who look as if they hope to earn a great deal of money fast come to this church to pray to the saint. But he is at pains to point out that the new devotion to St. Jude cuts across all social classes and occupations. "The other day a politician came here asking me to help him pray for victory in the elections. Just imagine!" he exclaims, amused, shrugging off the suggestion that St. Jude might be a narco-saint. "They say that when the statue of San Juditas shows him carrying his staff in his left hand, it means he's working for the drug traffickers, and nonsense like that." Father Jesús prefers to focus on the many new worshippers of true piety.

ON THE FACE of it, Mexican traffickers are the only ones who have no reason to feel desperate in the crisis currently obsessing their compatriots. Mexican traffickers, who are ideally placed to ship nearly all the cocaine consumed north of the border, also grow and smuggle much of the marijuana and an increasing percentage of the chemical stimulants US consumers favor. They use violence as a particularly effective means of communication, disfiguring their victims horribly and displaying their corpses for all to see, so that everyone will know how powerful the drug lords are and fear them.

Once a small group of country folk knit together by family relationships, the original traders hailed mostly from the small northern Mexican state of Sinaloa. Sandwiched between the Gulf of California and the Sierra Madre Occidental, at least three hundred miles from the US border and largely agricultural and poor, Sinaloa was an ideal location for a clandestine trade catering to the US market. The early traffickers' operations were restricted largely to growing marijuana in the mountains or buying it from other growers along the Pacific Coast, then smuggling it into the United States for a neat profit. For decades this was a comparatively low-risk and low-volume operation, and violence was contained within the drug world.

In the 1970s, the Mexican government, in coordination with the United States, carried out a series of offensives against the Sinaloa traffickers. It was like trying to get rid of a virus by flushing it into the bloodstream. A number of drug "foot soldiers," as they were beginning to be called, were imprisoned or killed, but most of their leaders escaped Sinaloa unharmed and set up operations in neighboring states and in the major cities along the US-Mexico border. With every new military offensive, the traffickers slipped into a new region and became stronger. As the stakes grew, so did armaments and the number of traffickers, and in each new city and region they bought off more politicians and police. There was no stopping the drug trade itself because it was run according to a perfect formula: sell illegal goods at a huge markup to consumers with money, and recruit your labor force primarily among young men with no money and no future, who are desperate to look sharp, act tough, and feel powerful. By the 1980s, a new order was in place. The drug lords controlled the underworld and key members of the security forces in cities like Guadalajara, Tijuana, and Juárez. In a shaky peacekeeping arrangement that nevertheless lasted for years, the drug lords parceled out each city to a particular family.

In the 1990s, the fragile peace among the displaced Sinaloa families broke down. They fought each other for control of the major border transit points and then began fighting sometimes with, and sometimes against, an upstart trafficking group with no Sinaloa connections. This was the self-styled Cartel del Golfo, from the Gulf Coast state of Tamaulipas. An offshoot of this group was the Zetas, a band of rogue military personnel originally trained as elite antinarcotics forces. Ordinary Mexicans had their first inkling of how much more brutal the drug violence was going to be in September 2006, when a group of men dressed in black walked into a roadside discotheque in the state of Michoacán and dumped the contents of a plastic garbage bag on the floor. Five severed heads came rolling out.

THE NEW ERA had arrived, and the foot soldiers in the escalated drug wars, facing the prospect of such a terrible death, increasingly turned to death itself for protection. It was during the first antidrug campaigns that the myth of Jesús Malverde, the original narco-saint, spread beyond the borders of Sinaloa.

According to legend, Malverde was a nineteenth-century outlaw who robbed from the rich and gave to the poor, was hanged for his sins, and then worked miracles from the grave. His cult took off in the 1970s, after a former street vendor, Eligio González, began praying to him. Sitting outside the Malverde shrine in Culiacán, González's sturdy, relaxed, and unsmiling young son, Jesús, told me the story of the miracle. Eligio had been working as a driver in 1976 when he was knifed and shot in a holdup and left for dead. He prayed to Malverde, whose only monument at the time was a pile of rocks where his grave was said to be, promising to erect a proper shrine in Malverde's honor if the saintly bandit saved his life. When he survived, he kept his word.

González appears to have understood that people would grasp Malverde's real importance only if there were an image of him they could worship, but unfortunately no photograph of Malverde existed—and, in fact, no evidence at all that he'd ever lived. In the 1980s, González asked an artisan in the neighborhood to create a plaster bust: "Make him sort of like Pedro Infante and sort of like Carlos Mariscal," Infante being a famous movie star from Sinaloa and Mariscal a local politician.

The Malverde shrine is a makeshift cinder-block temple directly in front of the Sinaloa state government office complex, and its green walls are covered, inside and out, with testimonials left by the faithful. The plaster bust is enshrined in a glass case and surrounded by dozens of flower bouquets, mostly plastic. Many accompanying photographs and engraved plaques feature the image of a marijuana plant or a "goat horn": an AK-47 rifle. No one seriously disputes Malverde's status as a narco-saint—in Sinaloa it is stated as fact that whenever a major trafficker wants to pray, the entire street is closed down so he can worship in peace. But as a warden of the Culiacán prison pointed out, Malverde is now so popular among Sinaloans in every walk of life that he is really more of an identity symbol.

IN MEXICO CITY, the director of penitentiaries refuses admission to reporters unwilling to sign a statement promising that they will not write "propaganda" in favor of the cult of La Santa Muerte. At the Center for Enforcement of the Legal Consequences of Crime, on the other hand, the director of the prison lets me talk without preconditions to some of the prisoners about their faith. Escorted by the prison guards past a series of checkpoints and corridors, I am startled to end up in a long open-air corridor whose left wall has been decorated with cheerful cartoon images of Snow White, Tweety Bird, SpongeBob SquarePants, and the like. These were painted at the prisoners' request, a guard explains, so that children might feel less terrified when they came to spend the holidays with their fathers. Facing the cartoon wall is a high-wire fence and behind it, a collection of hangarlike buildings surrounded by grass and even a few trees.

This is where Antonio, the accused kidnapper, writes *corridos*, or outlaw songs, a couple of which have even been recorded. And where El Niño, the convicted murderer, sticks pins into black velvet and winds brightly colored threads around them in elaborate patterns to frame cutout images of the Virgin of Guadalupe, Jesus Christ, and La Santa Muerte. He first learned of Holy Death through television, which might seem a strange source for such a spiritual revelation, but it was the path open to him behind his wire enclosure. Now nothing can break his faith in his new protector.

We talk in the shade of a leafy tree in the prison yard, several of us sitting around a rickety table a couple of prisoners have brought out and carefully rubbed clean. A host of other inmates who initially had closed loomingly around us eventually stand quietly, nodding in agreement as Antonio explains what gives La Santa Muerte her powerful attraction: "La Muerte is always beside you—even if it's just a little postage stamp that you put up above your cot, you know that she's not going to move, that she'll never leave."

El Niño's grandmother has told him that if he ever gets out of jail, she doesn't want to see him, and she doesn't want his daughter to see him again, ever. But unlike his flesh and blood, La Muerte needs him: "If you promise her a white flower, and you don't bring it to her, you feel bad," he says. "She weeps, and so you feel bad." And therefore he makes promises to her that he keeps.

Midday approaches, and the heat is rising fast. The men nudge each other, and one goes off to fetch a cracked plastic jug of water, which he serves with unexpected courtesy to the unusual guest. I ask about rumors flying around that the rituals for La Santa—the Santísima, the Little Skinny One, the White Child—involve human blood and even human sacrifice. A prisoner in another facility, where conditions were infinitely worse, had told me that this was true.

El Niño and Antonio say just that La Santa Muerte will grant your prayers— but only in exchange for payment, and that payment must be proportional to the size of the miracle requested, and the punishment for not meeting one's debt to her is terrible.

The men and I have been in conversation for a while, and despite temperatures that must be turning their cell blocks into furnaces, there is something about the openness of the prison, the grass, the trees, even the comradely way the inmates treat the lone guard on duty, that makes the place seem almost pleasant. ("He spends twelve hours a day here," Antonio says. "He's as much a prisoner as we are.")

As the men relax, their courteous ways with me even make it possible to imagine that they are not guilty of terrible crimes, that their faith in La Santa Muerte is merely a matter of preference and not born of desperate need. Then I ask El Niño if he thinks that when he gets out, it will be possible to lead a normal life.

His face twists into a bitter smile. "With everything I've done?" he says. "There's going to be people waiting to take me down the moment I walk outside the gate." We shake hands, and he and Antonio thank me for the chance to talk. I return to the other Mexico, where hope also requires a great deal of faith.

NOTE

First published in *National Geographic*, May 2010.

Risking Life for Truth

NOVEMBER 22, 2012

Let us say that you are a Mexican reporter working for peanuts at a local television station somewhere in the provinces—the state of Durango, for example—and that one day you get a friendly invitation from a powerful drug-trafficking group. Imagine that it is the Zetas and that thanks to their efforts in your city, several dozen people have recently perished in various unspeakable ways, while justice turned a blind eye. Among the dead is one of your colleagues. Now consider the invitation, which is to a press conference to be held punctually on the following Friday, at a not particularly out-of-the-way spot just outside of town. You were, perhaps, considering going instead to a movie? Keep in mind, the invitation notes, that attendance will be taken by the Zetas.

Imagine now that you arrive on the appointed day at the stated location and that you are greeted by several expensively dressed, highly amiable men. Once the greetings are over, they have something to say, and the tone changes. We would like you, they say, to be considerate of us in your coverage. We have seen or heard certain articles or news reports that are unfair and, dare we say, displeasing to us. Displeasing. We have our eye on you. We would like you to consider the consequences of offending us further. We know you would not look forward to the result. We give warning, but we give no quarter. You are dismissed.

1.

I heard the story of one such press conference a couple of years ago, shortly after it took place, and had it confirmed recently by a supervisor of one of the reporters who was present. It gives some notion of the real difficulty of practicing journalism in provincial Mexico, where dozens of reporters have been killed since the start of the century, some after prolonged torture. Different totals are given for the number of victims.

For example, Article 19, the British organization to protect freedom of expression, gives a figure of seventy-two reporters and photographers killed in Mexico since the year 2000, and of these, forty-five killed since the start of the administration of Felipe Calderón, in 2006. Other organizations give a total of more than eighty. The Committee to Protect Journalists (CPJ), among others, lists only twenty-seven killed since 1992. It does, however, keep a separate, open list of journalists' deaths in which the motive for each assassination remains unexplained by authorities. When these two sets of victims are added up, the total is sixty-five. "Mexico has the highest number of unconfirmed cases in the world . . . and the real reason so many cases we examine are unconfirmed is that there's no real official investigation [of these crimes] at all," the CPJ's director, Joel Simon, told me. "So we don't know why they were killed."

Whichever way one counts the total, those responsible for only three crimes against journalists have been tried, convicted, and sentenced since 1997, and in two of those cases there is widespread doubt that the convicted men were the minds behind the crime or even that they pulled the trigger.

In recent years, all the murders of journalists and all but a few of the threats against them, as well as disappearances and kidnappings, have taken place in the provinces. While covering the trial of Raúl Salinas de Gortari, older brother of disgraced former president Carlos Salinas, back in 1997, I learned that reporting for one of the hundreds of small media outlets that exist outside Mexico City is hard and often humiliating work. Raúl Salinas was a powerful and unpleasant character. He could and probably should have been tried for many things in connection with the hundred or so million dollars he had languishing in various Swiss bank accounts, but he ultimately served ten years' hard time on a murder charge for which the evidence was laughable. (The alleged skeleton of one of Salinas's supposed victims was unearthed on his property with the assistance of a self-described seer. Eventually it turned out that, at the request of the main prosecutor in the case, the skeleton had been planted by the seer's ex-son-in-law, who in turn had dug up his long dead father for the purpose.)

Farce or not, the judging of a former president's brother, in a country where the powerful enjoy almost total impunity, was unquestionably the trial of the century. Under Mexico's legal system, there was no jury, and the trial took place within a high-security prison a couple of hours' drive from Mexico City. I went out there every day for a week, to wait for hours at a time under a harsh sun for the one day when the authorities would, more or less arbitrarily, allow public access to the proceedings.

My colleagues from the country's principal news media turned out to be local reporters from the nearby city of Toluca, most of them stringers. I soon found out that they took turns among themselves covering the trial (or rather, waiting outside the prison for the occasional opportunity to cover the trial) so that each might have time to pursue the outside activities that allowed them to patch together a living. The reporter for one of the two principal television stations sold real estate in the mornings; another worked afternoons as a radio announcer. All were expected to recruit advertisers. (If memory serves, a commission on these ads was part of their income.)

Some arrived at the prison by bus. Several did not own computers. One had to borrow a tape recorder. They were not idealistic, but the job was exciting. They had clawed their way up the Mexican class system to find a career, and they were proud of themselves. It wasn't clear how many of them had graduated from journalism school or even college. For better or worse, many provincial reporters still have not. They worked fantastically hard, longed for career training and respect, and knew a great deal more than they published or broadcast.

GIVEN THE CIRCUMSTANCES, it would hardly be surprising if local reporters like the ones I knew back then were grateful for the envelope proffered by a drug trafficker as a sweetener to a death threat. Bribes, known as *chayotes*, are a long-established supplement to the income of journalists in Mexico.

Such payments were promoted and made primarily by the government itself since the early days of the Partido Revolucionario Institucional (PRI) and offered with greater or lesser subtlety according to the rank of the person to be paid. An editor from the provinces told me that the practice was more common in Mexico City, but an editor in Mexico City said it was the other way around. "Remarkably, [the *chayote*] has been impermeable to all the winds of modernity," said Luis Miguel González, the news editor of a business daily, *El Economista*, and a literate and dispassionate observer of the world he works in. "It's hard for foreigners to understand the lightheartedness with which the practice of the *chayote* is viewed in the general media," he went on. "Chayobribes, chayotours, chayomeals are all part of the joke."

Sometimes money is given to a reporter, a publisher, or an editor, specifically for the purpose of slandering a political enemy. Sometimes it is given in thanks by the subject of a particularly favorable story. Mostly, though, the money is handed out, like a regular salary, to beat reporters by their sources. In exchange, the writers are expected to publish government press releases as if they were news stories and to keep their own reporting within bounds delineated by the *chayote* giver. High-level reporters who pride themselves on their independence would be offended by such bribery. Instead, as González put it, they might be offered the chance to be lied to by a high-level government source.

It is hard to determine how immoral the *chayote* might seem to Mexican reporters, given that the practice was institutionalized by their own government. Not to accept a bribe or emolument from an official can be seen as a hostile act—a threat, almost. Few editors or publishers can be counted on to stand behind a reporter who refuses to play by the rules. Even fewer pay a living wage. (In the state of Tabasco, where the Zetas are powerful, the enterprising Salvadoran journalist Oscar Martínez found out that reporters are paid sixty pesos—about five dollars—per story.)

There has been a great burst of reformism and housecleaning in the Mexican media starting in the mid-1980s—there are now any number of superb, and fantastically brave, reporters who struggle to report and publish stories on all aspects of Mexico's difficult situation—but the practice of *chayotearing* beat reporters has gradually crept back to preform levels. As a working editor, *El Economista*'s González has to deal with these issues in often painful ways. "They will offer a free official trip somewhere. Then they'll tell you that on the trip there will be a good news story. Turn down the trip and you lose the story." My own very general impression over the years has been that the great majority of Mexican beat reporters see themselves as seekers of the truth who operate within extremely narrow confines. Or as González sums up their view: "Accept the bribe but don't get corrupted."

Which is to say that Mexican beat reporters' dealings with the menacing drug traffickers in their neighborhood are not so different from their historical relationship to government officials. The distinction between dead reporters suspected by international watchdog organizations of being on the take from the drug trade and dead reporters suspected by those in political power of *not* being on the take from anyone is perhaps less useful in this light.

Let us say that a Zeta press conference makes a deep impression on reporter A, particularly after reporter B is murdered for collaborating instead with the police. Reporter A decides to tailor her stories to what she imagines would be the liking of those who are watching her and even accepts specific instructions, guidelines, and requests. Let us say that one day she is murdered by enemies of the Zetas, who have spotted her as an enemy collaborator. In the unlikely circumstance that an outside observer could actually learn why and how it was that reporter A died, the question would remain: was she involved with the drug trade or a victim of deadly blackmail? In either case, the likelihood is that both reporters A and B were merely trying to stay alive.

2.

I went recently to the charming city of Xalapa, capital of the state of Veracruz, to talk with officials there about a recent wave of killings of journalists—eight dead in just two years, two of them dismembered, their heads left near the door of another newspaper. Xalapa has a lovely climate, an ambitious university, one of the best museums in the country, and, in the past two years, a raging war between powerful rival drug groups.

The state also has a notable spokesperson, Gina Domínguez, so famous that she was featured on the cover of a local society magazine that month. An enormous bouquet of roses decorates her spacious office. Her staff, friendly and highly qualified, speaks of her effusively. Thanks to a change in state law, she now oversees public relations for all branches of state government and not just for the governor. It is common to hear that she is the real power in Veracruz. More poisonous online rumors point to her tour of duty as press secretary to Mario Villanueva—former governor of the state of Quintana Roo, now extradited to the United States on federal drug charges—and accuse her of bribing the editors of local and even national newspapers.

On the day I arrived, all the Veracruz newspapers carried a front-page story—lifted more or less whole from the press release issued by Domínguez's office—about the arrest of four men and one woman. The headlines announced that with these arrests (which actually took place a week before the press conference), the killing of four of the eight reporters murdered in Veracruz since 2011 had just been solved. The detainees had confessed, saying that they had acted as hit men for the Pacific Coast drug group Cartel del Milenio.

Further, the press release and the media stories said, the accused had identified the killer of a fifth journalist, who, they said, had worked for the enemy camp, the Zetas. The suspects said that they had also killed "some" other reporters, which in turn had, according to the communiqué, "caused the deaths of still other reporters assassinated . . . by the Zetas." Better yet, the group of killers had freely confessed, or so it was said, to an additional thirty-one homicides. Thirty-six killings solved at a single blow!

In her office, Press Secretary Domínguez spoke in such perfectly even tones, with an expression so utterly unshifting, that I have no memory of her personality. She blinked once and changed the subject when I suggested that reporters used to the official bribe system were now being asked to choose between the frying pan and the fire, but otherwise she surfed smoothly over every question.

Could I interview the detainees? She listed the intricate legal impediments to that. Why was it that the wave of crimes against reporters had increased so sharply when the governor she now worked for was elected? In Veracruz, as in the rest of Mexico, she noted, drug group warfare was always shifting from state to state, and the murder of journalists was one of the accompanying phenomena. The government's record of successful struggle against violent crime was outstanding, she said coolly, and it had gone further than that of any other state in promoting more professional journalism. Had she in fact worked for the disgraced former governor of Quintana Roo, Mario Villanueva? Indeed she had, she said, for two months, and she had left that state long before his arrest.

Throughout the interview—she gave generously of her time—she stayed on message. "We have always maintained that the murder of these journalists had nothing to do with freedom of expression." The five detainees' confessions, she insisted, made it clear that the murder victims were only partially employed as reporters and that the actions of reporters on the police beat were furthering the interest of *los grupos criminales*. In every case but one, she stressed, all the victims were linked to the police beat.

The following day, both Article 19 and the Committee to Protect Journalists mentioned the dearth of evidence provided by the Veracruz state attorney general. A few days ago, when I asked Dario Ramírez, head of Article 19's Mexico regional office, if he knew how the case against the suspects was moving along, he explained why he didn't. The logic of the government officials, he said, "is to let the cases 'cool,' without producing an effective result. There is no access to the investigation, so we don't know what stage it's in."

3.

On November 13, 2008, the reporter Armando Rodríguez, who worked for the Juárez newspaper *El Diario*, waited in his car with his oldest daughter, then eight years old, while his wife got the youngest ready for preschool. She heard shots and for a moment thought that it was just part of the general Juárez soundtrack. When she looked out the window seconds later, it was too late. Riddled with bullet wounds, Rodríguez was slumped over his daughter's body, whom he died protecting.

Armando Rodríguez—known everywhere as El Choco (for "chocolate") because of his skin color—started out in journalism as the cameraman for Blanca Martínez, who was then a TV reporter. They married, and while Blanca became the editor of the local Catholic church weekly, Rodríguez persuaded a Juárez newspaper to hire him, and he transferred to *El Diario* as a reporter.

He worked the police beat hard, particularly at the time of a series of unspeakable *feminicidios*, or serial killings, of young Juárez women, and then again when the wave of drug violence started in 2008. An elder statesman on the police beat, Choco was respected by his editors and by his colleagues for his aggressive reporting.

"They said he was temperamental," his widow told me over the phone, "but it was just because he was so passionate about his work." The first time he got death threats, the paper persuaded him to take a break because he needed an operation. Many other threats followed. In the weeks leading up to his murder, Choco Rodríguez had published articles linking relatives of the Chihuahua state attorney general, Patricia González Rodríguez (no relation), to the drug trade. On November 12, he wrote a story about the gangland execution of two police officers who, according to Choco, worked directly for the attorney general, pointing implicitly to the possibility that the attorney general herself had connections to the drug trade. The story ran in the issue of November 13, which hit the street around 1:30 a.m. A few hours later, Choco was dead.

I asked Blanca Martínez how the investigation into her husband's murder was going and her voice got small. "That December they came to question me," she said. "I can't remember if they were federal or state police. They asked me about his work, they asked me if he carried a weapon. [He didn't.] One of them told me that they had precise instructions [from the federal government] to investigate the case. That was the first and only time the government ever sought me out." There were no arrests, she said. There were no new leads. The investigation was inactive. Years had passed before she was allowed to see the court files on her husband's murder, and then only briefly. There was, additionally, the fact that the main federal investigator had been gunned down a year after the murder. His replacement was killed shortly afterward.

Few murders in Mexico have been the focus of as much media indignation or pressure as Choco's. It has become a cause for Juárez reporters and editors and several media associations in Mexico City. The crime has also become a flagship case of sorts for the Committee to Protect Journalists, which is based in New York and is the most influential organization of its kind. In the fall of 2010, after many requests, the CPJ was able to meet with President Felipe Calderón, whose term in office is likely to be associated forever with the ill-fated decision to declare a military war on drugs and with the atrocious violence that ensued.

During his conversation with the CPJ delegation, the president emphasized that he was just as concerned with the fate of journalists in Mexico as his visitors and as determined to see justice done in the case of every crime against them. In fact, he said, the murder of Choco Rodríguez had just been solved; the culprit was a confessed hit man who had been under arrest for several months and had not previously mentioned murdering Rodríguez but who had recovered his memory of this crime.

Weeks before the CPJ meeting with Calderón, a reporter at *El Diario* was contacted by someone who claimed to have a brother, a convicted murderer, doing time in the Juárez penitentiary. This brother was the leader of a gang of killers and had confessed to several murders. But the source was concerned because the convict was being removed from prison every weekend and taken to a military base. There, he was being tortured mercilessly and told to confess to the murder of Choco Rodríguez. But he continued to insist that he had not committed that murder.

The day after the CPJ delegation's meeting with Calderón, the editors and reporters at *El Diario* were able to put the pieces of the puzzle together: the tortured hit man was called Juan Soto Arias, and it was he who had been identified by President Calderón as the confessed killer of Rodríguez. "Whatever limited confidence we had in the investigation disintegrated at that point," Joel Simon told me. "Someone was acting in an incredibly cynical manner. We don't know how high up that went. Regardless, the president told us information that was incorrect and easily confirmable as incorrect." The investigation has been dead since that incident, "like all investigations into the killing of journalists," as Simon pointed out. (Soto Arias reportedly remains in prison, serving a 240-year sentence for the murders he initially confessed to. He was never charged with the killing of Armando Rodríguez.)

ONE DAY RECENTLY I had a long phone conversation with Rocío Gallegos, who was Choco Rodríguez's editor at the time of his death. Since that first murder, reporters have received many threats, and a young intern was assassinated.

El Diario is unusual in that it is relatively prosperous and concerned for the welfare of its news staff, Gallegos said. Staff reporters are given fellowships to attend journalism school and seminars. They have health and life insurance, and most are on a salary. While journalism in Tamaulipas, homeland of the Zetas, has all but vanished, news continued to flow out of Juárez, and *El Diario*, even when it became the most violent city in the world. (Thanks largely to a deal that appears to have been struck between the Pacific Coast drug mafias and the local drug runners, similar to a reported deal in Tijuana, violence in Juárez has greatly diminished in the last year or so.) Even before Choco's death, the traffickers' hostility to the media was made clear: a week before that murder, Gallegos recalled, someone placed a man's severed head at the foot of a public statue honoring the city's paper delivery boys.

I asked Gallegos, who is currently the news editor at *El Diario*, how life had changed at the paper in the long years of bloodshed. "We understood that we had to give up on exclusives," she said. "Whether we got a scoop or not became irrelevant. [There were places] where you simply couldn't send a reporter out alone.

"We were so unprepared for this situation!" she said.

It overwhelmed us. We'd come in from a scene where the victims' mothers were crying, the families were crying, and then we had to sit down and write. Or it would be three in the morning and I'd find myself comforting a reporter who was weeping because she'd just received a death threat on her cell phone. You have to think: how have we been affected by all this? I think a great deal about those colleagues who have had to go out and photograph twenty corpses. How have they been affected?

I asked her what she would have wanted to see in these years of terror. "Justice," she replied. "Less aggression. Greater safety. But above all, I would have wanted justice, because the murder of our colleagues has received no justice. I would like to know who killed them and why."

POSTSCRIPT. Since the start of the war on drugs declared by President Felipe Calderón in 2007, and through 2022, the last year for which we have reliable figures, 240 reporters have suffered violent deaths in Mexico.

NOTE

First published in the *New York Review of Books*, November 22, 2012.

A Voice against the Darkness

MAY 18, 2017

Yet another journalist has been murdered in Mexico. It was the usual pattern: Javier Valdez, fifty, wrote a drug story, revealed too much information, said something someone did not want said, and was killed at noon on a busy street near his place of work. Six other journalists, none of them quite as prominent as Javier, have been killed in drug-infested cities since the year began, but because he was a friend of mine the details matter more to me this time. On reflection, I was grateful that, unlike many of the more than one hundred reporters killed in Mexico over the past quarter century, he was not abducted, tortured for hours or days, maimed, dismembered, hung lifeless from an overpass for all to see.

No doubt Valdez owed his comparatively charitable execution—he was merely pulled from his car and shot twelve times—to his prominence: he had received a Maria Moors Cabot Prize from Columbia University and the Courage Award from the Committee to Protect Journalists, published seven well-received books about the poisonous world he lived in, emerged as something of a hero for his younger colleagues, traveled, and talked endlessly about the fact that when a reporter was killed no one showed up at the protest marches except other journalists—no one seemed to think that it was important to have a free or unintimidated press. Since the vast majority of the reporters who have been murdered since the start of the drug wars work anonymously for tiny provincial papers, it has generally been assumed that someone like Javier Valdez would be safe. In fact, he survived for decades in the motherland of the drug trade, the northern state of Sinaloa. Why then was he finally not allowed to live?

Valdez grew up in one of the funkier barrios of Culiacán, the state capital of Sinaloa. Like most Mexican reporters, particularly in the provinces, he had clawed his way out of poverty and into a career. After graduating from a local university with a degree in sociology, he and Griselda, his new bride, found work as copy editors at a television station. This was thirty years ago, at the start of Sinaloa's second drug boom, the one that transformed the state from a simple marijuana producer into a major intermediary in the world cocaine trade and, subsequently, the world's second-largest heroin producer and exporter.

Javier was riveted by the story. Who wouldn't be? Beyond Culiacán, entire campesino communities were going through ridiculous economic booms and then surviving an onslaught of violent, unfocused, useless government repression. Humble campesinos who barely knew how to sign their names were rising to legendary heights, and an entire folk culture—the *narcocultura*—was taking shape around them. It was a great story, and it was all about the barrios Javier had grown up in, the kids he had played with, the families and society whose destruction he was witnessing. Plus, the only way he knew to cure the hemorrhaging pain it caused him to see his homeland destroyed was to write about it. In 2003, having already made a name for himself as a reporter for news organizations in Sinaloa, he and a group of colleagues founded a newspaper in Culiacán, called it *Ríodoce*, and gradually invented a kind of crime coverage radically different from provincial journals' standard scandal-sheet news-of-the-moment.

I met Javier five years later, on my first reporting trip to Culiacán. He swore like a lifer and had a rough face and a body like a Mexican bodyguard, paunchy and hard. When he smiled his face draped in folds. Understandably, he was paranoid for the first five minutes of any encounter with a stranger, but in my case he beamed and relaxed when I asked if he had thought of collecting his short weekly columns for *Ríodoce* into a book. As it turned out, he already had, but his most representative writing was still a work in progress. He was just refining the style that would serve him well over the course of countless *Ríodoce* columns and four more books; detectivesque, unafraid of clichés, and senti-mental, his voice was new to Mexican journalism and ideally suited to a broad audience. And what that voice told was a revelation. Here is my lightly edited translation of the column that ran on the morning of the day he was killed:

His uncle couldn't put up with him anymore. He was the shame of the family. So he decided to check him into a rehab center. He called some-one and the "flier" came right away: a windowless van with seven youths who kicked and shoved him to the ground, tied his hands and arms, hauled him into the van, and took him away.

When they arrived they hit him some more. Someone who seemed to be in charge strolled up. Well dressed, tall, deep-voiced. Everyone stopped when he approached, almost as if saluting him. Blackball, he said. And they all started the beating again. This time they split his head open and cut his back, cracked his collarbone. He lay there, flat on the ground. They gave him paracetamol and two days later they shouted get up, asshole. Speed it up, this isn't a hotel.

They shook him, gave him some powder, and he came to. Come on, we have to pick up two other new ones in the flier. That's what the Blackball was, and now it was his turn to inflict it on others. If not, they would apply it to him again.

He kicked and punched with the best of them and that's how he man-aged to get invited to the parties. A superior level. Beer, grass, and coke. Women were there for them too. They could dance and get high and then take them without asking for permission. There were other prizes waiting for him. He qualified for them with Blackballs. With yessirs to the boss, who was *el licenciado* [a Mexican honorific akin to the Italian *dottore*]. They taught him to become a criminal and smuggle drugs. His nickname was *el demonio*. When his uncle went to inquire about him they told him he was much better. But he didn't get to see him. Where is he? Well, he went to buy food and ask for donations at stoplights. But he's doing great, soon he'll be completely recovered. His uncle left, glad for the news but not quite convinced: not getting to see him left a bitter taste in his mouth.

No one liked him. The *licenciado* would say bring me *el demonio* and they would take him into the presence. He was good at hitting and fol-lowing orders. *El demonio* would show up and slam-bang. The victim wouldn't be able to move for days. A prize for him. He knew they'd give him any drug he wanted, and also the female interns in the next ward.

He lost his way in the dark clouds of the underworld. He smiled and drooled. And that's how they found him, sprawled on the floor, with his mouth full of gummy stuff. When they went to fetch him for another Blackball the *licenciado* said too bad. He was my favorite. And then he shouted, Blackball.

Over the years, his sketches filled in a world no one else outside the life had access to or could put into words. Thanks to this one, for example, his readers might be able to understand why a few years ago gunmen systematically raided the rehab centers in Tijuana and other towns along the border, killing some inmates and taking others away. They could speculate whether *el licenciado* was El Licenciado, otherwise known as Dámaso López Núñez, the former lawyer to Joaquin ("El Chapo") Guzmán Loera, now engaged in an increasingly bloody war with Guzmán's sons for control of the Guzmán drug empire. For clueless reporters from outside the life, like myself, Javier was endlessly generous with contacts, anecdotes, sources, tips, invitations to dinner, but it felt like we were in kindergarten, while Javier was poking around in the graduate chemistry lab, trying to find the secret formula before the evil professor realized that someone had been tampering with the chromatograph.

"He was the most imperfect of men," Griselda, his wife, said at the funeral. "But he had a heart as big as the universe." He caroused too much, he drank too much, or maybe he drank just the right amount to survive the tension of negotiating what he could and couldn't say about the deadly currents and shifting whirlpools of the Sinaloa drug world. His courage was always incomprehensible to me. Beginning in February, he started to write frequently about El Licenciado, in sketches like the one quoted here, and also parallel, deeply and anonymously sourced news stories for *Ríodoce* and a Mexico City paper, *La Jornada*. The threats he was used to getting became more frequent and scary. On the day he was killed, Javier had just come from a meeting with the *Ríodoce* staff about his security situation; he should leave Sinaloa, at least for a while, everyone agreed. He was intercepted by gunmen on his way home.

NOTE

First published in the *New York Review of Books*, May 18, 2017.

16

Making the Dogs Dance

JULY 14, 2015

Within a few hours of his relaxed escape from Mexico's highest-security prison early Saturday evening, Joaquín Guzmán Loera, better known as "El Chapo" for his stocky build, was back on Twitter, hopping about the ether, crowing and taunting like some sort of manic cartoon character. "Never say never," the world's most wanted drug trafficker cried at @ElChapoGuzmán. "There's no cage for this great Chapo!" He sent greetings to his family, thanked his collaborators, praised his sons, looked forward to working again with his compadre, Ismael "El Mayo" Zambada, who had run the Sinaloa Cartel since Chapo's arrest; and Don Rafa—Rafael Caro Quintero, a patriarch of the drug trade who was scandalously released from prison two years ago by a compliant judge and is now a fugitive. Lapsing momentarily into a bitter, mulling mode, Guzmán made rude references to President Enrique Peña Nieto: "And you, @EPN, don't call me a delinquent again, because I give people jobs, not like your piddling cheap government." Back in manic mode, the trickster taunted: "Tricks are more effective than brute force, that's what's worked for me."

Whether the tweets were typed by Guzmán himself, who is known to be barely literate, or dictated, with constant spelling errors, by minions, was hardly the issue. He and his equally boastful older sons have all had the same accounts for some years. The tweets were taken as authentic and provoked fervent responses from any number of young women twittering love emojis and young men praising his courage or crying, "Welcome, Great Lord!" Another form of tweeted submission was popular among men, who tuned in to exclaim "¡Eres la Verga!" ("You are the Big Penis!" or, more precisely, "You are the Mammalian Penis!") in response to their hero's missives.

There was a vengeful tweet early on from Guzmán—offering, to my mind, the first convincing evidence that he did not, in fact, turn himself in last year in the course of an arranged deal but was captured by army and navy special forces. [UPDATE: Another account suggests he may have been captured by US agents disguised as Mexican forces.[1]] "Now they're scrambling for a place to hide, those who put me on trial, the marine who took me to the helicopter, and the faggot *que me puso*," a narco expression that means, roughly, "(he) who betrayed me by positioning me so that I could be caught." Immediately afterward he quoted an old Spanish saying that sums up both his modus operandi and Mexico's present humiliating condition: "Money makes the dog dance."

"I put that escape at some fifty million dollars." This highly professional estimate came from a man called Jhon [*sic*] Jairo Velásquez Vásquez, more commonly known as Popeye, Pablo Escobar's closest bodyguard, contract killer, and go-between. Out of prison after twenty-two years behind bars, compulsively garrulous, a little tense, he discussed the case of Joaquín Guzmán with a reporter from Univision, the Spanish-language television network. "That's a very delicate case," he said. "In high-security prisons you can't make tunnels, because in the [control] room where they have the cameras they have sensors that detect immediately if there's digging going on. That escape was about money . . . [involving] the prison guards and a lot of people outside."

The high-security Altiplano Center for Social Rehabilitation, better known as Almoloya, has three-foot-thick walls and restricted communications, and, in fact, all the imprisoned heads of rival organizations to Guzmán's are still very much in residence in their own solitary confinement cells there. Guzmán, who is the head of the "Federación"—a loose assortment of drug clans who work together in the state of Sinaloa—was sent immediately to Almoloya following his arrest on February 22, 2014. There had been a week-long chase earlier in Guzmán's home state, ending at a beachside residential hotel in the pretty resort city of Mazatlán. It was the eve of the Mazatlán carnival, which features several beauty contests—Guzmán, partial to beauty queens, is married to one—and when he was asked what he was doing in such a public place, he replied simply that he hadn't seen his two little girls for quite a while. This was understood to mean that he had taken a heroic risk to see his family, but it could also mean that Guzmán was proceeding as usual, taking a little time off to watch the beauty queen parade from a hotel balcony in the company of his wife and kids, without fear of danger.

In the helicopter flying him to Almoloya last year—he had already escaped from a high-security prison once, in 2001—the world's most notorious trafficker commented off-handedly that he was responsible for some thousand or so murders, but he was in fact charged in several Mexican courts only with trafficking and organized crime. As the pretrial investigations began their lumbering progress through the legal system, the prisoner was confined to a windowless cell equipped with a twenty-four-hour video camera. He was taken to a patio for an hour of solitary exercise every day, and allowed family visits only once a month, each visit contingent on a judge's specific approval. Despite these restrictions, it is claimed that he somehow managed to organize a hunger strike last summer to protest the jail's appalling conditions, although the government, while acknowledging the strike, denies his involvement in it. But plans for his escape were well underway by the time of the hunger strike. In fact, they appear to have started almost as soon as he was arrested, and they were based, cheekily, on the very same device that has become Guzmán's trademark: a well-lighted tunnel equipped with a transportation rail.

One of the more entertaining photographs taken in the aftermath of Guzmán's larky escape shows Mexico's attorney general, Arely Gómez, squatting next to a neatly carved and reinforced, twenty-inch-square opening in the floor of an unfinished cinderblock house. The house is in the middle of a cornfield a mile away and in plain sight of the Almoloya guard towers, and less than a half mile from an Army regiment. In the photo, Gómez stares wistfully into the black hole, as if hoping that a white rabbit might suddenly pop out of it. The rabbit, however, had already hopped onto an unknown mode of transportation a good twelve hours earlier. "Up to that moment," according to the somewhat pleading official communiqué issued near midnight on Saturday, "the day had transpired in normal fashion. [Guzmán] had even been provided with his daily dose of medication."

One helpful detail Alejandro Rubido, the government's Commissioner for National Security, did not provide at the Sunday morning, no-questions-allowed press conference in which he confirmed Guzmán's escape is the precise time that the prisoner's flight was perceived by his guards. At 8:52 p.m., according to the official statement, the twenty-four-hour surveillance camera in his cell registered that Guzmán withdrew to the cell's shower area, "where he also regularly washed dishes." Conveniently, the camera's blind spot is in precisely this area. "Once the prisoner's long absence from view was noticed," the official statement reads, emergency measures were put into place "according to security protocol." Following protocol can consume long hours, and it may be that during the entire time it took Guzmán to reach his tunnel's escape hatch, clean up in a makeshift shower, select from a pile of brand-new clothing waiting for him in the safe house, and make his way over muddy, pitted, country roads to the main highway—or a waiting helicopter, who is to say?—the chase had not even started.

All that was left was for police and federal investigation units to marvel at the tunnel Guzmán's troops had dug unerringly from about sixty feet beneath this spot, under corn fields and pasture lands, beneath the prison compound and all the way across it, to the exact three-foot-square area occupied by the shower in Guzmán's cell. He and his engineers seem to have a thing for waterworks; access to his first major oeuvre, a marijuana-ferrying, two-hundred-foot-long creation that crossed the border from the state of Sonora to Arizona, was activated by means of a lever disguised as a water faucet outside a private house. Days before his arrest last year, he is said to have evaded his pursuers by means of a tunnel hidden under a spring-loaded bathtub in one of his many Sinaloa residences.

It took admirable skill to carve what may be history's longest escape tunnel, sixty feet underground. There was all that prison drainage, wiring, and pipes to avoid too. And Guzmán, who for all his pranksterism has revealed himself to be obsessively devoted to detail, no doubt insisted on the tunnel's inner dimensions: 5'7" high, so that he would not have to stoop (he is just under 5'6"), and seventy centimeters across. The tunnel was equipped with ventilation ducts and electricity as well as, apparently, a motorcycle hooked onto a sturdy rail, allowing Guzmán to speed under the muddy fields to the waiting safe house in a matter of minutes and in great style. *El Universal*, a Mexico City newspaper, has estimated that 291 trips by a dump truck would have been required to remove the 2,040 cubic meters of dirt and rubble extracted in the construction process. Praise songs retelling Chapo Guzmán's second escape from prison are already up on YouTube.

The most damaging consequences of Guzmán's latest great adventure will not be suffered by the government of the ever less popular Mexican president, Enrique Peña Nieto, or by those with whom Chapo has scores to settle, or the drug troops of enemy cartels he will necessarily do battle with, or the soldiers, journalists, judges, politicians, and police he may order hits on, though they may add untold thousands more to Mexico's narco graveyard. The Sinaloa drug clans have not suffered greatly during his time in jail, and business appears to be stable; the drug world has already reconfigured itself, and there is some small chance that we could be spared a major increase in violence even when, as seems inevitable, Guzmán is recaptured or killed.

"What's happening now with Mr Chapo Guzmán?" Popeye asked rhetorically. "When [Escobar and his people broke out of prison in Colombia in 1992] the CIA came after us, the DEA came after us. That's what's going to happen to Mr Chapo Guzmán. I give him eighteen months at large. Mr Chapo Guzmán must be feeling what I felt after we broke out of prison. Right now he's feeling good, Pablo Escobar was feeling good, but [Guzmán] knows that . . . they're going after his family, his wife. He's going to have to break with all his old ties. He's only going to be able to meet with his partners in the drug trade and with the people in charge of his military apparatus. It's going to be hard to catch him [but] the Americans are going to put a 20 million dollar price on his head. Anyone with [that kind of price] on his head will fall."

It was one of those sunny Mexico City mornings when it seems that the world is the way it is supposed to be, with schoolchildren on vacation skipping along the sidewalks and the traffic almost manageable, a mirlo bird whistling sweetly on the telephone wires. Emmanuel del Rey, the keyboard player for one of Mexico's most idolized rock bands, Café Tacvba, considered the damages of the grim joke played by the trickster drug lord over the weekend. Café Tacvba has huge drawing power among youths from Mexico's poorer neighborhoods, and it was these kids del Rey had in mind. "The message the escape will leave all those *muchachitos* who work with the drug trade," he said, "or who are thinking of making a life in organized crime, and who already think that Chapo is more intelligent, more astute, more powerful, more moneyed, and also a lot more fun, is that he is! They'll think Chapo Guzmán is proof that, just like in Star Wars, the dark side is more powerful. And this is a terrible thing."

It should be a simple matter to keep one dangerous criminal in prison, and yet Joaquín Guzmán Loera did not last even eighteen months in his cage. As one of the anonymous praise songs on YouTube says about his latest caper:

Money is very pretty
No cop can resist it
They just look at all those greenbacks
And they start to get the giggles.

One laughs only until the rage sets in.

POSTSCRIPT. Joaquín Guzmán was recaptured in 2016 and extradited to the United States the following year. Tried in a New York federal courthouse on ten counts of drug-related charges, he was sentenced to life in a maximum-security prison. In his absence, the drug trade has continued unabated, and the Sinaloa groups once led by Guzmán appear to have taken over even the cocaine trade inside Colombia itself.

NOTES

First published in the *New York Review of Books*, July 14, 2015.

1 For the theory that Guzmán was captured by US agents working without approval from the Mexican government; that his extradition to the United States was therefore deferred by stung (or corrupt) Mexican officials; and that his later jailbreak was propelled by the US official and public request for extradition, see my ""Guzmán: The Buried Truth," *New York Review of Books*, July 20, 2015.

A Lost World on the Map

DECEMBER 18, 2008

About two-thirds of the way through *Cave, City, and Eagle's Nest*, a new book of descriptions and interpretations of a sixteenth-century Indigenous paint-ing from Central Mexico, the historian of religion Vincent James Stanzione describes at some length a four-day voyage of initiation in the mid-1990s, on which he accompanied twenty-two young Maya men from their highland community on the beautiful shores of Lake Atitlán, Guatemala, to the lush lowlands and back again. All along the way, he reports, the pilgrims stopped for prayer, reflection, and ceremonial drinking at the very same spots where their fathers and forefathers before them had prayed and offered sacrifices.

The young men, who were members of a *cofradía*—traditional organizations that are linked to the Catholic Church but are devoted to a community's own religious practice—started their trip with empty carrying frames strapped on their backs. On their arrival in the tropics, they stole into lowland orchards to stage a symbolic hunt for fruit. Now pregnant, as Stanzione puts it, with their bounty, they began the punishing hike back to Santiago Atitlán. At the entrance to the village, as some of them cried with exhaustion and relief, they were welcomed by their young brides, whom they would be able to lie with now that they were men, able to offer the gift of their own fertility, as embodied in the fruit.

It is a beautiful story, beautifully told, but should any reader feel inspired by it to travel to a Maya community in order to serve an apprenticeship there in the deep ceremonies of life, Stanzione warns:

> Now that paved highways have been built [from Atitlán to the tropics], now that most of the town's residents are Evangelical Protestants, now that the *cofradía* system is all but dead, now that marriage is not as important to the people of Santiago as it once was, this *"costumbre"* or ritual of bringing home the fruit is no longer performed.

Stanzione, who arrived in Santiago Atitlán some twenty years ago and has lived there since, is fortunate to have been present for the last enactments of a ritual strongly rooted in the pre-Hispanic past, for it is precisely in the decades that he has been in Guatemala that, after centuries of existence, the *cofradía* system has finally collapsed. It embodied a vision of the order and place of things and humans in the world, with such strong roots in the pre-Hispanic past that epigraphers, like the groundbreaking Linda Shele, have been able to use Maya communities' rituals and daily practice to decipher pictograms carved in stone a thousand years ago.

The drastically increased rate of change is being felt not only in Guatemala: the religious vision, languages, dress, forms of production, daily round of duties, and network of obligations that bound together the Tzeltal, Otomí, Guaraní, Araucano, Inuit, Arhuaco, Ianomame, Ayoreo, Rarámuri, Kolla, Navajo, Arara, and Ojibway, to name a few, have been losing ground like the ice on the North Pole. Soon our only access to Amerindian modes of thought—and, too, Amerindians' only access to a record of their thought, their own recording of their history—may be through artifacts and accounts belonging to the past. We can be sure that few accounts will be more expressive and intriguing than the *Mapa de Cuauhtinchan No. 2*.

The *mapa*, a breathtaking tableau roughly 1 × 2 yards in size, was painted on the beaten bark of the native amate, or mulberry tree. It was created by painters who spoke the Nahuatl language from the nation-state of Cuauhtinchan—Eagle's Nest—in the decades immediately following the conquest of Mexico. Many postconquest maps were used by Indian communities to affirm their land rights before colonial authorities. Because much of the subject matter of the *Mapa de Cuauhtinchan No. 2* is unusual for this genre, we do not know this painting's original purpose; in fact, even what one-half of the *mapa* is a depiction *of* (a pilgrimage? municipal limits? a spiritual journey?) is a matter of intense discussion in several of the fifteen essays that make up *Cave, City, and Eagle's Nest*. But the artists' accomplishment is to have provided a thrilling, exquisite, and mysterious register of their spiritual universe as it was before conquest broke it apart.

1.

In the late 1990s, Ángeles Espinosa Yglesias, the extremely rich daughter of the Mexican banker Manuel Espinosa Yglesias, bought one of the few hundred surviving paintings produced in Mexico in the half century following the conquest. The painting that Espinosa Yglesias acquired from the private collection of a Mexico City family was richly detailed, but it was so damaged by moisture, rot, and vermin that large parts of it were impossible to read.

Nevertheless, it was clearly a drawing of a place, and, as the painting stated in careful Latin letters, it referred to the now vanished community or city-state of Cuauhtinchan ("Place of the Eagle's Nest"). Paths could be seen in the painting, represented by a trail of delicate footprints. Human beings, *chichimecas*—which means "barbarians"—bustled up and down the length of the map dressed in animal skins. Frequently, they appeared in the company of far more civilized men dressed regally in *tilmas*—one-shoulder cotton cloaks. There were dreadful scenes of human sacrifice—which a document destined for the eyes of a colonial authority might reasonably have avoided—and, oddly, a scene representing the ritual decapitation of a butterfly, a grasshopper, and a snake. Personified mountains were depicted, with devilish heads where their summits would be. There were naked men—perplexed-looking naked men—turned topsy-turvy by a whirlwind, and a flying goddess leading warriors out of a cave.

"Its beauty literally stunned me," Espinosa Yglesias wrote of the *mapa* a few months before she died last year. Thinking that the information locked in its images should be decoded, she asked John Coatsworth, who was at the time the director of the David Rockefeller Center for Latin American Studies at Harvard, for help. In addition, she commissioned restoration work on the painting from the Mexican conservator Marina Straulino, who, using state-of-the-art imaging techniques, made visible many sections of the painting no longer accessible to the naked eye. Straulino also created a digital version of the newly legible map.

Meanwhile, Coatsworth turned to Davíd Carrasco, a historian of religion who is the head of the Moses Mesoamerican Archive at Harvard. Carrasco put together a team of scholars of history, anthropology, ethnobotany, and archaeology, among other disciplines, and included in the group the estimable Keiko Yoneda, who has spent decades studying and identifying each figure in an early reproduction of the painting. The team met once in Mexico to examine the document and a second time at Harvard. The result is the magnificent volume *Cave, City, and Eagle's Nest*, which, in addition to the fifteen essays, contains copious illustrations, a poster-size image of the *mapa* itself, and life-size fold-out reproductions of each of sixteen portions of the whole.

HOW DO WE KNOW that a person is Indian? How does that person know himself or herself to be Indian? Some academics argue that there is no such thing as a common Indian heritage throughout the Americas; others point out that in most of these countries a great many people *are* native Americans, genetically speaking, even if they dress like punksters or in business suits. Liberals in the nineteenth century, including the Indian president of Mexico, Benito Juárez, equated cultural Indianness with backwardness, while an all-too-modern world treasures the idea of museum-quality Indians who will remain forever untouched by time, greed, or mall culture. Regardless of the arguments for or against Indianness, it might be generally agreed that a culturally distinct Amerindian will have inherited significant elements of a view of the world that antecedes the conquest and the arrival of Catholicism. It seems clear, as well, that many of the surviving elements found in different ethnic groups and cultures throughout the hemisphere coincide tantalizingly with each other—enough to be seen as distinguishing characteristics.

One such element is the notion of a world in which all living beings have animal and/or spirit counterparts endowed with magical powers. These beings, and the universe they occupy, can be seen with our own eyes, provided we know how to read the signs. Frequently, a reader of the signs will have recourse to fasting, dance, or hallucinogens to reveal the parallel universe. This shaman, most often a man, is frequently titled the Speaker, and what he speaks when he is in a trance are messages from the parallel world as well as the history of the tribe and its heroes, all of which form the chain of continuity that holds the community together—a community that includes both its present members and the ancestors who created it.

It would appear that on the left-hand side of the painting, the *Mapa de Cuauhtinchan No. 2* describes the story of the ancestors' journey to establish the community, and, on the opposite half, the physical and magical borders of the Cuauhtinchan state they founded. Thus, the *mapa* would be not so much a map as an epic narrative, an evocation of the barbarian ancestors and of the divine beings who guided them on their journey: first, out of the primal cave of Chicomoztoc, from which the Nahuatl-speaking people believed that human beings emerged; then, through the holy city of Cholula, where they would become civilized (and perhaps learn to sacrifice butterflies and snakes instead of people), and finally on to the sacred Nest of Eagles, where they would stake their claim.

In the closing essay, the book's two editors, Davíd Carrasco and Scott Sessions, point out the importance of the city that occupies a central space on the map—the sacred center of Cholula—as a "changing place": a place where identities are transformed. They describe the circuitous path traced on the left-hand side of the painting as a ritual labyrinth of a type common both to initiatory ceremonies and to voyages of discovery. Vincent James Stanzione, evoking the four-day pilgrimage from Lake Atitlán that he participated in, argues that the right-hand side of the *mapa* could well be a real map—a guide for pilgrims who traverse every year a ritual path in the real world. The left-hand side re-creates the initial voyage that the ancestors make over and over again in the parallel word.

The Cuauhtinchan of today is a small town in Central Mexico of some eight thousand people, not far from the city of Puebla's atrocious industrial belt. The lovely colonial cities of Tlaxcala and Cholula are also near, and, visible behind them, the snow-capped volcanos Popocatépetl and Iztacíhuatl. It is a highland region whose fertile plains, pine forests, and spiky vegetation are depicted in the *mapa* and described with close attention by the modern ethnobotanists whose essays are included in the book.

We know from a sixteenth-century written history from the same area, which was guarded for centuries by the people of Cuauhtinchan, that in the twelfth century the Toltec people of Cholula fought a rival ethnic group for control of the city. Under siege, they looked for assistance. The *mapa*'s narrative starts in the center of the painting, in Cholula, where two shaman-lords of the besieged Toltecs set out for the barbarian regions of the North, looking for military assistance from the fierce Chichimecas, who are renowned for their skill with bow and arrow.

In the upper left-hand corner we see the beginning of the epic journey of the Chichimeca ancestors of the Cuauhtinchan people from their northern lands to Cholula. A warrior goddess carrying a human trophy-leg flies out of a primal spirit-cave, a mythical spot generally known in the Nahuatl-speaking world as Chicomoztoc. It is depicted in the *mapa* in traditional style, as a womblike mountain with seven inner hollows. Chichimeca warriors equipped with bows and arrows follow the goddess. The lords from the embattled city of Cholula wait outside, ready to lead the savage Chichimecas to the city. The *mapa*'s left-hand narrative is limited to this journey from Chicomoztoc to Cholula, and what is striking is that, unlike most such epics, there are no battle scenes or images of conquest and triumph, or mourning and loss. Instead what we see most frequently are the rituals performed at stops for prayer along the way.

2.

For many years I put up a Day of the Dead altar every November 1 in my Mexico City apartment. I did this in collaboration with the woman who used to take care of it and me: Señora Jacinta Cruz Ilescas, a Zapotec woman from a village in highland Oaxaca where traditional dress has long disappeared and only Spanish is now spoken. In a fever of creative ambition, we would find new ways each year to suspend cloth backdrops on a bare wall. We would pin paper cutouts to the cloth; wrap and stack shoeboxes to create small free-standing altars on the larger one; surround portraits of the departed with fruits and the fruit with flowers and small plates of the favorite traditional foods of the deceased. Then we would fit a dozen prayer candles among the dense display of offerings and try to make the whole thing fireproof.

Finally, after we had admired the result and pointed out the current altar's virtues with regard to the previous year's, Señora Jacinta would invariably say, "Ah, señora, but if we were in my pueblo, we would be able to uproot a vine chock-full of jicamas, and make an arch for the altar with it. That way it would be right." Years ago, I read that the Maya people of southern Mexico also make a ceremonial arch from jicama vines, and they still remember why. The radish-like jicamas, which hang down from the vines and have brown skins but are white on the inside, represent the stars of the Milky Way.

One year, a few weeks before the Day of the Dead, I fretted that I would have to be abroad for that hospitable feast, but Señora Jacinta reassured me: she would prepare my mother's favorite foods and place them on her own altar—"It's a good thing she liked her mole Oaxaca-style," the Oaxacan Jacinta noted—and my mother would no doubt know to arrive at her door rather than mine. "She knows she will be very welcome there," the señora said calmly, even though the two had never met.

The all-important Day of the Dead festivities in La Paz, the capital of Bolivia, coincide with the week in November during which the sun at the equinox is most directly overhead. This means that at high noon on those days, and particularly on November 8, human beings walking about under the stark blue bowl of the sky cast no shadow. Throughout the world, people without shadows have been identified, often spookily, with the dead, but this association is seen as a great opportunity by the urban Aymara and Quechua who make up a large part of the population of La Paz. On the day of no shadows, they pack the cemeteries, and they bring with them their *ñatitas*, or household skulls. These skulls have been procured on the sly from a potter's field, or the forensic institute, or the family grave—some questions are better left unasked—and they are household helpers. (I heard from a celebrant that if a house is empty and robbers try to break in, for example, the *ñatita* will turn on all the lights and make it sound as if a blowout party were going on inside.)

On their day of days, the *ñatitas* are reunited with their fellow dead and feasted and thanked. Mariachis and native huayno groups and guitar trios serenade them, while their owners, dressed in their most impressive finery (and the amount of gold a prosperous Aymara woman can display is very impressive indeed), prop coca leaves or lit cigarettes between the skulls' teeth, crown them with flower wreaths, and shower them with petals, make them a present of, say, a brand-new pair of Ray-Ban sunglasses or a leather motorcycle cap, and then drink to their health.

Traveling this path of ritual through the recurring time of the calendar year—feeding the ancestors, blessing the animals, asking for blessings from the river and stream forces, keeping an infant all but immobile until its soul has had time to catch up with its body—Amerindian peoples have kept themselves whole even as the world has whirled uncontrollably around them, and indeed even as their rural communities have broken up, sending their members into the great diaspora of the cities and far abroad. (There are living in the United States today a not insignificant number of migrants from Chiapas, Oaxaca, and Puebla who speak Maya, Mixtec, Zapotec, and some English, but no Spanish.) For centuries, Indian community struggles centered on the right to the land taken from them. In these days of exodus, they fight, in ways that are often confused and contradictory but determined, for their ritual life.

ONE DAY IN 1993, while waiting in line in a government office in Bogotá, I struck up a conversation with a group of beautiful, cinnamon-skinned men dressed immaculately in flowing white robes. They said they were Arhuacos from the Sierra Nevada de Santa Marta—a snow-capped range on the Colombian Caribbean—and they invited me to visit their home.

The drug traders who have murdered so many of the Arhuaco leaders seemed to be in retreat at the time, and it was possible to make one's way up to the communities without danger. I stayed a couple of days in a peaceable village of perhaps two hundred people, in the midst of orange groves and cornfields, and the inhabitants explained the cultural projects they were trying to get off the ground—a community library, a radio station, and a historical archive of some sort that would be a depository of their history and self-knowledge.

The Arhuacos suffer greatly because mestizo land invaders, illegal loggers, drug traffickers, and government officials have deprived them of their ancestral land—not only their farmland but the land on which are located the sacred places to which they must make a pilgrimage every year. The attrition caused by religious conversion, forced exodus, and recruitment by coca and marijuana growers has been great, but lately the Arhuaco population has been growing (they number around fifty thousand). The Arhuacos are extraordinarily skilled and imaginative bureaucratic infighters; they are able to move in and out of the modern world more easily than many other Amerindians. They send their children out into the world to study things like computer programming and medicine, and it would seem that, like the young man who was my self-appointed guide for the visit, at least a few have actually chosen to return, their sense of community and self intact.

On my last night in the Sierra, the villagers gathered at a cluster of boulders a short way beyond the last of the rectangular thatched houses. There was no moon, and the stars were huge and near. Not wanting to intrude, I hung around the edges of the meeting and listened as a man's high voice beautifully recounted an epic involving the voyage the stars had once made to be in the company of humans. Then my guide escorted me back to the guest room in the village school.

The following morning I asked to be introduced to the wonderful speaker who had told this tale, and I found myself shaking hands with a tiny, grinning man with an easy giggle whom I had earlier taken to be the village fool. He had not told his story in Spanish for the simple reason that he did not speak the language. My hosts could not be convinced that there was something remarkable about the fact that I had thought I was listening in Spanish, nor is it clear to me that the narrative I thought I had heard was in fact related to what the giggling shaman actually said that night, although they seemed to think so, or else didn't find the question relevant. They walked me to the road and waved goodbye as I climbed into the back of a pickup truck, suddenly and inexplicably in tears. Years later it was a wonderful surprise to learn that despite the continued killings and other offenses against them, many of the projects my Arhuaco hosts had been putting together—a historical archive, their own videos and publications—were being carried out.

3.

On the first day of 1994, many, if not most, of the Tzotzil and Tzeltal Maya Indian communities of the central Chiapas highlands in southern Mexico staged an uprising against the *cabrón gobierno*, the son-of-a-bitch government. The fighting, such as it was, took place mainly in the town of Ocosingo and in the vicinity of the charming former state capital, San Cristóbal de las Casas. Then it stopped on the twelfth day, when Mexican president Carlos Salinas de Gortari called a unilateral ceasefire. It had, in any event, been a completely chaotic and ineffective war, which was not altogether surprising once it was learned that the rebels' improvised training was provided by Subcomandante Marcos, a white-skinned revolutionary with no fighting experience himself who also wrote the Zapatistas' (much more successful) communiqués.

It was clear, though, that the couple of thousand insurgents, in their homemade uniforms and with hopelessly inadequate weapons—some machine guns, lots of old hunting rifles, and quite a few carved wooden representations of rifles as well—thought that they had a serious chance of victory. Many reporters were struck by the wooden rifles, instruments that seemed somehow linked with the fighters' idea of the power that oppressed them. "Let the *cabrón gobierno* leave his palace and come and sit here among us!" the rebels who spoke some Spanish used to say, and it was hard not to think of the Mexicas at the time of the conquest, putting on their most magically power-filled masks to do battle with the Spaniards, who had guns.

Some of the ski-masked fighters who appeared in the background of interviews with Subcomandante Marcos were quite possibly among the slight, quiet men who before, during, and after the heyday of the uprising slipped into San Cristóbal every market day and spent hours squeezed together on the sidewalk in front of the electronic goods store, watching the silent images of a telenovela flicker on the television screens in the display window. The question arose then, as the rebels in the villages struggled to express their conflicted longings both for a return to tradition and for computers, for unthreatened *comunitas* and for higher education for their children, of what a good definition of a future for the Amerindian communities might be. Is it possible to be

Indian and be modern? Or, rather, is it possible to enjoy the benefits of modern technology and survive an omnipresent market capitalism without destroying an inner life full of meaning, and of meanings?

THIS MAY, A SEQUENCE of aerial photographs taken by employees of Brazil's Indigenous peoples' protection agency—the Fundação Nacional do Índio (FUNAI, National Indian Foundation)—was broadcast throughout the world. The images showed a clearing where members of a last, uncontacted, tribe of Amerindians live. In the past twenty years or so, aerial photography has helped upend the general conception that the Amazon has always been sparsely populated by hunter-gatherers. Along the Amazon River and its tributaries, neatly ordered dwelling mounds, built above the seasonal floodline, indicate that the Amazon was actually quite densely populated before the arrival of Europeans and their devastating epidemics, and not by Stone Age nomads but by highly inventive farmers who lived in villages and towns like their fellow Indians in Mesoamerica and the Andes.

Today, though, the last of the Native tribes that live in the Amazon basin—numbering perhaps 1.5 million people in all—are largely hunter-gatherers. Their habitat is shrinking at an alarming rate, and the past twenty years have seen an exodus of tribes like the Ayoreo, whose last malnourished dwellers in the wild reluctantly made their first contact with the modern world only in 2002. They reported that they were being attacked by jaguars even as they slept by the bonfire in their *malocas*, no doubt because the big cats were themselves being starved out of their environment.

The people in the aerial photographs taken in May don't seem malnourished, but they do look very scared of the enormous roaring object—a helicopter—flying above their heads. Painted from head to toe in red and black and making ferocious faces, they brandish their strung bows and spears at the horrifying intruder. José Carlos Meirelles of the FUNAI explained that the agency decided to take the photographs in order to prove the existence of isolated tribes because loggers and farmers and miners often deny that there are such tribes even as they tear down their environment.

How much the images will actually protect these last of the First Peoples is much in doubt. At some point they will most likely be forced to join the rest of their brethren in the reservations and rough, dusty frontier towns on the jungle's edge, where they might whittle arrows for tourists or prostitute themselves in exchange for a few coins, and give up on the struggle to make sense of their nightmare new world.

For the moment, though, the roaring flying thing has come and gone, and perhaps the fear it provoked is fading, turning into stories the shaman will tell over and over again by the fire. Perhaps the hallucinogenic leaves of the *yahé* vine will reveal the apparition's real meaning to him or to another seer who will be moved to paint what he has learned on a soaked and flattened strip of bark, one that might endure and be treasured for centuries, like the *mapa* from Cuauhtinchan.

NOTE

First published in the *New York Review of Books*, December 18, 2008. Reviewed: David Carrasco and Scott Sessions, *Cave, City, and Eagle's Nest: An Interpretive Journey through the Mapa de Cuauhtinchan No. 2* (Albuquerque: University of New Mexico Press, 2007).

The High Art of the Tamale

APRIL 28, 2011

Diana Kennedy was born in England some several decades ago (she does not like to be precise about such things) and grew up high-spirited, feisty, and no-nonsense. In 1957 she came to Mexico with her soon-to-be husband, Paul Kennedy, who was a foreign correspondent for the *New York Times*, and then she *really* fell in love—with her new life and with a universe of flavors, colors, textures, shapes, and aromas several light-years removed from her own. How could she have resisted? She was coming from the drab kitchens of postwar England, and in Mexico City just a short walk through any neighborhood market was enough to make her swoon: armfuls of blossoms the color of gold, the smoky perfume of dried chiles gusting through the corridors, the racket of a dozen vendors vying for her attention, waist-high pyramids of unheard-of vegetables, pumpkins of every description, gourds, melons, purple amaranth plants, shocking-pink cactus fruit, blood-red hibiscus flowers, and, above the general din, the metallic cries of the vendors . . . *¡cómpreme, marchantita!* Buy here! Buy here!

And then to huddle at a market stall and wait for an industrious woman in braids to chop up some *barbacoa* and onion and cilantro and spoon it all over a tortilla and hand the steaming morsel into her eager hands . . . Heaven.

Then there were the cooks, brown-skinned women with hands calloused from a lifetime of direct contact with fire—shoving kindling into the stove, turning over dozens of tortillas on a baked earthenware griddle, or *comal*, grinding and chopping and kneading all day for their husbands or in the kitchen of the *patrona*, the she-boss. With an empathy that often shocked the society ladies she lived among, Kennedy found a natural home in those back kitchens, and with a formidable tenacity she may not have known she possessed, she set about learning how to cook Mexican. She devoured recipe books, but she also learned to observe and imitate the cooks' every gesture.

Here she is in her masterpiece, *My Mexico* (1998), at the end of a two-page account of how she learned to make *tamales de espiga*, flavored with the dried toasted anthers, or pollen sacs, of the male corn flower. After harvesting the flowers and setting them to dry, they had to be winnowed:

> The winnowing was not . . . done with the wind or by tossing [the anthers] in the air but by drawing the fringe of a *rebozo* [traditional shawl] slowly over the surface so that the husks adhered to the fabric. But it wasn't quite as easy as that. Catalina said she had forgotten to bring her *rebozo*—actually she had lent it to her daughter, who had lost it. We sent across to some neighbors to borrow one. Elena, who had two, we were told, sent back word that she couldn't find hers; Esther had just laundered her *rebozo*, and it was still damp. I produced a woolen one and thought it worked quite well, but it did not pass Catalina's stringent test. The most efficient fringe for their work, so it turns out, is that of an ordinary *rebozo de hilo* (a common *rebozo* made of a more commercial thread).
>
> The cleaned anthers, mixed with some of the brilliant yellow pollen that had been shaken from them, were a luminous pale green but needed to be dried for two extra days.

One can only dream of reproducing the recipe provided next for fragrant, spongy tamales made with those luminous green anthers, but what matters as much to many non-Mexicans is the zooming view Kennedy provides of small-town Mexico, with its agricultural seasons and its kitchen life and gossip. (Of *course* Elena hadn't lost that rebozo!) Not very many years from now, when all the traditions are gone and all Mexicans have substituted bouillon cubes for heady, healing chicken *caldo*, sandwich bread for *bolillos*, and Tetra Pak orange juice for the palate-dazzling real thing, the Kennedy oeuvre will allow Mexicans, too, to revisit that place of infinite nostalgia called *la tradición mexicana*.

KENNEDY'S BOOKS WERE a logical extension of her fervent evangelizing on behalf of her New World discoveries. Following the untimely death of her husband—the other great love of her life—she lived in New York, and in the dismal food landscape of those days, which I remember clearly, the two or three Tex-Mex outposts in Manhattan sold glutinous, revolting, pasty glop that no one in their right mind wanted to touch. Sometimes I felt that I was the only Mexican in the city, pining simply for a little fresh coriander or a mango. If only I had known Kennedy back then! Now the city is full of hardworking migrants with refined palates from the states of Oaxaca and Puebla, who have filled local markets with the freshest vegetables and herbs. But Kennedy created the first receptive audience for those products. In her kitchen, foraging ingredients from here and there, Kennedy taught what she had learned. Craig Claiborne, the great, benevolent food critic of the *New York Times*, had suggested that she give classes in Mexican cooking, and with one of those life-changing bits of advice offered casually over dinner, also prompted her to do a book.

Characteristically, she went at it like fury, compiling, testing, teaching herself to write, and then waging an all-out campaign to promote it by cooking her way into the affections of the sales force at Harper's and then hauling food for booksellers at their yearly convention. Her first book, *The Cuisines of Mexico* (1972), was revelatory from the very title, emphasizing as it did that Mexican cooking is a high-art form and that it is as regionally varied as that of China or France. It was immediately successful.

She moved back to Mexico. In the beautiful state of Michoacán, she built an adobe house far ahead of its time in its ecological obsession, started an organic garden of edible plants, and, with a camp kitchen fitted into the back compartment of a rattling little truck, she began her endless pilgrimage up and down the República Mexicana. A description in *My Mexico* of a hair-raising excursion to Mascota, Jalisco, in pursuit of the perfect fruit sweets shows her determination. Following a collision with an oncoming truck and a long negotiation with the local police, the last two and a half hours were by far the worst. At first the road was shaded by trees along a small river and there were some homesteads and a few children playing while their fathers gossiped over a beer. . . . We were held up twice by huge machines trying to clear the road of a recent fall of rocks and earth and then began a precarious descent when the road narrowed considerably as it hugged the side of the steep slope. The loose stony surface made it slippery, and the bends were closed and blind. . . . As we descended, we had a distant view of the broad valley below and soon caught sight of the tiled roofs of Mascota . . . the Emerald of the Sierra, as it is known locally.

It was by then late afternoon: the restaurant that we had heard so much about was closed for a wedding party, so we hurried along to the lady who was famous for her conserves. She had gone to Mass, a long one, her son said, but he finally took pity on us and showed us in to buy her much acclaimed wares.

Where were the stuffed peaches that we had particularly come to buy? There was no peach harvest this year. . . . But what a variety of sweets there were: [thick jellies] of local fruits—pears, apples, guavas, and *tejocotes*, a type of crab apple—thin layers of fruit conserve rolled up with a coating of sugar, the most delicious being a pale green color and sharper than the others, made of steamed green mangoes.

Of course, Kennedy works alongside the cook to learn how to make this last treat, a perfumed concoction that plays on the tongue with so many tingling, contrasting shocks of sweet and tart, mellow and barely ripening, that I once consumed a large block of it in the course of a single day and felt only sorrow that there was not more.

VORACIOUSLY, KENNEDY COLLECTED every recipe she came across: from other books, from her friends, and, increasingly, from women all over Mexico whose names she provided above each list of ingredients, often followed by little vignettes. Some of her best recipes are so simple that the name of the dish is also its description, like "Tortillas stacked with guacamole and tomato sauce" and "Eggs scrambled with chorizo" (you have both the complete ingredients and the process right there).

Her consuming interest in the exotic life all around her made it inevitable that the seven cookbooks she ended up writing would range far from the standard recipe collection, but one can see that in each successive book she veered farther from the mestizo, or mixed-blood, cuisine of the cities, toward the rural, Indian roots of Mexican culture. She evolved into a sort of historical ethnobotanist very much in debt to the nineteenth-century writer-explorers.

It was probably inevitable that someone as constantly aware of the landscape as she is, and familiar with every part of the country, would become incensed by the ecological and cultural devastation Mexico has been undergoing. I could go on at some length about our garbage-lined highways, the almost daily loss of native species, the forests logged by lumber black marketeers, drug traffickers, and landless settlers, the slow attrition of our beautiful markets thanks to the likes of Wal-Mart, and the takeover in local Wal-Marts of everything fresh by everything processed—for one small example, the replacement of locally grown raisins by imported dried cranberries—but I won't. Suffice it to say that Kennedy's latest work, *Oaxaca al Gusto: An Infinite Gastronomy*, is an homage to one of Mexico's economically poorest and culturally richest states, and to its Indigenous people, whose immense poverty and fragile, stubborn beauty scald the heart.

The book itself is beautiful, chock-full of photographs, many of them lovely, and most taken by the author. But though it looks ready for the coffee table, it clearly aims to be the definitive work on the subject. To shore up that claim, a few Oaxaca experts have been rounded up to provide essays that could just as easily have been left out. (Although what inexplicably *has* been left out is an alphabetical index.) What counts is the collection of recipes. Gathered by Kennedy over the course of a lifetime, they reveal a universe in which food is ritual and sustenance and where agriculture and cooking are part of a single, perpetual cycle of transfiguration.

Perhaps not everyone will feel like making the wasp's nest salsa that Kennedy collected in the Puerto Escondido area of the state, but what an astonishment it is to read a recipe that seems to come through the millennia straight from the time of the hunter-gatherers. Step one: find your wasp's nest. Step two: munch on a few of the grubs. Step three: invent corn, develop the tortilla, grind the nest—the part with the wasp eggs in it—in a hollowed-out bit of volcanic rock, and roll yourself a few tacos. "Interesting and delicious" is how Kennedy cheerfully describes the result.

THE WINDOW KENNEDY most often opens to the past looks not onto the Stone Age but onto the dazzling era of the great preconquest kingdoms, with their elaborate court life and ongoing exploration of the exquisite world of "flower and song." Flowers were for holding to one's nose while strolling about in a princely fashion and for munching. The book abounds in recipes for squash flowers and fragrant plumeria blossoms, for maguey flowers and palm buds, which I am not aware of ever having tasted.

Then there are the numerous recipes based on masa, or dough, made of ground corn. Corn is all, or nearly all, in Mexican food culture: a drink (atole), a bread (tortillas), a thickener (*chilpachole*), a dough (tamales). The middle classes are increasingly switching to wheat flour products at home, but most Mexicans still eat some manifestation of corn at least once a day. Take, for example, the typical working-class breakfast of a bread roll stuffed with an enormous, spicy, scalding-hot tamal (*torta de tamal*), served with a cup of steaming strawberry or vanilla atole, a combination available at dawn for less than two dollars outside every metro stop in Mexico City. As Kennedy might say, "Delicious!" Tamales alone deserve a book or so: fluffified by means of generous additions of lard, and yet with an addictively grainy texture, the masa surrounds fillings as simple as beans or chopped-up leaves of some kind, or as complicated as mole, or, my favorite, chunks of pork in a tongue-stinging sauce of serrano chilies and tomatillos. For the snooty there are now things like lobster tamales in green pumpkin-seed sauce (*pipián*), and they're actually not bad.

Then there is the tortilla, deserving of a dozen tomes, of which Kennedy has already written one. Unless you are extraordinarily lucky, you never have eaten a fragrant, hand-patted tortilla made with freshly ground local corn, and you should add this to your existing list of painful regrets. Homemade tortillas are vanishing as women join the workforce, and commercial tortillas have been all but ruined by the industrial tortilla barons, who have substituted masa made of sawdust for the glorious real thing. These crude imitations don't roll up well, which makes enchiladas difficult, and I suspect the current rage for tortilla soup and chilaquiles has to do with the fact that the easiest way to make today's tortillas palatable is to fry them and dunk them in something else. (There are few things better than a good tortilla soup, but that's beside the point.) For the home cook, Kennedy recommends the standard modern method of placing a ball of commercial masa in a tortilla press covered with two sheets of plastic, and it works well enough.

Masa-based dishes in Mexico are generally prepared with a hominy-like corn that is first "cooked" in lime to soften the grain and loosen the hull. But Kennedy found that many traditional cooks in central Oaxaca insist that corn for thickening moles and preparing tamales be soaked in wood ash, for reasons that seem related more to ritual than to taste. She includes instructions for this method in the book. Also in central Oaxaca, she discovered cooks who made eggs cooked in wood ash, and, obsessively, she sets that recipe down too.

"These eggs have a distinctive flavor, but the slightly gritty texture is not to everyone's taste," she admits, adding, ever undauntable, "but they are healthy!" For those equipped with a gizzard, perhaps.

AND YET . . . THIS is one of several recipes in the collection that takes us back to the beginning of time. Suddenly we are hunched around a fire we are just beginning to learn how to manipulate. Step one: roast the hunted things—tapirs, monkeys, birds—on a stick above the flames. Step two: bury the foraged things—yuca, squashes, eggs—in the ash. Step three: invent clay and make a flat baked-clay griddle (comal) and eat the foraged things (at last!) without the grit.

Step four, who knows how much later, involved inventing the pot, and much of the Oaxaca book is devoted to food made in pots—not exactly soups or stews but brothy moles: meat or chicken and many wonderful vegetables cooked in a stock brought to life by the addition of various combinations of finely ground chiles. (Mole, pronounced *moh-leh*, means food that is ground, as in guacamole.) Throughout Mexico, these pot foods are frequently crowned with little masa dumplings, and Kennedy tells us how to make their characteristic indentation by pressing a thumb into each ball of dough before placing it in the boiling pot. Known in Kennedy's book as *chochoyotes*, they are also called *ombligos*, or navels, and here, if readers will be indulgent, is a thought: in the pre-Hispanic world there were not four directions but five; north, south, east, west, and up-down. Up-down was the *axis mundi*, and the navel of the world, and in this dimension lived the ancient god of fire. But since everything in pre-Hispanic thought is joined to its opposite, the axis the god of fire inhabits is made of water. Perhaps the "navels" in these dishes commemorate the union of water and fire that takes place inside a pot.

Such are the fancies inspired by the world so beautifully represented in *Oaxaca al Gusto*, with its plunging immersion into the very heart of an ancient food culture. But what, you must be wondering by now, about the eating part? We do not wish to eat eggs baked in grit, and we are tired of all this philosophizing. Well then, there is an eating part in the book too, and because moles are what Oaxaca does best, there are fifteen different recipes for them alone. Moles are famously complex in flavor and time-consuming to make but not really technically difficult. I am not an accomplished cook of Mexican food— or indeed of any other—but I decided that I might as well test the book with one of its moles, a classic red one from the isthmus: *mole rojo Ixtepequeño*. As an indispensable first step, I consulted Kennedy's *The Essential Cuisines of Mexico*

(2000), which provides clear instruction for selecting and prepping the various ingredients. Going back to the recipe, I worked slowly and did as instructed, except that I substituted cooking oil for the required pork lard, and Mexican chocolate for the less sweet Oaxacan kind, which I couldn't get.

I deseeded and deveined a mixture of chipotle, ancho, and guajillo chiles (all available quite easily in the United States), fried them very carefully and quickly, then ground them into a velvety paste with some chicken broth. I put a few thick slices of onion on a comal over a medium fire and let them char a bit, then ground them with a mixture of garlic, thyme, bay, pepper, cinnamon, and a couple of dried and lightly toasted avocado leaves. I fried this mixture quickly in oil hot enough to spatter, then added the ground chiles. I charred a few very ripe tomatoes on the comal and boiled them in some more broth, blending tomatoes and cooking liquid together thoroughly at the end. Finally, I added a couple of fistfuls of crumbled, slightly sweet Mexican breakfast rolls and the Mexican chocolate. I let everything cook and marry, and then I tried it.

Delicious!

POSTSCRIPT. The indomitable Diana Kennedy, defender of the marvelous and varied cuisines of her adopted country, died on July 24, 2022, at the great age of ninety-nine. She was still traveling abroad and in Mexico, giving talks and cooking, in 2019.

NOTE

First published in the *New York Review of Books*, April 28, 2011. Reviewed: Diana Kennedy, *Oaxaca al Gusto: An Infinite Gastronomy* (Austin: University of Texas Press, 2010).

Works referenced: Diana Kennedy, *The Cuisines of Mexico* (New York: Harper and Row, 1972); Diana Kennedy, *The Essential Cuisines of Mexico: A Cookbook* (New York: Clarkson Potter, 2000); Diana Kennedy, *My Mexico: A Culinary Odyssey with Recipes* (Austin: University of Texas Press, 1998).

The Twisting Nature of Love

Alfonso Cuarón's Roma

FEBRUARY 7, 2019

Water comes over the screen in waves for long minutes as the film opens. Off-screen, we hear the scrubbing of a straw bristle brush, as soapsuds float in and out of the frame, and at last the shot widens to reveal a young woman, tin bucket in one hand, long-handled squeegee in the other.

The tiled area under the brush is the carport of a home in one of the older parts of Mexico City, and if you're a Mexican viewer you'll know without thinking that the person with the bucket is a servant, doing the daily morning clean-up. You'll know her occupation even before you really see her face because she is dark-skinned and too poorly dressed to be anything else in a house of that size and because she exudes an air of calm and ingrained patience. What you won't necessarily realize is that she, Cleo, is the protagonist of the film, because no Mexican film, other than the farcical and offensive comedies featuring la India María, has ever had a household servant at its center.

(It is only later that we'll understand that what Cleo is so busily scrubbing away is the filthiest of all filth: dog shit, supplied in large quantities by Borras, a cheerful mutt who is the house dog but not exactly the house pet. American-style pets didn't really exist in Mexico back in 1970, when the film begins.)

For an American viewer—or at least for those viewers who have never met or been a domestic employee, known anyone who employs a full- or part-time servant, or hired a woman to provide domestic help—reading the character of Cleo, and by extension those of her employers, is possibly even more complicated. But start by looking carefully at the house: it is in the no longer elegant Roma neighborhood. Large but not enormous, and somewhat run-down, it's certainly not luxurious. In addition to Cleo and her best friend, the household cook, seven people live here: four children, who share two bedrooms; their father, who is a doctor, and his wife, a chemist; and the wife's mother. The furniture, heavy and dark, most likely belongs to the wife's mother, as, in fact, the whole house probably does. (How do I know this? Because in the 1960s professionals like Cleo's employers lived in newer, more comfortable houses in the suburbs, or in apartments that were cheaper and easier to care for.)

This is the house that Alfonso Cuarón, the director of *Roma* (2018), grew up in. Or at least it's the re-creation, meticulous to the point of madness, of that house. And this is the story of Cuarón's memory of a turbulent time in his childhood. The movie is shot parallel to the action, as if the camera were the ghost of Cuarón revisiting his childhood and looking on it silently, with the compassion and distance we are sometimes lucky enough to muster for our sinning youth and that of our parents. The hero, though, is Cleo, the nanny whose affection, unlike the parents,' is never wavering or disconcerting, and who, unlike a different, infinitely tiresome nanny on other screens around the city, performs true miracles. She had been on Cuarón's mind for years: in his early masterpiece, *Y tu mamá también* (2001), one catches a glimpse of Liboria Rodríguez, the real-life model for Cleo, carrying a tray of food up a long flight of stairs to the rich kid played by Diego Luna and handing it to him with an affectionate pat. (The Luna character is nearly oblivious of her care, her effortful journey up the staircase, her love for him, her hard work. Almost, but not quite; later in the film, as the car he is riding in passes a road sign pointing to Tepelmeme—Liboria's hometown in real life—the Luna character notices it and reflects that this is the place the nanny he once called *mamá* came from.)

SO WHO IS CLEO? The subtitles tell us that the language she speaks with Adela, the cook, is Mixteco, so we know she is from a desperately poor highland area of southern Mexico comprising parts of the states of Puebla and Oaxaca. Her small size and the shape of her face tell us so, too, because the dozens of nationalities, languages, and customs of the first peoples in Mexico were as highly distinct as those of Europeans; there were, among others, long-boned Apaches in the north, Purépechas and Mexicas in the middle, and delicately built Zapotecs, Mayas, and Mixtecos in the south. (Both the real-life Liboria and the first-time actress who plays her, Yalitza Aparicio, a recently graduated preschool teacher, are Mixtecas. Aparicio was living in her native village in the highlands of Oaxaca when Cuarón recruited her to play Cleo.)

Lastly, Cleo is part of a family, or rather two. She belongs to a family back home, of course, but *Roma* is about the family she works for and lives with. Nannies everywhere are often considered part of the family, and families tend to reflect the societies of which they are the building blocks. In this particular case, Cleo is and will remain throughout the film—and, we understand, beyond it, as the real-life Libo has remained to this day—part of a hierarchical, exploitative, unequal, unstable, and nevertheless unstintingly loyal and, yes, loving, Mexican family.

Cleo and Adela (played with relaxed authority by another Mixteca nonprofessional actress, Nancy García) are probably kin. Adela, the older of the two, may have emigrated first to the city, in search, like Cleo, of a life better than the parched subsistence she and her family eked out back home, with its grueling workload of endless days that transformed women into hags before they turned forty. But Cuarón is not interested in portraying Cleo anthropologically; he wants to show us what she was to him and to tell the story of Mexico City and what happened to Cleo the year that his own family shattered.

Life in *la capital* is both exciting and pleasurable for the shy Cleo and her more forward friend. They share a crowded room at the back of their employer's house—how lonely to sleep by yourself! The work is delightfully easy compared to the punishment they left back home, the money better—they can buy a sandwich and drink soda whenever they want! And they are lucky to have stumbled on good *patrones*—they get a day off every week. Like any live-in nanny—like any full-time housewife, for that matter—Cleo's days are as long as those of the four children she cares for. She sings them to sleep, nuzzles them awake, is nourished by the way their eyes melt with love when they say goodnight. Cleo doesn't say much when she is around them, in part because her Spanish is hesitant, but alone with Adela the two chatter and giggle endlessly in Mixteco about boyfriends, the *patrones*, and the children.

The thrill of going regularly to the movies in one of the ornate movie palaces that dotted the city back then is superseded only by the excitement of romance. Cleo falls for a wised-up *capitalino*, Fermín. We should know he's bad news from the moment he guzzles her soda on the sly before rejoining her on their date, but, like her, we are dazzled by his grace and sheer beauty. Fermín tells Cleo what Cuarón needs us to know; he is a child of a shantytown on the city's eastern outskirts, Nezahualcóyotl. Today, it is a full-blown city of one million people, but back in the movie's time it was a vast expanse of reeking mud—no paved roads, streetlights, water, or phone service—where immigrants from the desperate countryside often found a first foothold.

Fermín drank too much, huffed glue, was generally a mess, he tells Cleo, but then he discovered the martial arts of which he has just given us such a ravishing demonstration. He is a different, more powerful man now. Of course, he gets Cleo pregnant. Of course, he walks out on her the moment she breaks the news to him. Of course, the day she travels all the way to Nezahualcóyotl, where he is part of a kung fu stick-fighting group, he denies that the child could be his and calls her a whore. Meanwhile, seeing garbage trucks parked behind the field where he has been training, we realize that Fermín is a garbage worker.

And so, now that we have been introduced to *Roma*'s main characters, calmly and in some, but not too much, detail, the action lumbers forward like a tank that takes a fair amount of time to roll up to cruising speed but then is almost impossible to stop. The crucial events take place on Corpus Christi, a movable feast in celebration of the transubstantiation of the body of Christ that, in 1971, fell on June 10. An extremely pregnant Cleo and the matriarch of her employers' family go together to a furniture store, to buy a crib for Cleo's expected baby. In Cuarón's obsessive re-creation of the real-life events of Corpus Christi, we see the two women pass through a street scene that the inhabitants of Mexico City have come to know well: roads lined with military armored cars, police vans, heavily armed police, and tense men in civilian clothing carrying not-so-concealed weapons.

Also walking toward broad Ribera de San Cosme Avenue are increasing numbers of young people, on their way to join a march that is gathering at a crossroads a couple of blocks away. In real life, less than three years had passed since the gruesome Olympic Games massacre at Tlatelolco Plaza, and the Corpus Christi march was the largest protest since that event. At the start of the march, demonstrators sang the national anthem, which, in the movie's brilliant soundscape, we hear approaching offscreen. A growing murmur of panic rising from the street draws the shoppers in the furniture store to the windows.

Dazed, they watch the protest break up under the assault of men wielding heavy sticks and firing guns. Marchers scatter like a column of ants threatened by a torch, and now their utter panic is brought inside, into the store, to the very threshold of Cleo's body: a clutch of murderers in civilian clothes has burst into the showroom, guns pointed at a terrified protester. The young man is shot and falls dead; another gun is pointed at Cleo, and at the other end of it is a face whittled by adrenaline to a feral point: Fermín. Of course: those of us who remember the Corpus Christi massacre's history know that many of the men who attacked the demonstrators, killing dozens, were garbage workers controlled and trained for the occasion by goons from the ruling party (and, the movie implies, by US operatives). In the shock of recognition, Fermín retreats, Cleo's water breaks, chaos ensues.

WHEN I WAS A CHILD, there was always a nanny. My parents were broke more often than not—breakfast and supper might frequently be a bread roll and black coffee—but there was always a nanny, and no matter how sporadically we paid her, she never left: it was the order of things. Carmela fed me breakfast when my parents weren't around. She took me with her wherever she went: to market, to shop for the day's meal; to the shoe repair shop; to the park, where we sat on a bench to watch the pigeons while I clung to her, blurting questions; and even to faraway Xochimilco, where she had relatives, and where, on a dusty road in the middle of cornfields and narrow canals, I saw my first funeral—a quavering chant in the air, a dozen mourners, the men in straw cowboy hats, the women wrapped in rebozos, everyone holding a flower or a candle in the late-afternoon light, and at the center, a small white coffin bearing the *angelito*, the dead child.

There is a dead child in *Roma* too, stillborn but perfect, that an exhausted Cleo watches as it is carefully wrapped in its little shroud. In the past, *angelitos* flew from their mothers so often as to make it an ordinary occurrence. My own grandmother gave birth to twelve children, of which six survived. Women were always pregnant, and it was up to the father, if the marriage was stable, to find ways to feed five, or eight, or twelve children. Or the woman might die young, frequently in childbirth. There would most likely be a second marriage for the father, and the new wife might want to ensure sustenance for the new family by attaching the husband more to her own brood than to the one from a previous union.

Families are fragile and even dangerous things, as Cleo learns: throughout her pregnancy she has watched the breakdown of her employers' marriage. The husband, whom we first see arriving home in an ostentatious Ford Galaxie almost too big for the driveway, has found a new love: his heart commands him to abandon his wife and family, and he follows its orders. (Cuarón, directing the film of Cleo's life, which is also that of his life as a child, has his little revenge: the Galaxie drives straight into a neglected pile of dog shit, and the father himself steps on another of the dog's efforts as he leaves home for the last time.)

As *Roma's* producer, writer, cinematographer, editor, and director, Cuarón may have asked himself as he began to conceive this film how much of his love song to his nanny would be understood outside his country, or whether a commentary—a translation, really—would be a necessary complement for some viewers. What is evident is that he has made no concessions to foreign audiences, for whom every second of the movie is unavoidably not as transparent as it is to Mexican viewers—or for whom the film might not provide enough background to see that the central problem Cuarón is dealing with is the twisting nature of love.

I once interviewed a couple of dozen domestic servants about their work. It was hard to get young *empleadas* to talk to me, particularly if they were from the countryside: the fear of sounding ignorant, of saying the wrong thing, of losing their job, of *speaking*, made most of the young women I approached simply turn away from me. But the older women had plenty to say. A surprising number stated that they were happy with their families; an overlapping majority had loud complaints about their salaries. But what I heard most frequently was the rage they felt at previous employers who had fired them with no warning or thought for their feelings. *What about the children?* they would ask. *They fire us, we have to abandon them, and then you have to learn to love a new set of children, and you're always afraid you're going to be fired all over again and lose them.* One woman cried as she explained this. "They never think about the fact that we love the children," she said.

What no one talked about, unless I asked, and then not much, was the fact that, if they were live-in nannies, most of them had their own children, who were being raised at home in faraway Oaxaca, or Hidalgo, or Guerrero, by grandmothers or aunts.

How, I wondered afterward, does a woman's heart unravel once she is in this impossible fix? She is working to guarantee her children a better future than the one she faces, but while her child might be at home eating stringy meat and watery soup, she herself eats like an empress. The children she cares for loudly demand the latest-model cell phone every year, while at home a single phone with a cracked screen might be shared by an entire family. Her employers' children will go on to top universities, learn smart things, move easily through the world; her children try to get enough education to graduate from the menial jobs their parents hold. She knows the household children intimately; her children do not know her very well at all. Does she resent her employers' children for this monstrous difference? Or—let us face the thing squarely—does she love them more than her own? That the women I interviewed could love the children they cared for—and love them, in fact, to the point of heartbreak—was to me nothing short of miraculous.

And thus does Cleo love her family's four children. She performs a miracle for them, even, saving two of the four from drowning during a trip to the beach, although she has never seen the ocean before and does not know how to swim. But here's the thing that Cleo can admit at last: she did not want to bear her baby, Fermín the assassin's stillborn child, and the guilt has been threatening to drown her. She did not want to give birth to her, *pobrecita*, poor little thing, she blurts out after she has performed her redeeming miracle. *No la quería.* She loves the four children more.

So much happens in *Roma*. It is so bursting with life, Mexican life! Geese copulate at a New Year's party, men fly out of cannons, dogs shit and jump for joy, street vendors call out their wares, Norwegians sing, corn grows, young men are murdered, rich people dance the conga, and a poor girl from the Mixteca region loses a baby she did not want to have, saves two children, forgives herself, and climbs a rickety outdoor staircase to a rooftop sink to do the family laundry after a transformative trip. When I saw the movie in New York, the entire audience sat in silence as the credits rolled over a long, meditative shot of the staircase and the sky, until the screen blacked out over the title, and they sighed and moved on.

NOTE

First published in the *New York Review of Books*, February 7, 2019. Reviewed: Alfonso Cuaron, dir., *Roma*, Netflix, 2018.

A Hundred Women

SEPTEMBER 29, 2003

Long before her current troubles began, Cynthia Kiecker de Perzábal knew that Mexico had changed her life. When she was growing up, in Minnesota, she vacationed with her family here year after year. When she was a freshman at the University of Minnesota, she told me proudly, she traveled to Mexico City with the college marching band and played her saxophone at Aztec Stadium. In high school, she had wanted to become an actress, but instead, in 1979, after a year of college, she moved to Mexico and studied art in San Miguel de Allende. As she entered adulthood, her sense of what was important in life appears to have changed; she adopted the name Cheyenne and took up a wandering sort of existence, moving from one city to another, from plaza to plaza, selling bead-and-wire jewelry she made. In 1985, at the age of twenty-six, she met a Mexican street musician named Javier Perzábal, who had adopted the name Ulises; a few months later, she married him, and he began making jewelry too. Eventually, the couple wound up in Chihuahua City, the capital of Chihuahua, a vast desert state abutting the Rio Grande, whose most famous city is Ciudad Juárez.

A small, wiry woman with long blond hair and clear blue eyes, Kiecker looks lovely in a photograph taken three years ago, fair skin glowing in contrast to that of the handsome Ulises, who has dark skin, piercing Aztec eyes, high cheekbones, and waist-length jet-black hair. Kiecker says that she sees herself as an *artesana*, a craftsperson, and not as a hippie, which is how conservative-minded Chihuahuenses had grown used to thinking about her and her husband over the years—a weird but inoffensive long-haired hippie couple.

In recent years, the couple's life seemed to be acquiring greater structure; improved sales of their wares—something to do with the current vogue in shoulder-length earrings, perhaps, or a loosening of Chihuahuan mores—allowed them to move their enterprise off the street and into a curious little slat-board store downtown. The couple also rented a small house on a quiet street in a working-class neighborhood near the center of town, where they had a cordial relationship with neighbors who, like them, are not prosperous enough to have a phone. Chihuahua City is a prim and orderly place, with neatly laid-out streets and parks, well-run public services, and a low crime rate. High temperatures can be a problem, and boredom too, but the Perzábals liked their house and their livelihood. In general, life was good.

According to the Perzábals, shortly before midnight on May 29 they were at home, working on their jewelry. They had recently received a shipment of new supplies, and Cynthia says that she was sitting in the bedroom with Ulises, admiring a beautiful jade butterfly and imagining an appropriate setting for it, when they heard ferocious shouts and crashing noises at their front door. Within seconds, they saw an axe, or a bludgeon of some sort, break through the door and, behind it, five or six men wearing civilian clothes, all armed with submachine guns. The intruders shoved the couple, kicked them, swore at them, and attempted to gag them with the clothes lying around the room. Ulises says that he tried to protect Cynthia, but he was thrown to the floor and immobilized almost immediately. Cynthia, panic-stricken, was shoved into a waiting van; Ulises was dragged out by the hair and dumped into the back of a pickup truck. Cynthia struggled to breathe after the men placed a sack made of some sort of plastic over her head. She heard a neighbor try to deter their abduction by shouting, "I'm videotaping you!" (a bluff, she assumes), and then the couple were taken to a place they subsequently identified as the former Chihuahua State Police Academy.

No one knew where they were. By their account, they were held in adjoining rooms and were kicked, beaten, and tortured for the next forty-eight hours. In the end, they signed documents confessing to the murder of a sixteen-year-old girl named Viviana Rayas, the daughter of a prominent local labor leader.

Willy-nilly, the Perzábals were now leading characters in the most shameful human rights scandal in Mexico's recent history: a string of brutal killings of young women that came to be called the Juárez murders because they seemed to be confined—in the public imagination, at least—to one seedy border town.

A GRACELESS, SPRAWLING city more than two hundred miles north of Chihuahua City, Juárez is as garish as the capital is straitlaced. There are highways, fast-food stops, drab shopping malls, a couple of parks, and, everywhere, the *yonkes*—junk yards—where mountains of battered cars are piled so high on either side of the road that one seems to be driving through a canyon. In winter, the plywood-and-corrugated-plastic shacks on the outskirts provide no shelter from the frost. In summer, the heat melts the asphalt. The cheesy night clubs and topless bars along the main highways are where Stateside boys go when they come over from neighboring El Paso to get wasted.

The rootless nature of Juárez is like a mold in the atmosphere. About half of its million and a half residents came from their native towns and villages sometime in the past quarter century, looking for work in the foreign assembly plants known as maquiladoras. The uprooted immigrants live in sullen shantytowns—where a high number of households are presided over by unmarried, divorced, or abandoned women—and seem to have lost the essential inner compass that points back home. In the early 1990s, the international drug cartels decided that Juárez, with its border location, its table-dance joints, and its floating population, was a good place for an outpost. Within a few years, and as the violence that accompanied the drug racket escalated, people began finding the decomposed or calcified bodies of young women and girls along the city's desert outskirts—victims of a murder spree that has resulted in more than a hundred deaths so far, first in Juárez, but now, frighteningly, in other parts of Chihuahua state.

Among the first victims to be noticed in the crime pages of the local press was a thirteen-year-old girl from a poor background, Alma Chavira Farel, whose death is still used as the marker of the official count. Her corpse was found in January 1993 in an empty lot in a middle-class neighborhood—she had been raped, beaten, and strangled, the brief news story said—but there is to this day no explanation of why a young girl's violated body might have ended up in such a place. The following May, the body of another raped and strangled victim, name unknown, was found. She was discovered on the slopes of the Cerro Bola, a high hill with the words "Read the Bible" lettered on it, which overlooks Juárez. A third corpse appeared in June. This girl had been stabbed and set on fire. Another anonymous victim, found on the banks of the Rio Grande, had been raped, impaled, and knifed to death; her head had been bashed in. In 1993, Esther Chávez, who had recently founded a human rights lobbying group and had a weekly column on feminist issues in the Juárez daily *El Diario*, read accounts of the murders in the paper's crime pages. She began to take notice, keep count, and write about the killings. It was the first time that the murder of women in Juárez had been treated as an issue of public concern. It was years before the rest of the country paid attention.

I went to Chávez's tidy middle-class home in Juárez late one afternoon to rummage through a few of the boxes of files she keeps in her study. The press clips made it clear that the victims were for the most part maquiladora workers, high school students, and shop clerks. They were invariably young: the largest cluster of victims were between fifteen and twenty years old, and they were slender, dark-skinned, dark-haired, and pretty. Their most important characteristic, however, had to do with race and class: dark-skinned, long-haired young girls waiting at a bus stop or emerging from a factory are likely to come from families that are poor and nearly defenseless in a bureaucratic, overloaded, and user-hostile legal system. I found a dearth of credible suspects in the clips, or even police sketches of possible assailants, but there was a numbing quantity of photographs of victims' relatives, holding banners and demanding justice in endless marches and demonstrations or denouncing the offensive treatment they had themselves received at the hands of the police—the jokes, the laughter, the obscene insinuations about the victims' secret lives. When I left her study, Chávez, a petite, even-tempered, and self-possessed woman of seventy, was in the living room in a favorite chair, nursing her daily treat of a whiskey-on-the-rocks. Since she began keeping track of the murders in Juárez, she has counted ninety-six "feminicides," or sexual homicides—women whose deaths didn't seem to be part of a larger wave of killings by husbands, pimps, gigolos, neighbors, stepfathers, and the like. The bodies of the victims—strangled or beaten to death, often raped and, sometimes, hideously mutilated—are found in the desert days or months after the girls fail to come home. Their faces are often disfigured, the skulls crushed. The autopsies sometimes reveal that they were kept alive for days before being killed. "You know, when I first started looking into these murders, and I found out how these girls had died, I didn't sleep for days," Chávez recalled. "I kept thinking about how, in their final hours, they must have prayed for death." She pondered for a while. "I thought that it was just a question of getting the information out, so people would know what was happening, and then it would stop. I thought it would all be over after a few months. And now it's ten years later and nothing has changed."

JUST THREE YEARS AGO, Mexican voters, electing a new president, decisively overturned a seventy-year-old authoritarian regime. The victor, Vicente Fox, has continued the policy started by his immediate predecessors, Carlos Salinas de Gortari and Ernesto Zedillo, to greatly reduce federal power and devolve both tax monies and authority to the state and municipal levels. One result has been stronger local governments—or, where citizens are passive, stronger local rulers—and a weakened presidency. Vicente Fox, a gifted campaigner, as president has shown himself indifferent to the actual business of governing. Only after years of pleading by human rights lobbying groups like the one founded by Esther Chávez in Juárez did the federal government agree, in July, to intervene in what it has long insisted was a purely local law-enforcement situation. In a damning special report issued in August, Amnesty International decried the lack of progress in human rights issues in general under President Fox and, in particular, the federal government's mishandling of the unconscionably long list of Juárez murders. At the state level, the report focused specifically on police indifference to the plight of victims' families, a trail of confessions obtained through torture to gain questionable convictions, and incidents in which disfigured corpses have been returned to grieving parents—only to have the parents subsequently conclude that the corpse, though dressed in recognizable remnants of their daughter's clothing, isn't their daughter. Irene Kahn, the Secretary General of Amnesty International, told me that the murders "are just one example of the failure of justice in Mexico. We see all the delays, torture, negligence, fabrication of evidence, open discrimination against women that we have seen in many other situations in Mexico, but here it's very clear and blatant, and that's why it's so important. And it's been going on for the last ten years."

There are many theories about these killings. According to opinion polls, most Mexicans believe that the girls are murdered so that their organs can be extracted for transplants for wealthy patients in the United States. None of the recognizable remains found so far have been missing internal organs, but this theory has great symbolic weight. For many years, more serious speculation centered on an unnamed group of *narcosatánicos*, who might be using the girls in atrocious rituals. Recently, greater attention has been paid to the possibility that members of the various police forces are murdering the girls for sport. Perhaps, as some well-informed observers on both sides of the border believe, the killers are what are known as "Juniors," scions of Mexico's ruling elite, out on a hunting spree. No theory is sufficient to explain all the crimes, and none necessarily excludes the others. And, if all the theories seem inevitably to lead to paranoid and convoluted conclusions, it must be said that no theory is as demented as the crimes themselves. There is to date no legal evidence, in any case, pointing convincingly in any particular direction.

IN JUÁREZ, MANUEL ESPARZA, who is the official spokesman for the Chihuahua investigative police—the *judiciales*—received me in a bare, uncomfortable office in the former Juárez police academy, not far from a stretch of desert where the bodies of eleven victims have been found over the years.

Esparza, who is surprisingly young—thirty-two—and garrulous, is also the chief of agents for the special investigative branch of the *judiciales* in charge of murders of women. He told me that since 1998, when Patricio Martínez was elected governor of Chihuahua and appointed Jesús Solís as his attorney general, police work has become in all ways more efficient. A map is being put together to match all the information about each victim with the site at which the body had been found. A special unit for crimes against women has been created. The FBI has been invited to provide training and advice, and has done so.

The careers of Solís and Martínez have been linked at least since 1993, when Martínez was elected mayor of Chihuahua City and appointed Solís to head the municipal police. Published rumors regarding Solís's possible involvement in the drug trade have hounded him (and been angrily denied) since then, and over the years numerous complaints have been filed accusing him of participating directly in acts of police brutality against the citizenry.

According to Esparza, one serial murderer, or an association of murderers, was responsible for twenty-five of the crimes in Juárez to date. Even though it is well known that serial killers are hard to find, Esparza said, his people had arrested all the criminals involved in those twenty-five murders. The other murders, he went on, including the recent ones, could be attributed to imitators.

The most notorious arrest took place in 1995, three years before Martínez's election, when Abdel Latif Sharif Sharif, an Egyptian resident of Juárez with a long arrest record in the United States for assault and battery of women, was accused of seven of the Juárez murders. He was tried in 1999 and in the end convicted only of one, the murder of seventeen-year-old Elisabeth Castro. In the view of human rights activists and journalists who have examined the Sharif trial record, there is no substantial evidence linking him to Elizabeth

Castro's murder—a conclusion that Amnesty International concurs in. Sharif, throughout his years of imprisonment, has insisted that he is innocent.

In 1999, with Governor Martínez and Attorney General Solís in power, a thirteen-year-old girl managed to escape from a bus driver, employed on one of the maquiladora routes, who had tried to rape and kill her. He and some of his fellow drivers were subsequently accused of killing several young women on Sharif's orders (the prosecution argues that Sharif, who was in jail at the time, commissioned the murders in order to prove his own innocence), but these cases, too, seem to be full of holes, and none of the accused have been sentenced. Just last month, Sharif was charged with seven more of the Juárez murders—also carried out from jail under his orders, the accusation says.

Two years ago, two other bus drivers were detained and accused of killing eight young girls whose bodies had been found days earlier near a well-traveled avenue in Juárez. The suspects were not allowed to talk at their perp walk, but they removed their clothing to reveal burn marks and bruises, which the prison medical examiner subsequently identified as evidence of torture. When the press questioned an official from the attorney general's office about this, he explained that the wounds had been self-inflicted. One of the drivers died in custody in February. His lawyer, Mario Escobedo Anaya, who was outspoken in his denial of his client's guilt, had been killed by police a year earlier; the officers involved said that they had confused the lawyer with a fugitive criminal, though it is not clear why they would have. (Escobedo Anaya was talking to his father on his cell phone at the time of the shooting.) The police were cleared of all charges a few months later, on the ground that they had acted in self-defense. Innocent or not, the surviving bus driver, after three years in jail, still has not been sentenced.

The media and the human rights activists who monitor these cases had assumed that the killings of young girls were a phenomenon defined by the Juárez border mentality, its transient and economically deprived population, and a burgeoning drug culture. Then the killings spread from Juárez to the capital. In the past four years, fifteen young women and teenage girls have disappeared in broad daylight from the streets of Chihuahua City, having been last seen leaving the maquiladoras in which they worked, or the schools where they studied, or their homes to go shopping. Nine corpses have been found in the mesquite desert around the city, strangled and disfigured and possibly raped, and police say they have identified six of them.

ON SUNDAY, MARCH 16, at about four in the afternoon, a Chihuahua City labor leader named José Rayas dropped off his daughter Viviana at a park near the city's downtown area, where she was going to do homework with some classmates. Viviana, a quiet, thin, and childish-looking sixteen-year-old with long dark hair and big Mexican eyes, was last seen by her classmates an hour and a half later as they left her at a bus stop near the park. When her parents returned home from a family visit at eight o'clock that evening, they learned that she hadn't come home.

José Rayas is a stocky man with sad eyes whose face and body seem to be puddling at the bottom. His voice is soft, he wears no diamond jewelry or gold chains, and his demeanor is modest. In other words, he does not look like what he is: the general secretary of the Chihuahua section of the Workers' Union of the Communications and Transport Ministry—which controls the nation's highways and airports and its radio and television networks. Before the murder of Viviana Rayas, the killers had preyed on poor families, but her case was different: in a state that is about as large as Oregon and has barely three million inhabitants, and whose numerous foreign-assembly factories rely on an efficient and well-maintained highway network, Viviana Rayas's father is an extremely powerful individual and skilled in playing hardball.

Viviana was the youngest and most cosseted of José Rayas's three daughters. He and his wife, Columba Arellanes de Rayas, called her Baby, until she begged them to stop, and they switched to Bibis. They doted on her delicate ways and her love of poetry. After her disappearance, Rayas hardly bothered with the police; he mobilized his entire union chapter instead. Truck drivers reported any suspicious movement along the highways, repairmen in the city set up lookout posts, investigators fanned out through the downtown area chasing even the flimsiest clues. Mostly, Rayas told me, he concentrated on a string of anonymous phone calls that started after he went on television to ask for help in finding his daughter. He followed through on every tip. Young women called to turn in their estranged boyfriends. Children denounced strict parents. On the face of it, the police were cooperative: Rayas says that they hardly ever came up with their own leads, but they always investigated whatever information he supplied. In the long weeks between Viviana's disappearance and the day he was called to the morgue to identify the body, Rayas had dozens of people interrogated or detained on the basis of anonymous tips.

Not one of the leads panned out. Rayas invited the members of Justicia Para Nuestras Hijas (Justice for Our Daughters)—a small women's group that has aggressively and effectively called attention to the murders in Chihuahua City—to participate in a May Day parade, in which, according to Mexican custom, all labor organizations march past the balcony of the highest local authority, in this case Governor Martínez. For the event, Rayas had five hundred yellow T-shirts emblazoned with Viviana's photograph and the words "Help me find her," and distributed them among the paraders. Governor Martínez, presiding over the march, at one point shouted to Lucha Castro, an activist lawyer and one of the founders of Justicia Para Nuestras Hijas, that she get a real job and "stop profiteering with the mothers' pain." He did not address Rayas directly, but it may be that the march influenced his decision, on a weekly radio broadcast, to refer to members of Rayas's union who had left loose gravel on a highway as "assassins." The remark was widely reported.

Perhaps, too, the radio incident had something to do with the vehemence of Rayas's growing conviction that the government was sabotaging his efforts to find his daughter. By the time of the May Day parade, both Rayas and his wife, who works in the cafeteria of the public high school where Viviana was enrolled, were frantic. An anonymous caller who spoke "as if he were talking through a voice distorter" told Rayas that if his wife would consent to dress as a prostitute and walk around the red-light district he would see to it that their daughter was released. Twice, Columba complied. Another caller said that on the evening of March 16, her eleven- and twelve-year-old sons had seen a young girl they subsequently recognized from press photographs as Viviana sitting in a pickup truck, apparently fighting with a young man. The girl was crying and looked as if she wanted to get out of the truck. Rayas notified the police; later, they told him that nothing had come of the lead.

One evening in late March, an unusually savvy informant, who announced that she was calling from a phone booth in order to avoid the caller ID on Rayas's phone, told him that he should check out a store in the downtown area: the owners were a strange, long-haired couple covered with tattoos who sold hippie jewelry. Their store stayed open until all hours, and perverted things seemed to be going on there; one of the owners, Ulises Perzábal, liked to take photographs of the young girls who went to the shop, the caller said. Rayas contacted the police.

LIKE SHARIF, THE MAJOR suspect in the Juárez murders, who has dark skin and peaked eyebrows, Ulises Perzábal, with his long hair and jewelry and tattoos and scraggly beard, looks the part. Like Sharif, Perzábal, who is forty-five, could be difficult: ordinarily a peaceful and sociable man who waved to his neighbors and chatted with whoever dropped by the store (in contrast to Cynthia, who is always described as a quiet presence behind the counter), he had moods. When I talked to him briefly at the Chihuahua state prison, he was sweetly cheerful and then suddenly hyper and conspiratorial. "This isn't about a murder," he said. "It's an attack on our politics. We're in the eye of the eagle, man! In the eye of the eagle!" He irritated Chihuahuenses with his endless harangues and fixations and exhortations. He was obsessed with a return to a noble Aztec past and lectured his hapless audiences on the need to improve their brains by eating more beans—or so his listeners recall. He sang rather tuneless protest songs, accompanying himself on a guitar, and had been a fixture of the small, sporadic radical demonstrations held around town. Eventually, he was no longer invited because he tended to drive audiences away.

Perhaps none of this was important when the police weighed whether to question him. What really counted was the fact that, like Sharif, he had been arrested in the past for a sexual offense. In 2001, at a time when Cynthia was traveling, he had had a brief affair with a minor, and her family filed suit. ("He probably thought he was the rock star and she was his groupie," said someone who knows him well.) The family dropped all charges two months later, but the record stayed (and Cynthia moved out for a time). After Viviana Rayas's father received the anonymous phone call and reported him to the police, Ulises Perzábal was detained on four occasions, beaten, and interrogated by *judiciales* regarding the murder of Viviana and the other disappeared girls from Chihuahua. After the fourth detention, Perzábal sought out Miguel Zapién de la Torre, the lawyer who had represented him when he was arrested in 2001. Zapién and his law partner, Adrián Alzate, filed for an order of protection from police harassment, and the cops left Perzábal alone for several weeks.

There were fewer leads for José Rayas to follow after the *judiciales* appeared to turn their attention away from Ulises Perzábal. The Rayas family remained convinced that Viviana had been abducted and had not simply run away. She went home after school with her mother every day. She loved to write, and her grades were good—she had recently got the equivalent of an A-plus on one of her poems. She had "little friends," who, according to her father, were allowed to court her only in the safety of the Rayas home. Her father had seen a large pink cross that Lucha Castro and other activists erected two years ago in front of Governor Martínez's office. There was a nail embedded in it for each of the Juárez and Chihuahua victims. On May 26, at the climax of yet another demonstration, José Rayas addressed the governor's controversial attorney general directly.

Initially, Rayas had intended simply to marshal his union brethren and some of the women activists for one more walk to the governor's office, he says. But as they prepared to set out, he and his friends looked around and asked each other, "Which way should we go?" They decided to take a longer, less direct route that took in a busy downtown street where fruits and vegetables are sold. On the way, bystanders joined the procession, and by the time the marchers had passed the fruit and vegetable stalls and returned, nearly a hundred women—shoppers and venders both—were walking behind them. Rayas and his fellows led the demonstration to Attorney General Solís's offices and there called a halt. Rayas knew the controversial Solís well enough to call him by his nickname. "Chito!" he yelled over a megaphone. "Give me back my daughter! I know you know where she is!"

In the union's headquarters recently, Rayas explained to me what he had meant by this statement. "I am the head of my family, and I know where my children are at all times," he said. "As attorney general, Solís has the obligation to know what is going on in the state of Chihuahua." But those who heard him at the time interpreted the challenge differently: Rayas's listeners seem to have felt that he was in some way accusing Solís of playing a role in the murders.

Beneath Solís's window, Rayas issued an ultimatum: either his daughter was found, and those responsible for her fate were arrested, or he would see to it that all the road workers in the state walked off the job, including the toll-booth operators, who collect a significant portion of Chihuahua's highway income. Two days later, around noon, the head of the Attorney General's Special Office for the Investigation of Sex Crimes and Crimes against the Family, a woman named Rocío Sáenz, phoned Rayas at work and told him that two women who were on their way to a local pilgrimage site had spotted a body some five kilometers off a desert highway and called the police. Sáenz asked Rayas to come to the morgue to identify it. The following evening, Cynthia Kiecker and Ulises Perzábal were taken to the former police academy for two days of intense interrogation. Then they were formally charged with the murder and shown to the press.

THROUGH THE GLASS SEPARATION wall of the visiting room in the Chihuahua women's prison center, Cynthia Kiecker, who is forty-four, doesn't look like a hippie kid anymore. Her skin has been raked by the sun, her mouth drawn thin by tension. But there is still an emotional haziness about her—and a lack of anger—that could have been the product of traumatic reaction but seemed to me more likely the result of a generally dreamy and benevolent view of the world. Often in our conversations, I felt like shouting, "Listen up! Focus! Don't you realize you're in terrible trouble?" But I could imagine that in a different situation—as she offered a slice of home-baked banana bread to a visitor to the shop, say, or gazed at her husband while he sang and played the guitar—there would be a graceful charm in the seemingly willful vagueness.

Why, if she was now insisting that she and Ulises were innocent, had she confessed to murder? "I held out as long as possible, but I didn't know how far they would go with my husband," she said. "The only thing I was sure of is that I wouldn't make it out of there alive." During the forty-eight hours that the couple's de facto abduction lasted, they had been kicked and beaten repeatedly, she said. Every once in a while, someone would throw a bucket of water over Cynthia's shirt and then apply electric shocks to her back and legs. The one concession her guards had made in those two days was to remove the plastic hood so that she could breathe more easily. Eventually, she told me, several of the couple's friends and acquaintances were brought in, and they were tortured too. Ulises was held separately. At the end of the second day, Cynthia was taken to see Ulises. He was naked and badly beaten, she said. Electric shocks had been applied to his back and genitals repeatedly throughout those forty-eight hours. "And they had tried to stretch me out on a cot," Cynthia told me, "and they threatened to rape me, and they said, 'We're going to shove this stick up your ass' and"—her voice trailed off— "oh . . . all that stuff. And then I saw Ulises"—here for the first time her voice quavered—"and he said to sign, just go along with the story, and it sounded to me like the best solution."

Cynthia testified that on Sunday, March 16, around 5:30 p.m., after closing down the store, she and Ulises headed home to get ready for a party at which they would listen to rock music and drink tea that she likes to make from peyote. (Cynthia said that the confession was videotaped while several *judiciales* and Sáenz observed the proceedings out of camera range.) She said that on the way home the couple ran into Viviana Rayas, a young girl who had at some point bought rings or bracelets at the store, and that Ulises invited her to the party. Cynthia then testified that after drinking the peyote tea she became jealous of Ulises and Viviana and quarreled with her husband; that Viviana became sick from the effects of the tea and fell, injuring herself; that Ulises "andaba bien loco"—was acting pretty crazy—and that sometime after 9 p.m. he grabbed the short iron rod that jewelers use to size rings and struck Viviana once on the back of the head.

In Ulises's confession, which differs from Cynthia's in some critical respects, he narrates at length how he had befriended Viviana long before the night of the murder and how he had decided to prepare a special "ritual" for her, inspired by her "Aztec features." At the party that evening, during which the "energizing ritual" would take place and at which abundant quantities of cocaine and marijuana were consumed, *he* prepared the peyote tea. Viviana became ill, Ulises became solicitous, and Cynthia became jealous and, in an uncontrollable rage, attacked first Viviana and then Ulises with a baseball bat, then with a rebar, and finally with the ring sizer. At some point, Cynthia let up on Ulises, but then Ulises, "pursued by rage and confusion," was moved to strike Viviana himself. (The initial forensic report on Viviana's body lists the cause of death not as a blow to the head but as "crushed vertebrae due to violent strangulation," which is consistent with many of the previous feminicides.) Realizing that Viviana was dead, the statement goes on, Ulises, his wife, and three friends took the body out to the desert, dumped it, and covered it with a sheet of metal roofing. And then Cynthia and Ulises drove their accomplices home.

Whether the authorities who took down the statements were troubled by any of the striking discrepancies between the two accounts—however they may have been obtained in the first place—is not known. The friends who had been hauled in as witnesses signed approximately similar versions of the events at the Perzábal home on the evening of March 16 and then were released.

Cynthia and Ulises were transferred to the state prison, just outside Chihuahua City, where their arrest was announced to the media. Cynthia says it was a huge relief to be in jail: "I felt safe: I was somewhere where the *judiciales* couldn't come and get me. Only prison guards are allowed in here." A few days later, having seen the stories about the *narcosatánica* Cynthia Kiecker in the local press, the United States consul stationed in Juárez came to visit. His assistant lent Kiecker a cell phone, and Kiecker called her family.

IN CHIHUAHUA CITY, I talked to Manuel López, one of four acquaintances of the Perzábals who testified against them. López makes his living sketching pencil portraits of passersby on the streets of downtown Chihuahua and was not really a friend of the couple, but they had been kind to him, agreeing to show some of his work on consignment at the store. Once, when he couldn't pay the rent in the transient hotel where he was living, they took him in for a couple of weeks. López has astonishingly light-colored blue-green eyes and a haunted, even terrified expression. How prosecutors found him is a mystery, but he says that he was taken to the former police academy the same night as the Perzábals and beaten for hours. He signed a witness statement and got out of town, but when the Perzábals' lawyers, Zapién and Alzate, found him, he agreed to retract his statement at the trial. López feared for his life, he told me, and to judge by his startled movements and trembling hands he was not exaggerating. He has no family, no fixed address; who would care if he was discreetly disposed of?

Still, he was willing to recant. After Zapién and Alzate brought him back to Chihuahua, and after the trial judge refused to set a date to hear López's retraction, the lawyers called a press conference at which López and another acquaintance of the Perzábals both spoke. "I used to see Cynthia and Ulises in the news every day after I denounced them, and I would cry," López told me. "When I came back and talked to the press, I felt at peace again." Immediately after the press conference, a white helicopter began hovering over the two lawyers' downtown offices. Six other partners at the firm quickly moved out, and Zapién and Alzate had to vacate the premises, at their landlord's request. They decided to send López into hiding.

The press conference at which López spoke seems to have marked a turning point for José Rayas. The more carefully he looked at the state's case against the Perzábals, the more he began to wonder if the real killers were still at large. Rayas has wielded power and dealt with the state for many years, but when I talked to him he seemed curiously innocent and forlorn, as if during the preceding weeks he had been robbed not only of his daughter but of all certainty. His doubts now extend even to the identification of his daughter's body; among the many large issues facing the officials dealing with the Chihuahua feminicides, perhaps none is more confounding than the question of why they have, on several occasions, turned over to a grieving family what appears to have been the wrong body. In the case of the two bus drivers accused of murdering eight young girls in 2001, DNA tests did not match samples taken from the relatives of five of the girls the suspects had named. Two tests were inconclusive, and only one body tested positive, according to Oscar Maynez, who was then the head of the Juárez forensic department. Maynez told me that he had refused to plant some of the bus drivers' hair as evidence, and that he simultaneously resigned and was fired a few weeks later.

In another instance, the mother of a seventeen-year-old Juárez victim named Sagrario González demanded that a DNA test be performed in Mexico City on the body that the police had delivered as her daughter's, and the results revealed that the dead girl was no relation. When the mother insisted on an exhumation of the girl's remains, police managed to dig up the wrong coffin. In the case in which Sharif was convicted, the family of Elisabeth Castro received a corpse, dressed in Elisabeth's clothing, that was approximately five feet four inches tall; Elisabeth was five feet seven. More recently, in Chihuahua City, Patricia Cervantes, the mother of Neyra Azucena Cervantes, refused to accept the body offered to her by the prosecuting attorney's office and continues to claim her daughter as missing.

At the morgue in Chihuahua City, *judiciales* and Sáenz showed Rayas and his two older daughters a number of garments displayed in a long glass case. Rayas didn't recognize many, but a blouse, a brassiere, and a short jacket were undoubtedly his daughter's. Sáenz showed him photographs of a corpse, swollen and bruised from the waist down, a skeleton from the waist up. Did he recognize Viviana? he was asked. Rayas fumbled for words. A dentist was brought in, and she told Rayas—as she told the press shortly afterward—that she had filled two of Viviana's molars back in October and that she recognized the teeth. Would you like to see the body? Rayas was asked, and was told that he could spare himself a great deal of pain if he identified his daughter from the photographs alone. Rayas decided that he would rather remember Viviana as she had been in life. He signed the identification warrant and authorized the burial.

For weeks, Miguel Zapién pleaded with the Rayas family to authorize an exhumation of the body. Viviana's mother was so horrified by the request that she stood guard over the grave. And yet José Rayas's doubts have grown: a bloodstain on the Perzábals' wall turned out to be maroon-colored vinyl paint; according to dates that appear in court records, police notified a ranch owner that a body had been found on his property the day *before* the two women stumbled onto it and called the police. In the original press story reporting the discovery of a corpse, a spokesman for the *judiciales* denied that it could be any of the missing girls; it belonged to an older woman, he said. Two days after the Perzábals' arrest, Rayas had taken a video camera out to the area where Viviana was supposedly found and filmed Ulises Perzábal as he demonstrated to some *judiciales* how he had dumped the victim's body. In the video Rayas showed me, Perzábal is limping badly, and when the *judiciales* realize that they are being filmed they form a shield around him. In July, Perzábal phoned Rayas from jail to tell him that he was innocent. On August 5, Rayas agreed at last to meet with Zapién and with Cynthia's mother, Carol Kiecker, who, with her former husband, Burton, and other family members, takes turns traveling to Chihuahua to visit Cynthia in jail.

THE PERZÁBALS' prosecutors may have found it surprising that a middle-aged hippie turned out to have such loving and protective parents. The Kieckers come from Bloomington, Minnesota—Carol is a retired vice president of a major West Coast HMO, Burton is in real estate—and José Rayas, too, may have been inclined to see Cynthia and Ulises Perzábal in a more favorable light after talking to them.

Carol Kiecker has a lively gaze, a face that, like her body, is comfortably rounded at the edges, and a fast, purposeful stride. She is sixty-eight and anything but unfocused. When she retired, a few years ago, she took up backpacking, and since then she has traveled in Ghana, Togo, and Benin, and along the Silk Road in China. Before her amicable divorce from Burton, in 1983, the couple and their three children vacationed in Mexico many times, and she can speak a little Spanish.

Carol Kiecker appears to have thought that the drug-murder-by-bludgeoning episode involving her daughter would soon be declared a mistake by the Mexican justice system—President Fox had already heard about Cynthia's travails from a few Minnesota congressmen and both senators, thanks to the family's efforts—and that Cynthia and Ulises would then be released. But Carol now stays in a budget hotel in Chihuahua and eats her meals at modest restaurants because she has begun to see that the trial may turn out differently, or at least take much longer than she ever feared. The full impact of Cynthia's situation seems to have descended on Carol the day that her daughter and Ulises were scheduled to testify for the first time. By then, Carol had learned enough about the Mexican legal system to know that there is no such thing as a jury trial; that the court session would take place in private, before a presiding judge and a transcriber; and that the proceedings might take a long time (though not, it must be said, by the standards of the woefully laggard Mexican justice system, in which prisoners can wait in jail for years for their first trial date). Testimony in the Perzábal trial was scheduled to begin on Friday, August 8, with Cynthia's interrogation to be followed by Ulises's. Manuel López and a friend of the Perzábals who had also been detained with them were scheduled to retract their confessions the following day. Carol expected to be given access to the sessions; she was not aware that third parties—especially the press—might not be allowed in. There were only a few reporters there in any event: a British television crew, an AP reporter from the Mexico City bureau, and me. There were no local press people except for a couple of eager kids from a tiny radical periodical.

A few minutes after the hearing was supposed to begin, Zapién was called into the office of Judge Bernardino Medina. Zapién, who is thirty-four, is reserved and polite in an old-fashioned, provincial sort of way and, in the perishing Chihuahua heat, wears blue suits and immaculate white shirts without breaking a sweat. He is personable but not quite handsome, and he could probably be convincing before a trial jury, I thought, were there ever to be such a thing in Mexico. But when he emerged from the judge's chambers half an hour later, he was furious. He said that the judge had rescheduled the session for the following Monday, perhaps mindful that by then the journalists who had flown into town to cover the trial would be gone.

Carol Kiecker was unusually quiet, suddenly looking older and struggling to regain the chirpy poise that in previous days had allowed her to take on with aplomb foreign laws and lawyers, hundred-degree-plus temperatures, and press interrogations. But when the trial resumed, under a different judge, a few days later (Zapién had demanded and, astonishingly, obtained a change of venue), Carol was back on form. She and Zapién had met with José Rayas, and he had agreed to consider the family's request that he appear as a witness for the defense at the trial.

The witnesses were permitted to retract their confessions on August 15, and on August 25 Rayas appeared before the court. He stated that he did not believe the Perzábals had murdered his daughter, and he said that he and his wife had agreed to authorize an exhumation of the corpse so that a DNA sample could be taken. Even if the body Rayas and his wife buried does turn out to be Viviana's, the family's pain will never find relief. Like dozens of other families who have lost a daughter during the past ten years in the state of Chihuahua, they may never believe that justice has been done, that the government has thoroughly prosecuted the crime of their disappeared child and arrested the murderer. José Rayas may never find out what happened to his daughter when he dropped her off at the park that afternoon—and, indeed, it may be better for him if he never does. As for Cynthia and Ulises Perzábal, long months and numerous judicial procedures lie ahead of them before they are sentenced or acquitted by the presiding judge. Meanwhile, on September 7 the body of another girl was found on the outskirts of Chihuahua City.

POSTSCRIPT. Since the first wave of murders in Ciudad Juárez, a succession of suspects has been arrested on the basis of no evidence, but not all have been as lucky as the Perzábals. As far as can be determined, a number of those arrested still languish in jail, and in a country where an estimated nine out of ten homicides are never prosecuted, or involve arbitrarily selected suspects, or fail to convict an obvious guilty party, this is not surprising. The epidemic of feminicides in Ciudad Juárez at the turn of this century was horrifying, but the numbers have only gone up since then, and the murder of women because they are women was revealed to be a nationwide phenomenon. The murders are concentrated in a few states, and of those states, in a few cities. With two or three exceptions, they are cities where one or another major drug clan holds sway. (There are no figures for gender-related crimes in Indigenous communities, and it is taken as given that feminicides in the countryside are underreported.) In large part, the higher numbers are the result of much improved reporting, thanks to the tireless efforts of feminist groups. Thanks to feminists, too, feminicide is now a category in the penal code, and six out of ten feminicides are prosecuted today. All this is cause for optimism, but the hard fact remains that 2,802 gender-related murders against women were recorded in 2022, more than seven women a day dying a violent death. Feminicide is a significant and specific aspect of the landscape of violent crime in Mexico.

The heroic Esther Chávez died on Christmas Day 2009, her role in calling world attention to the murder of young women in Ciudad Juárez largely unrecognized. The Perzábals, acquitted, live in the United States.

NOTE

First published in the *New Yorker*, September 29, 2003.

Forty-Three Students Went Missing

What Really Happened to Them?

MARCH 11, 2024

1.

In February last year I drove south from Mexico City, along the highway toward Apango, a hillside town in the state of Guerrero. The highway ends at Acapulco, but there were no palm trees and no glamour where I was going. On a silent two-lane road, I rode past villages where Náhuatl, Amuzgo, or Me'phaa are still spoken. It was the dry season, and the scrub-forest hills had turned every shade of dust and brown, punctuated only by the soft white flowers of the casahuate trees. In Apango, an orderly place with a pretty square of greenery in the middle, I asked for Estanislao Mendoza Chocolate, or don Tanis, as he is respectfully known. I wanted to ask him about his son, who vanished one night in 2014, taken away along with forty-two other students from a rural teachers' college, never to be seen again.

Don Tanis was already waiting anxiously in his doorway when I arrived—a round-faced, neatly dressed man who looks younger than his 65 years, with a lively manner, and eyes so haunted it was hard not to look away. He showed me around his house, a collection of bare cinder-block rooms with a light bulb in the center of each one, built over twenty years as a seasonal migrant in California. There was a storage room for the year's supply of corn—to sell, or to grind for the family's tortillas—and, untouched all these years, the room where his son had lived: a sagging cot, a chair, some fading photographs and posters on the wall. "I wanted a ranch, with *animalitos*, and he was helping me set it up, but it's all abandoned now," he said, studiously avoiding his son's name, as he would throughout our conversation.

His son, Miguel Ángel Mendoza Zacarías, was older than the rest of the first-year cohort at the Ayotzinapa Rural Teachers' College: a tall, full-grown man of thirty-three, with a shock of hair he was proud of, to judge from the amateur self-portrait he drew on the outside wall of the house, advertising the haircuts he offered the neighbors. I asked why he had applied so late to the school. "It's never too late to learn!" don Tanis said brightly. "He loved children, and he always wanted to teach." I suspect he might also have wanted an opportunity away from cheap day labor as a construction worker, with a sideline as a barber. For Indigenous and/or campesino communities—in Mexico these are neighboring categories—Ayotzinapa provided free tuition and board and a chance at a better life as a rural teacher. In 2014, the semester started on July 20; the first week famously involved privations, strenuous self-defense training, and living rough. Suspicious outsiders claimed it was guerrilla training, but it struck me rather as a projection of the view that survival, in a world not made for students like the school's, was a nonstop struggle.

Impoverished students find a sense of belonging and purpose at Mexico's nineteen rural teachers' schools, but they learn quickly that their diplomas will go nowhere toward closing the chasm between their country selves and the people who rule, and many become radicalized as a result—usually in the old-fashioned Marxist-Leninist sense. In the state of Guerrero, one of Mexico's very poorest, multiple campesino guerrilla movements had flourished in the 1960s and 1970s, and two of their leaders, Lucio Cabañas and Genaro Vázquez Rojas, campesinos themselves, had close ties to the school. Although their respective movements were exterminated by the army in a "dirty war" that lasted through the 1970s, their portraits appeared on a red-and-black mural that overwhelmed a school wall, along with Lenin, Guevara, and Marx.

The Ayotzis were generally tolerated, but hardly loved, in the region: a rowdy bunch, aggressive, *revoltosos*, people called them—troublemakers, punks. They often carried sticks and wore bandannas or ski masks when they took over highway toll booths and demanded payment "for the revolution." Whenever they needed to travel as a group—to a protest march somewhere, or a meeting at other rural teachers' schools—they were in the habit of taking over buses on the highway, leaving the passengers stranded on the asphalt at night or under the burning Guerrero sun.

On Friday, September 26, the students went searching for buses. There were about a hundred of them, mostly first-years, traveling in two recently requisitioned buses. Their need for more transportation was especially urgent that afternoon because October 2 was approaching. On that date, in 1968, dozens of demonstrators were gunned down by army troops, on orders of a government seeking to suppress a weeks-long, and escalating, antigovernment student movement. At a recent meeting with the other teachers' colleges student unions, the Ayotzinapa delegation had agreed to provide for everyone's travel to the capital: staying away from the yearly commemorative march in Mexico City would have been inconceivable. *Dos de octubre no se olvida* (October 2 is not forgotten)! They set out to find buses.

Because the state capital, Chilpancingo, was a fifteen-minute downhill drive away, its central terminal was the Ayotzis' favorite place for bus takeovers—so much so that it was a frequent, even negotiated, event. But on this day the students were chased out of town by police. By nightfall they had failed to take over a single bus, and in their search they ended up far from their home turf, on the outskirts of the flatland town of Iguala. It was going on nine o'clock when one small group of students finally managed to take over a bus bound for the Iguala terminal. The driver convinced them to let him deliver the passengers to their destination before returning with them to campus. Foolish students! Once in Iguala, the driver let the passengers out and swiftly locked the students inside. Minutes later, the rest of the Ayotzi search group arrived to rescue their mates. Shouting and banging on the walls and doors of the terminal dock, they took over three buses, for a total of five, and prepared to head back to their school in triumph.

That was when the killings started.

It was a busy night in town; the mayor's wife had just hosted a lively ceremony in the central square, cafeterias were still open, there were people strolling or hurrying home. And yet half a dozen or so members of the Iguala police, in uniform and well known to many by sight, opened fire on the buses minutes after they left the station. A statewide electronic monitoring system registered the fear as hundreds of messages zipped through the social networks: *Stay at home, there's a shooting. Two people are dead. We've turned out the lights and put the lock on.* People fleeing the area saw how police cars closed off the roads, blocking all possibility of escape for the buses. The rumors and fear flew back and forth: *The army is out, the police aren't hiding. They killed last night, they were drugged.*

The ayotzinapos are here, they say they kidnapped three buses. By dawn of the following day, police from Iguala and two smaller towns had killed nine people, including three students, and left another in a coma. But the worst of the terror was still to come: in the days and weeks that followed, dozens of families would come to understand that forty-three of their children were missing.

THERE'S A LOW-RANGE official estimate that more than eighty thousand people have been "disappeared" in Mexico since 2006, when then-president Felipe Calderón ramped up the so-called War on Drugs by bringing in the army to fight Mexican citizens. Backed by the DEA, police and army focused on what was called "the kingpin strategy," betting that if the leadership of the drug groups were captured, their organizations would disappear: "Poof!," as an agent once put it at a drug conference. In reality, the effort has been about as effective as trying to get rid of ants by breaking up one nest: over the years, handfuls of the most notorious drug clan leaders have been captured or killed, allowing Mexican presidents, and their drug-enforcement allies in the United States, to boast of many victories. But they rarely mention that each drug leader's death or capture leads to the rise of several more small would-be lords. In the struggle, paranoid traffickers turn on close business associates, and underlings look to consolidate their own spot in the sun by killing each other. With murder as an increasingly common and deadening practice, traffickers exert ever more grotesque forms of violence on their enemies and on the civilian population; abductions leading to disappearances are now a fact of life throughout the country. The War on Drugs also forced the price of cheap, fast-growing crops like marijuana and poppies to absurd levels, which only enriched the drug groups. Military patrols assigned to destroy crop fields get corrupted by drug money. They uproot the poppy plants from a field or two and file a report: mission accomplished. The situation is stable, as long as no one oversteps the boundaries of a delicate tacit agreement. The drug groups are increasingly entangled with regional economies and with officialdom at every level. A bar owner I know in Mexico City was having trouble with a drug group that was demanding the right to sell drugs in his bar. Eventually he was invited to have lunch with a local authority and discovered that the other guest was the drug boss of the group that was threatening his life. Governors of the states of Quintana Roo, Veracruz, and Tamaulipas have all been convicted of drug-related crimes in Mexico and abroad. Judges and the security forces are all too frequently in the pay of drug groups, and as a result, justice for the relatives of the *desaparecidos* is rare.

According to the investigative reporting group Quinto Elemento Lab, for example, the town of Ursulo Galván in the state of Veracruz, with barely 30,000 inhabitants, produced, among other clandestine burial sites, one mass grave that held a hundred bodies. Between 2018 and 2020, more than two hundred clandestine graves were found in Tecomán, Colima, which has little more than 100,000 inhabitants. Not all these deaths were produced in a single year, but we are talking only about the graves that have been found. It is up to the relatives of the disappeared to look for their loved ones, and teams of searchers can be seen throughout the land, scratching the ground for any sign that it has recently been disturbed. Each new batch of names floats in the news cycle for a day, or a week, and vanishes into the air. *Ya nos acostumbramos*, people will say. We have become accustomed. Or, you might translate the phrase as, *It has become part of our customs.*

If it were not for don Tanis Mendoza and the other relatives of the missing Forty-Three, none of the politicians, drug traffickers, security forces, and military personnel who participated in the mass disappearance and/or ongoing cover-up of that crime would be the subject of successive investigations now, nearly a decade later. Unforgiving, stubborn, and extremely vulnerable, the families march once a month through central Mexico City, sticking themselves in front of television cameras, shouting, gathering at the entrance to government buildings, refusing to budge, demanding the return of their sons. Because of them, within weeks of the boys' disappearance the number 43 was painted on walls, buses, windows, and doors everywhere in Mexico and, for a time, throughout Europe and the Americas. As far away as Australia, people marched. "We are missing forty-three," they chanted. And "Alive they were taken; we want them returned alive."

"I used to come across protest marches by students or workers and say 'lazy bums, get back to work,'" don Tanis reflected. "Now I say, 'I understand.'"

2.

Before dawn on Friday, September 27, 2014, Don Clemente Rodríguez, the father of an Ayotzi named Christian Rodríguez Telumbre, raced to the Tixtla campus when he heard that his son was in trouble. "The student leaders had told us that there had been an attack on our boys. I wanted to grab a machete and go fight whoever was harming my son, but I was told that it wasn't the prudent thing to do," he said. He waited until morning to go down to Iguala from his home in Tixtla. "We looked for our sons everywhere in Iguala—the hospitals, the courthouse. I thought 'if my boy's done something wrong, they'll be holding him at the jail.' But no one gave us any news there or anywhere." By dawn, Vidulfo Rosales, a sturdy man in his fifties who is a lawyer and human rights defender at the Centro de Derechos Humanos La Montaña Tlachinollan (La Montaña Tlachinollan Center for Human Rights), in the mountain region of Guerrero, also heard what was happening in Iguala and hitched a ride from the owner of a beat-up VW Beetle for a four-hour drive over a gutted dirt road. Rosales has years of experience at the crossroads of human rights and violence, but his volunteer driver refused to go any further when they reached Chilpancingo. "News of what had happened in Iguala had spread fast," Rosales explained. "There were roadblocks everywhere; people were riled up." He got in touch with four other Tlachinollan staffers possessed of a car and used to flammable situations, and continued to Iguala. He and his colleagues worked frantically all that Saturday, locating student survivors who had spent the night in hiding, checking the morgue and hospital, finding official escort to take the students they could locate safely back to their school. It was only after days of anguish, as a handful of stragglers made their way back to the school, that the extent of the tragedy became clear. Dozens of students remained missing.

Within days, protest marches erupted all over the country. The United Nations and other international organizations expressed their concern about what had happened in Iguala. Pursued by the scandal, President Enrique Peña Nieto, a slick but empty politician, was forced to call for an investigation. "After Iguala, Mexico must change," he declared, and one month after the crime his attorney general, Jesús Murillo Karam, discussed the investigation with the press. The students, Murillo Karam stated, had been abducted by a handful of rogue municipal police from the towns of Iguala and neighboring Huitzuco and Cocula. Following orders from the mayor, the police had handed their captives over to members of a local drug group, several of whom had already been arrested and confessed. (The mayor was later convicted of an unrelated kidnapping and other charges.) Here Murillo Karam displayed photographs of a few men—shabby, dejected, filthy, and, as seasoned reporters immediately suspected, tortured. The goons had taken all forty-three missing students to a trash dump near the town of Cocula, Murillo Karam said, and killed those who weren't already dead. Subsequently, the murderers built an open-pit fire with tires, gasoline, and wood to burn the youths' bodies down to ashes so small they would forever remain unidentifiable. No member of the armed forces, or the federal police, high-ranking or low, had been involved. The parents of the dead boys should resign themselves, the highest-ranking justice official in the country implied. As for the perpetrators, every one would be caught. "This is a call to find the formula so that this, which should never have occurred, will never be repeated," Murillo Karam concluded.

This version of events—which Murillo Karam later took to calling "the Historic Truth"—is what has stuck in the minds of most people today. But the evidence shows that Ayotzinapa students did not die at the trash dump, the Iguala mayor was not the one who gave the order to kill them, and the military was indeed involved. It was only years later, in 2021, that the attorney general's own involvement became clear, when independent investigators gained access to a hard disk with a series of drone images taken by the Mexican Navy early on the morning of October 27—exactly one month after the disappearances. The images show two Navy pickup trucks parked on the edge of the dump next to three large white sacks. It's 6:30 a.m. A group of men hurry back and forth between the packages and the pickups. They light a fire, and the smoke rises high from it for nearly an hour. When we see the trash dump again—it would appear that some images were either deleted from the sequence at this point or were never taken—the sacks are no longer in view. At 8:31, Murillo Karam, the attorney general himself, arrives to supervise the scene, while at least two dozen men scurry about in the reeking garbage. Forensic experts from the attorney general's office descend to the garbage and displace or discard small objects. There is no image of it, but we know what happened next: Mercedes Doretti, a founding member of the renowned Argentine Forensic Anthropology Team, who was searching for any trace of the students at a site a few miles away, was summoned to the dump. Indeed, Doretti and the other members of the Argentine team did find human bone fragments, but they would spend weeks at the site, looking unsuccessfully for fragments large or whole enough to be used for DNA identification. Replaying the drone video over and over years later, I couldn't help wondering why two Marine SUVs arrived first at the dump without authorization from the attorney general's office, took things to the trash pit and lit fires, and kept the record of their actions hidden in a digital file marked "Top Secret." (Murillo Karam, currently under house arrest and seriously ill, has publicly defended his investigation, and his lawyers maintain his innocence.)

"From the beginning I knew it wasn't true," said don Tanis when I asked him about Murillo Karam's version of the event, which the government took to calling the Historic Truth. Always soft-spoken, don Tanis lowered his voice even more. "When you roast a pig," he explained carefully, "there is always a pool of grease at the end. But at the trash dump there was nothing." There was other easily available evidence to contradict the Historic Truth version of events: the vegetation around the dump was unsinged, and besides, it had rained buckets that night. Don Tanis and the other suffering families knew that their children had not died at the trash dump. They wanted them back alive, but how would their insignificant voices be heard against the government's roar? Now, years later, sitting with don Tanis in his home, I asked him how it was that he and his wife had gone from lying awake at night, wondering if their child had been fed that day, to running through the endless possible ways he could have died, to uniting with all the other parents and relatives, marching together over and over to this day, each relative holding an Ayotzi's image, shouting that they want their sons back alive. "It was love for our children that brought us together." he said. "We'd never even met before." And it was also, he added, support by the human rights community.

"By the fourth or fifth day, we realized in Centro Tlachinollan that we couldn't do this work by ourselves," Vidulfo Rosales told me when we talked online. Rosales is from the highland Guerrero town of Totomixtlahuaca (pop. 1,200), where he was one of only a few students to make it past ninth grade. He went further, graduating from law school, joining Centro Tlachinollan and working on cases involving the disappearances, torture, and murder of Indigenous and human rights activists. When we talked about the mayhem following the disappearance of the Forty-Three, he told me that he initially believed Centro Tlachinollan knew what to do. "We had certain procedures in place for those situations," he said when we talked. "But slowly we saw that this was more than we were prepared for. There were the dead, dozens of disappeared, the whole question of the buses, the aggressors, and the families." Rosales called on other organizations in Mexico City—chiefly, the Jesuit-founded Centro de Derechos Humanos Miguel Agustín Pro Juárez A.C. (Miguel Agustín Pro Juárez Center for Human Rights A.C., known as Centro Prodh), which in turn called the Interamerican Commission on Human Rights and the Argentine Forensic Anthropology Team. In November, President Peña Nieto was obliged to accept the mandate of the Interamerican Commission on Human Rights, of which Mexico is a member. The commission recruited an international team with expertise uncovering and prosecuting human rights violations and baptized it with the cumbersome name Grupo Interdisciplinario de Expertos Independientes (GIEI, Independent Group of Interdisciplinary Experts). In April 2015, the GIEI arrived in Mexico. It was the parents' first great triumph.

3.

One afternoon this spring, I met with two of the four GIEI investigators, Carlos Beristain and Angela Buitrago, at a park-side café in Mexico City. Beristain, a physician and psychologist, has worked with trauma victims for human rights commissions throughout Latin America. Buitrago, a Colombian prosecutor, put a number of generals responsible for monstrous human rights violations behind bars. The pair remembered the moment of the group's first visit to the Ayotzinapa campus. "Even before we entered the school grounds, there were people waiting to escort us in," Buitrago said. "Parents, students, the school's marching band. They placed one garland of flowers after another around our necks. Every one of the speakers who welcomed us repeated the same thing: the one thing they asked of us, they said, was to always tell them the truth, not to lie and not to sell out. I'm a lawyer, I believe in institutions," Buitrago concluded, "but when I heard that phrase, 'don't lie, don't sell out,' repeated so many times, I thought that this had to be the ultimate expression of a citizenry that no longer believed in anything at all."

Soon, the GIEI members were learning the Mexican lesson. At the café, Beristain and Buitrago chuckled as they remembered the staffers at the prosecutor general's office, who said things like "You will never see a more complete investigation than the one we have carried out" when they handed over their report. "They told us with a straight face that a drug gang had incinerated forty-three corpses with only tires, branches, and five gallons of fuel," Buitrago said. After the GIEI expressed doubt, Beristain added, "they took us to the site and showed us a tree from which two branches of very green wood had recently been cut," claiming that the branches had also fed the fire. "And then," Beristain and Buitrago chortled in chorus, "they said, '*Now* we have it right!'"

That was the head of the Mexican investigating attorney's office on organized crime they were quoting, proud to have overcome an objection so neatly, even if it involved altering the evidence almost before the GIEI commission's eyes.

The GIEI and the Argentine Team were forced to spend much of the twelve months of their mandate proving that the government's account of events was impossible. They were blocked at every turn, principally by the military, which refused to grant access to most of the documents the teams requested. The secretary of defense, Salvador Cienfuegos, refused the GIEI's request to talk to anyone from the local Iguala battalion: "I will not permit soldiers to be treated like criminals," he declared, and denied the investigative teams access to the two military battalions in Iguala. Buitrago has a striking Andean profile—high cheekbones, a sharply defined nose, very black eyes that tilt slightly upward—and it was almost fun to watch her at the GIEI's periodic news conferences because she called out lies and spelled out facts in a way that is all but unheard of in Mexico's official discourse. "We were given statements signed by personnel from the prosecutor general's office that were false," she would say about their first months in Mexico. "Information obtained from legal documents was not true. There were investigative proceedings in which all the information was tampered with." At the end of their first year, their contract was not renewed, and so in April 2016, there was a farewell gathering in a packed Mexico City auditorium. Flower wreaths were placed once more around the GIEI members' necks. Each parent hugged the members tightly. "Right at the end one man stood up and shouted 'Don't leave!'" Beristain said. "And then another stood up, and then they were all chanting, '*No-se-va-yan!*' Don't leave us. We nearly died then, all of us."

In 2018, Andrés Manuel López Obrador became the first independent candidate to be elected president in more than seventy years, and he promised to clean up the mess left by his predecessor. It was a new day of victory for the parents of the Forty-Three, but they had learned to be mistrustful. They reconfirmed the Centro Prodh as their legal representatives and insisted on the return of the Argentine Forensic Anthropology Team and the GIEI. A new investigative unit was created, headed by Omar Gómez Trejo, a headstrong young lawyer with a deceptively easygoing manner who was the *secretario* for the GIEI when he was chosen to head a new investigative unit under the attorney general's office. All the teams came under a new umbrella commission headed by Alejandro Encinas, a Santa Claus-y man always handy with one of those loud, flapping hugs Mexican men give each other. Encinas was not only a longtime political ally of López Obrador but also a former mayor of Mexico City and immensely powerful in his own right. He would prove to be a key intermediary for the various teams throughout the following years, leaning on López Obrador to intervene whenever a government office—notably the armed forces—refused to allow investigators access to official documents or installations. Beristain, the psychologist in the GIEI team, was elated as the teams resumed their work. "Of course I knew what the landscape we were moving through was like," he told me recently on a video call, "but I trusted the direct commitment [the president] had made to the families, and to us. They had agreed on our return, knowing the kind of work we did." Gómez Trejo was excited too. "You had the attorney general's office, the president, the GIEI, the Inter-American Commission on Human Rights, the United Nations, and, principally, the families' legal representatives, all working to ensure that justice was done, to know what happened to the boys," he told me. But not even the president's ukase was enough to overcome the barriers to the investigation set up by the military.

In early 2023, I found myself in the surprised possession of a confidential document: the more-than-six-hundred-page court filing presented before a judge in August 2022 by the special prosecutor for Ayotzinapa, Omar Gómez Trejo. It was the product of two years of tireless digging in files and collecting evidence, and hours of interviewing hundreds of suspects, survivors, government officials, bystanders, and relatives of the disappeared. Thanks to the intricacies of the traditional Mexican legal system, which in organized crime cases still does not involve jury trials but relies instead on ritualistic arguments presented to a judge in writing, the document had proved all but incomprehensible to me at first pass. But beneath the legalese, it's packed with information, particularly regarding a drug-trafficking organization based in the state of Guerrero: the Guerreros Unidos (GU, United Warriors) responsible for the disappearance of the Forty-Three.

Guerreros Unidos was born because a major drug boss, Arturo Beltrán Leyva, was shot and killed by Mexican Marines in Cuernavaca in 2009. As generally happens, Beltrán's underlings then split into several small, family-based clans. One of these called itself los Rojos—the Reds—and took over the hillside town of Tixtla, home to the Ayotzinapa campus. The Rojos ran a nice little business, buying crystal meth and poppy gum from an allied drug group that controlled the production end of things in the highland fields of Guerrero state. But it wasn't long before the Rojos, too, splintered and joined with a handful of brothers, half brothers, and cousins, several of whom had grown up in the Chicago suburbs, and formed the breakaway Guerreros Unidos. A story in the *Chicago Sun-Times* revealed that two of the siblings had at one point delivered pizzas for a Chicago restaurant called Mama Luna's; a cousin of theirs, Pablo Vega, had worked in local factories, and all had done jail time for minor drug offenses. By 2012, the pizza boys and their homegrown cousins set up shop in Iguala, a town equipped with a bus terminal big enough that unusual activity might go unnoticed but not so large that it would call attention to itself. This was key to the group's success because the gang's specialty was fitting invisible compartments into passenger buses traveling the admittedly unusual route of Iguala–Chicago. The compartments would be stuffed with drugs and the bus sent on its way. At its destination, Pablo Vega would unload and distribute the merchandise, replace the product with cash, and send the bus back to Iguala.

In 2022, the DEA allowed Gómez Trejo and an assistant to spend time in its Chicago office, reading the transcripts of twenty-three thousand messages sent by Pablo Vega and an array of other clan members and relatives. As it happened, the agency had stumbled across Vega in the course of a money-laundering investigation in 2014 and put a sting on him and two other GU members in Chicago. The sixty-character Blackberry phone texts, which were first reported in the Mexican press and later in English by the *New York Times*, make stupefyingly boring reading on first pass, consisting as they mostly do of terse discussions about where to park the "aunt"—the bus—and how many "vases" to deliver, but as Gómez Trejo speed-read his way through the print-outs, he told me when I sought him out, he became dizzy with joy. There were messages in which Vega and his pals chatted about the military and government officials who were on the take from them. They mentioned specific visits, dates, demands for money. It was, the special attorney told me, "objective and resounding proof—not just a declaration by a witness—tying an authority of the state to organized crime. In other words, it was objective confirmation of key aspects of our own investigation in Mexico." He could build a case.

Other texts gradually reveal an inept, all but illiterate bunch, destined to fail. On one of the group's first shipments from Iguala to Chicago, the bus crashes, loaded with product, "because it was raining." Someone leaves a loaded car illegally parked and it gets towed, but no one can find the spare keys, and because the boy who was driving the truck gets picked up by immigration, Pablo's guys have no way of reclaiming it from the impound lot. A key collaborator vanishes in Mexico, and days go by while the group makes a lame attempt to understand what happened to him. ("What's his name?" "I just know him as *el cuate* [the guy].") Vega's wife harangues him constantly, and when she does he messages a girlfriend and asks for *una foto sexi*. A shipment succeeds and tens of thousands of dollars get distributed, but two months later the water is cut off at Vega's Mexico home because he can't pay the bill. Vega's team is always hungry for work because there's never enough product: it would appear that the competition has the market cornered. Vega's sister-in-law, widow of the presumably height-challenged GU founder known as "El Minicooper," brother to Vega, complains endlessly that she's always the last to be taken into account. Someone announces that he's selling tennis shoes to make ends meet. Worst of all, the cousins, who are supposed to be united by mystical links of shared lineage, constantly suspect each other of treason. And then there is the real danger: the big players on the national scene—the Sinaloa group, the Familia Michoacana, the Jalisco Nueva Generación—who have been trying for years to win control of the opium-rich state of Guerrero.

Perhaps because the competition wasn't that bright either, Guerreros Unidos managed to consolidate its fledgling operation and even imbue its hold on Iguala with a sort of mystique. By then the state prosecutor is allegedly on the payroll, and so is the Iguala coroner, happy to pass along the names of the day's take of corpses. As "Juan," a boastful and cold-blooded GU member who eventually turned state's witness, explained to Gómez Trejo and the GIEI in a sworn deposition, "The purpose of every person who belongs to the organization" is "to send drugs to Chicago, and to keep watch and do what is necessary . . . that is why there should be support by public officials—like police officers—at every level." The GU often cleaned its cash through public works contracts and other traditional money-laundering methods. There was also the convenient resource of a chain of jewelry stores operated by the mayor's energetic wife, who was, in turn, the sister of two Beltrán Leyva gangsters killed years earlier. The clan saw to it that yet another associate—Francisco Salgado Valladares, a pig-eyed man who was in charge of a ferocious group of Iguala police tied to the cousins and known as the *bélicos*—was appointed vice chief of the force.

By August 2014, according to witnesses cited in the court filing as well as the SMS chats, a cousin in charge of government relations, a man who went by the name of "El Güero Mugres," or Filthy Blondie, appeared to be on visiting terms with an officer in Iguala's Battalion 41, and he'd also established friendly relations with a certain José Martínez Crespo, a newcomer to Iguala Battalion 27 with the rank of captain and "a great guy," even if the messages among the cousins complain about the *putos* in the military and their inexhaustible appetite for money. Others are brought in—a butcher here, a carwash owner there, all on salary from the clan, in addition to dozens of gofers, petty drug peddlers, and lookouts who keep an eye on the whereabouts of every resident, visitor, and passerby in the GU's areas of control. Their bosses wanted reports, particularly on army movements—long sequences of the twenty-three thousand messages are devoted to minute-by-minute reports on the exact whereabouts of the army's daily patrol movements—and above all, on any sign of the presence of rival groups, referred to as "contras." Unfamiliar cars entering the group's control area are stopped and searched for signs of the enemy. Pursued by fear of their rivals, GU killed senselessly, adding by the month to Guerrero's awful body count.

4.

It was nine o'clock on the night of September 26, 2014, when the hundred or so Ayotzinapa students rode into the bus station in Iguala on the two buses that had transported them from their campus. According to the text messages the students sent that evening, it was 9:16 when they emerged victorious: they had rescued their fellows and, in addition, acquired three more buses, bringing their count to a total of five.

"Unfortunately," a survivor from that night told me, "in the heat of the moment it seemed easy to take over a few buses." Luis, as I'll call him, is one of more than twenty Ayotzis who agreed to testify anonymously before the GIEI and Special Prosecutor Gómez Trejo. Luis was a second-year student back then, and is a teacher now; self-contained, serious, task-oriented. Talking to me in a café in downtown Chilpancingo was one more thing he had on his schedule that day, but he rarely says much to anyone, particularly about the night he survived. I struggled to hear him over the café's pounding music and the roar and screech of traffic. "The police started shooting immediately as we left the station," Luis said. "They . . . ran after us, firing in the air. I got scared then, but then I thought well, they're leaving, they've left. But when I turned around I saw that there were more police, and they were shooting directly at us." The youths shouted that they had no weapons, and they threw rocks at their aggressors, but the police had guns.

Luis talked with visible effort about the many terrible things that happened next: frightened students throwing rocks and shouting defiant insults at the cops who were firing their guns at them, pedestrians running away from the gunfire, screams of panic. Two of the buses trundled along single-file at a snail's pace along a narrow downtown street, and, just as they were about to leave the central Iguala area to take the ring road, they were forced to stop. Luis slipped out from the second bus, to check what was blocking their progress, and saw a patrol car screech to a halt in the middle of the next crossway, blocking the caravan. The driver raced away. (In one of those incongruous details the mind captures during trauma, another student remembered that the driver was a policewoman with streaky, unpleasantly red-dyed hair.) Under fire, Luis and several other students, including a boy named Aldo Gutiérrez Solano, tried to move the car off the road, but the wheel was locked. In the mayhem, the students yelled at the police that there was a wounded comrade. "He's dying!" they yelled, asking for help, still not grasping the situation. Luis remembers looking dumbly at the red-hot spent casings all around. "They're fireworks," he thought. "Maybe they're throwing fireworks at us." No help came. A student somewhere screamed, bleeding from a bullet wound to the hand, and the students who were still on the bus texted over and over for an ambulance—for him, for the boy lying on the street, and now for a first-year student who had a collapsed lung and therefore was known as Pulmón—Lung—who was in the throes of a severe panic attack, turning blue, unable to breathe. In a moment of mercy that would not be repeated—or perhaps simply because an ambulance appeared at last and the paramedics were uncomfortable witnesses—there was a break in the shooting, and Lung was hauled onto a patrol car and delivered safely to the ambulance. (Aldo Gutiérrez Solano was also removed from the scene. He remains in a coma to this day.)

Luis crouched between the first and second buses and looked back in the direction they'd come from, searching for a way out. Instead, he saw that the bus he had been on when they left the school was just arriving behind him. "It rolled back and forth, dancing, as if it had a punched tire," he recalled. "The group of police split in two and started firing at it from either side. Then we saw how they started bringing the compañeros down from the bus. I counted twelve or fifteen of them." (Others counted twenty or twenty-five.) A half-dozen military-style police pickup vans had moved into place behind that bus, lights flashing. Other survivors who testified before Trejo and the GIEI think some of the boys may already have been dead at that point, and it would seem that many were unable to walk. "I saw several that had been on that bus with me, come out of the bus," Luis recalled. "The police ranged them all along the sidewalk, face down, and then they stacked them in the back of the pickup vans." He would never see them again.

At long last, the police captain from a nearby town, Huitzuco, who Luis assumed was in charge of the operation, made a circular "let's go" gesture with his hand at the cops firing from the back of the convoy, and Luis knew he had survived.

Minutes later, at a police checkpoint almost directly in front of the municipal court building, police stopped the other bus that had come down from Tixtla, which had attempted a different escape route. (A fifth bus was stopped later near the same spot, and the students were ordered out and told to flee but were otherwise unharmed.) At the court building, police lobbed tear-gas canisters through the windows to force those students out. An anonymous witness cited in the court file saw a policeman tear off a slender branch from a nearby sapling, strip it of leaves, and then whip the students with it as they staggered off the bus, while other police kicked and beat them. There were not enough police units left in Iguala to carry all the student prisoners, so more municipal police from Huitzuco and the nearby town of Cocula were called in. These Ayotzis were also bound and stacked and loaded onto police pickups. Members of the federal police arrived in uniform, parked, and stood by as the scene on the ring road unfolded. An intelligence agent from Battalion 27 rode his motorbike down to the ring road, took a few photos with his cell phone, and headed back to headquarters. It was pouring rain as the police vanished into the night with their cargo: real human beings last observed by witnesses sometime around 10:30. By the early hours of September 27, the students had become ghosts: invisible, untraceable, nonexistent.

And yet the violence was still not over. In town, the shooting had stopped, and the students who had escaped from the attack were frantically looking for safety and texting for help from their schoolmates. A handful of Ayotzis raced down from the campus into Iguala. On the way, an older student called reporters based in Chilpancingo. As an improvised street-corner press conference got underway at midnight, a reporter's voice recorder registered gunshots: several cars had arrived, and armed men dressed in black jumped out, opened fire, climbed back in, and sped away. Two students lay on the ground, killed instantly. At around the same time, on the ring road, municipal police from Iguala and neighboring Huitzuco attacked a bus that was carrying the members of a Chilpancingo junior league soccer team, heading home after celebrating their victory over the locals. Before the police realized that they were attacking a non-Ayotzi bus, they shot and killed the bus driver, a fifteen-year-old team member, and a woman in a passing taxi.

A final victim would be discovered late that morning lying outside a soccer field, identified later as a first-year Ayotzi, Julio César Mondragón, twenty-two. Like many of the students trapped in Iguala, he had texted his family an ongoing account of the night. His last message to his pregnant wife was a farewell: "Take care of yourself and of my daughter. Tell her I love her. Bye." When he was found, he had been severely beaten and had multiple broken bones. Much of his face was missing.

Patrol cars roamed the streets in the predawn silence of Saturday the twenty-seventh, tauntingly calling out to the Ayotzis. From a rooftop where he had found safety, Luis heard them whistle for them. (*We know you're hiding!*) One panicky group scrambled from building to building downtown, trying to get help for a schoolmate who had been shot through the jaw. Eventually they found themselves inside a small private clinic, begging the staff on duty to help a severely wounded comrade. (They refused.) The Ayotzis cowered in the waiting room and on an upper floor, terrified that the police might find them. Instead, when they answered a loud knock at the door around midnight, a cluster of soldiers armed with machine guns muscled their way into the waiting room, fanned out, and pointed their guns at the students. They were followed by an imposing man in uniform: José Martínez Crespo, the captain from Battalion 27. "Frankly, I felt joyful when we saw him" a student testified, thinking he would help.

"Get the others the fuck down here," Crespo commanded a soldier. He ordered a photograph taken of the scene—twenty-five despondent, exhausted young men staring at the floor. "You sons of bitches, you think you're so tough! Now you're faced with a real motherfucker, let's see how tough you really are." Crespo made them strip to the waist, ordering someone to take headshots of each one and write down their names. "Make sure you give the real ones,"

Crespo said. "Otherwise they'll never find you later." At last he left, saying he was "off to see about some corpses"—most likely the two students killed at the press conference—but he'd be back. The students fled and survived the night. (Crespo is currently in military prison, accused of collaboration with the GU.)

What Crespo was doing, or thought he was doing, and on whose orders, is unclear. He later told his superiors that he was checking a report that there were armed men at the clinic and that he and his men showed the students every courtesy, but he didn't mention the photographs. Were they taken to show to the GU, so they could see if there were any Rojos infiltrated among the students? Or was he taking the information back to his battalion, where the statewide monitoring system showed clearly where armed men in fact were? But it would have been almost impossible for the officers at Iguala's two military battalions to ignore what was going on outside their gates: Battalion 27 regularly sent out armed patrols into the city; they had a long established practice of infiltrating soldiers into the student body as informants (one of them would perish with the other first-years that ended up in Iguala); both bases constantly monitored a state-wide system of video surveillance of streets and highways, and the Mexican Defense Ministry had been among the first agencies in the world to purchase Pegasus, a virus-like program that allows its owner to monitor the entire contents of a victim's cell phone in real time. Even as the attack was taking place, army intelligence was linked via Pegasus to the phones of several GU members. But no one in the military intervened. This is the part that guts Gómez Trejo. "If they knew, why didn't they save those boys?" he asks himself to this day.

Why the military did not save the boys is perhaps one of the most important unresolved questions of the investigation, the other being why the GU found it necessary to carry out a nightmarish persecution of some one hundred students and murder nearly half of them. Perhaps, as the GIEI believed, one of the five buses was loaded with product, or weapons, but that would not explain why only the Ayotzis who were in the two buses that left from the school campus that morning were disappeared. Another theory—there are many—holds that the GU was convinced that the Ayotzis had been infiltrated by the Rojos. There is some evidence to support the idea. The GU had been fighting with the Rojos the week before, and perhaps it expected a counterattack. There is also one small piece of evidence to support this argument. The day after the Iguala attack, a GU cousin who liked to call himself "Silver" sent a text to Pablo Vega in Chicago. "Cousin, the contras came into town all mixed up with the Ayotzinapos. And the shit came dooown!" A massacre on defenseless youths carried out by paranoid, inept, and bloodthirsty goons: that makes sense.

We have one last glimpse of the forty-three Ayotzis before we lose sight of them forever. A driver from one of the commandeered buses told investigators that he saw a number of the students at the Iguala police station, lying prone on the floor. Another witness, who happened to walk into the station the following morning, testified that he saw a photograph of the students on a screen and heard the magistrate on duty (in this case, a position more like that of a hoosegow sheriff) joking about how the Ayotzis had been roughed up and boasting that he himself had participated in their beating. (The magistrate, who was granted asylum in the United States in 2020, has denied that the students were brought to the police station that night.)

Investigators pulled this account together slowly over the course of many months, cross-checking hundreds of interviews with survivors, eyewitnesses, and participants in the events. But the answer to a key question sought by the students' parents—what happened to their children after they were last seen that night long ago?—remains elusive: of those seven or eight missing hours, only fragments can be pieced together, and the story behind them guessed at.

At approximately 11:30 p.m., according to a document released by the Mexican military that investigators were unable to corroborate, the Iguala vice chief of police messaged Gildardo López Astudillo, known as "El Gil," who was the head of Guerreros Unidos for Huitzuco, Cocula, and environs. "I've got 21 packages (tied-up people, or corpses) . . . inside the bus that's leaving," he wrote. To which El Gil replied, from his base in an area known as Loma de Coyotes, 'OK, land them here.'" By this time, some of the students may already have been dead from injuries sustained during their beatings. The survivors could talk, create problems. What should be done with them?

According to the state's witness Juan, GU members received an order from one of the high command: *"pártanles su madre."* The slang phrase can be translated either as "beat the shit" out of the students or, given the context, "do away" with them. What appears likely is that as many as half the students were taken to El Gil, where—and this is a ghastly thing to have to write—they were bludgeoned and hacked to pieces. (Why not shot, one wonders. Why not that one small mercy?) Juan says that he doesn't know the victims' names, because it did not occur to any of the murderers to inquire. A lowly gofer testified that he and a partner were sent to get cleaning supplies and pick up the mutilated corpses, which were stuffed into black plastic garbage bags.

The bodies of five or six other students were delivered to a different GU member, who probably dissolved them in vats of acid. The remains of the boys who died at Loma de Coyotes were taken to one or more funeral homes equipped with cremation ovens. Juan told investigators that it took several days to make sure the remains were so thoroughly incinerated that no one—not their grieving families, certainly—would be able to identify them. Normally so careless with their victims—during the same time period and in the same region, different groups of mourners searching for their own relatives have found 150 bodies, none belonging to an Ayotzi—the GU was at pains to make the students truly disappear. "We didn't think that this business would be so *mediático*," says Juan, irritated by the publicity.

5.

Eight years later, on August 18, 2022, María Luisa Aguilar, from the Centro Prodh Father Pro Center for Human Rights, accompanied the families to a meeting with the president, called only a short time before. López Obrador had met with the parents several times over the years, always courteous and friendly, sitting at a round table with them to hear their suggestions and concerns about the investigation, and Aguilar, who handles international relations for the Father Pro Center, had always been there, along with the parents' legal representative for the center, Santiago Aguirre Espinosa. Aguilar is a slight, uncannily youthful woman, who must have learned the art of remaining calm during the six years she spent working at the Tlachinollan human rights center, in what was then one of the most drug-violent areas in all of Mexico. When she walked into the meeting at the National Palace together with the parents, she knew something was wrong: the president entered and stood behind a podium, flanked by a good part of his cabinet, including his attorney general and the defense minister—figures the parents distrusted. The families were ushered to chairs in the audience.

The hail-fellow-well-met Alejandro Encinas, the president's appointee as overseer of the entire Ayotzinapa effort, read the government's official "conclusions" on the investigation thus far. Encinas disagrees, but the Argentines, Gómez Trejo and his group of investigative police, the GIEI, Aguilar and Aguirre, and certainly the parents all say they had not been advised earlier of the contents of the report. Using the information gathered over the previous two years by the various teams, Encinas narrated the crime and the subsequent investigation. He spoke of judicial participation in the abduction, murders, and cover-up, and he denounced police and military participation "by omission or commission" in the disappearances. For the first time, he defined what happened in Iguala as "a crime of the state"—a historic acknowledgment by a Mexican administration. But as the GIEI, Gómez Trejo, the families, and their lawyers listened and looked at each other in increasing distress, Encinas also presented a series of WhatsApp messages purported to be screenshots of SMS messages sent by local officials and by members of the GU. To anyone familiar with the GU clan's brutal and near illiterate forms of communication, these well-spelled messages read as fake. And in contradiction to everything the GIEI and Gómez Trejo had learned, they harked back to the cover-up's Historic Truth version of events, sidelining the military's participation and ascribing the order to kill the students to a relatively minor figure: the Iguala mayor. (Encinas denied pushing the "historic truth.") Worse, because they were WhatsApp screenshots, they were impossible to trace and verify. Toward the end of the meeting, Aguilar listened in shock as Encinas told the families that, after all those years of hope, all the evidence pointed to the fact that their children were dead. The families and their defenders squirmed in their seats in dismay as they first heard what Aguilar describes as "the very graphic details" of how, to the best of anyone's knowledge, the forty-three sons of the families present had perished at the hand of the Guerreros Unidos clan. López Obrador ended the meeting without taking questions. "The families were utterly undone" (*trastocadas*), Aguilar said. "The mothers were distraught; men who do not allow themselves to cry in public were weeping."

"The president closed by saying that he was sorry for the parents' suffering," Aguilar remembered. "And he told them that their movement had not been in vain." The words were meant as a consolation, but the event destroyed the families emotionally and marked the beginning of the end of the Ayotzinapa Special Investigative Commission.

Up to that moment, it had seemed to the families and their teams that justice, the long-sought object of Gómez Trejo's efforts, was at last within reach. While Gómez Trejo was at the meeting at Palacio Nacional, his investigators were presenting their long, arcane court filing before a judge and requesting warrants for the arrest of eighty-three participants in the events at Iguala and/or the subsequent cover-up. Among those indicted were GU members; soldiers; police officers; the magistrate at the Iguala police facility; the judge in Chilpancingo who ordered the destruction of state surveillance footage of the night of the event; the state attorney general at the time, Iñaki Blanco; Captain José Martínez Crespo; and the commanders of the two Iguala battalions. Gómez Trejo arrived at the disastrous meeting with the parents feeling joyful and left in an altogether different mood for Israel, seeking to obtain the extradition of former attorney general Murillo Karam's chief of criminal investigation. A week later, he returned to a different world. His team of investigative police had been sent away for "retraining." A team of auditors took possession of every file in his office. In a meeting with his boss, the attorney general, he was told that he would not be allowed to open any new lines of investigation. Days later, and on the authority of the attorney general, the same judge who had approved Gómez Trejo's eighty-three arrest warrants rescinded twenty-one, including those for Blanco, fifteen military, and the judge in Chilpancingo who had erased the videos from the Iguala street videocams. A few days later, Gómez Trejo resigned and his security detail was removed. Two of the four members of the GIEI, feeling that they would be legitimizing a fraud if they stayed, also resigned and left the country. The remaining two, Angela Buitrago and Carlos Beristain, stayed because they could not bear to leave the parents so defenseless. Later I would learn that, as Gómez Trejo weighed his resignation, a high-ranking official took him aside, draped an arm confidentially over his shoulder, and said, more or less verbatim, that Gómez Trejo had really managed to piss off the president. López Obrador had negotiated the arrest of five military with the armed forces high command, the official told Gómez Trejo, "and you, *cabrón*, went and issued orders for fifteen!" (The attorney general and President López Obrador did not respond to requests for comment.)

It was a startling indication of the real power of the Mexican military, beneficiaries of López Obrador's unprecedented generosity. The president has turned over the construction and administration of airports, roads, railroad lines, customs offices, tourist agencies, and more to the Army and the Defense Ministry. Most seriously, he has given the Defense Ministry oversight of what was once the Federal Police, now restructured as the National Guard. In 2020, retired general Salvador Cienfuegos, who had stopped GIEI investigators from interviewing members of the military, was arrested in the Los Angeles airport on charges that, as secretary of defense, "with [the members of a drug clan from the state of Nayarit] he did knowingly and intentionally conspire to manufacture and distribute one or more controlled substances," including cocaine and methamphetamine. Part of the indictment unsealed in Brooklyn's Eastern District of New York alleges that he sent his troops to attack the Nayarit clan's rivals. But after President López Obrador threatened to suspend DEA operations in Mexico if Cienfuegos were not cleared of charges and sent home, the US Justice Department intervened and prosecutors returned Cienfuegos to Mexico. He walked off the plane a free man. "We view this not as an act of impunity, but of respect toward Mexico and the Armed Forces," Secretary of Foreign Affairs Marcelo Ebrard declared then. Four months later, Mexican justice officials decreed that there was no evidence of the general's ever having had any relationship with the Nayarit drug-smuggling group. In October 2023, López Obrador gave him a medal.

Gómez Trejo moved to the United States with his wife and child, fearing for his family's safety. When I had lunch with him in New York recently, he looked rested—not as haggard as when he first left Mexico. He's working as an international consultant on human rights issues. Carlos Beristain and Angela Buitrago, the two members of the GIEI who initially felt that some small things could still be accomplished if they stayed in Mexico, held a press conference in July 2023, demanding answers they believe only the military can provide. Then they resigned and left the country. The president appointed a new special investigator, who quietly reinstated several of the twenty-one arrest orders that had been revoked and left it at that. There is now a sense that, for all practical purposes, the investigation into the disappearance of the Forty-Three has come to an end.

One recent afternoon, I spoke with Centro Prodh's Santiago Aguirre Espinosa, as slender and cheerful as his colleague Aguilar and as permanently in haste to get to the next appointment and take on the next crisis. Aguirre too spent years in Guerrero at the Centro Tlachinollan. I asked him what he made of their last nine years of effort. "Some progress has been made," he began. "To have the military—Crespo and the commanders of the two Iguala battalions—accused of organized crime is very important. It means the government accepts that they were involved. But from the point of view of the families," he went on, sounding uncharacteristically grim, "their main objective was to find their sons, and that was not achieved. They are angry and sad, and some of them have doubts as to whether their fight was worth it." For his part, Beristain, who has now returned to his home in Spain, lamented that the extent of the military's involvement in the saga remains unclear. There are hundreds of pages of military records that are still missing, he said—pages the GIEI believes can shed light on what exactly happened to the students and why two administrations have felt the need to cover it up.

These days, the president has taken to denouncing Centro Prodh and Centro Tlachinollan's Vidulfo Rosales at his daily press conferences. Their phones have been repeatedly infiltrated by Pegasus. (When Encinas told López Obrador that his phone was also being monitored by the military, the president confirmed at a morning press conference that he had told his longtime ally "not to give it any importance.") In September, Encinas left the commission to join the campaign for President López Obrador's designated successor, Claudia Sheinbaum. As his six-year term draws to a close, the president's relations with his perceived adversaries grow more fraught. Recently, the *New York Times*' Mexico

City bureau chief, checking out a now closed US investigation into the drug trade's possible dealings with close associates of the president, sent him the mandatory questionnaire asking for his response to such claims. His reaction was to lash out at the reporter, reading her name and phone number out loud during his morning press conference. This may be illegal, but "I would do it again," he said the next day; the president's "moral authority is above the law." (The *Times* felt that after this outburst it had no option but to publish the story.) In an exceedingly rare interview—two hours with a Russian journalist from a minor Spanish cable channel—he recognized that Ayotzinapa remains a pending assignment. "There is still time," he affirmed. "The most important thing is to find" the students.

Six years after the massacre, Clemente Rodríguez and his wife, Luz María Telumbre, received a visit at their home in Tixtla from Special Prosecutor Omar Gómez Trejo, Encinas, and Centro Prodh's Aguirre and Aguilar. The group was there to tell them about a two-inch fragment of bone that Gómez Trejo's team had found in a dry gully. The Argentine Team had certified that the shred of recovered DNA in the fragment belonged to Christian Rodríguez Telumbre, one of only three positive identifications that have been made in all this time. "We tried to bring some dignity and a sense of ceremony to the event," Gómez Trejo told me about that visit, but it was a hopeless attempt to replace a twenty-year-old boy who skipped gaily around his parents' house, practicing steps from the folklore dances he was crazy about, with a broken and charred bit of bone. When I met doña Luz María in Mexico City last spring, at the start of one of the parents' Mexico City marches, I asked her about this moment. She is a beautiful woman with an easy, affectionate manner, but there was no hiding the paper-slicing edge in her voice when she answered. "I said thank you," she told me, "and I asked what part of the body this *huesito*—little bone—was from." She was informed that it was part of Christian's right heel. "But I've seen people who lost a foot and are still alive," she said, not raising her voice. "I am not satisfied. I want my son."

IT WAS DAY of the Dead in Mexico City when I ran into don Clemente Rodríguez again, a year later, at Centro Prodh. I asked if he was going to place a picture of his son on the family altar in Tixtla that night. There was a long silence before he finally said, "I can't." Don Clemente was in town to give a talk at a local school, and as usual he had brought some of his friends' and family's handicrafts to put out for sale. He used to sell five-gallon jugs of purified water for a living, but the constant traveling to agitate for their sons' return has ruined the families' livelihood, and now many make a little money weaving straw, or baking bread, or embroidering textiles to sell whenever they march. Don Clemente has a sidelong sense of humor, but he is wound so tightly, and is so permanently exhausted, that it rarely comes through. Now, I watched his face crumple as he tried to find words to explain his son's absence on the altar. "I don't have a body to mourn," he said. "I don't know the place where he is. I have nothing to hold that is him."

The hope that their children would be returned was at the center of the parents' movement. It was the motivation that kept them going through years of doubt, and fear, and struggle, away from their families and their fields. *Alive they were taken away. We want them returned alive.* What parent wants to kill his own child in his heart? Don Tanis gently corrected me when I referred to his son in the past tense.

Last year, I drove to Guerrero once again, down the same long, parched highway to Acapulco, but this time I took the Tixtla turnoff, in order to visit with Rafael López. His son, Julio César López Patolzin, was one of the three students the army infiltrated into Ayotzinapa and the only one of those three to be killed in the massacre. Unavoidably, the father became something of a pariah among the other families once his son's role in the school was made public, and it seemed to me an unusually cruel fate to lose a son and then be unable to seek the comfort that the other parents obviously find in each other's company. Don Rafa, square-set and curmudgeonly, and limping from a wounded foot, took me to see the bit of land he can no longer farm without his son. He showed me a picture of Julio César at his high school graduation, a dark-skinned boy stiffly uncomfortable in his formal shirt and vest, holding a diploma. He handed me a sheet of paper with the words "Life Project" written with bright blue ink in careful block letters at the top of a list of goals. Don Rafa found it among his son's things once he was gone. "I would like to travel around the country learning different things and meeting new people," it began. Further down, Julio César—named after the boxer Julio César Chávez—stated that he would like to study at Ayotzinapa so that he could become a physical education teacher. He would also like to join the military, said another starred goal, so that he could study to become an army doctor. And he would like to earn money, "so that I can help my parents the way they have helped me."

In the end, having tried to make a decent living at whatever crappy forms of underemployment are available to a poor boy in a small town—working at the market, selling candy, or giving a shoeshine—he did join the army, and he spent his time patrolling poppy fields in the mountainous region of Guerrero.

Eventually, his father said, Julio César injured himself and could no longer go on patrol. He wanted to leave the army and study, but giving up the salary of a foot soldier was not easy. One can imagine his commander zeroing in at that point to offer him a deal: *Go to Ayotzinapa if you want, and keep your salary. But help us.* He must have protested at the unfairness of his fate before he was killed.

Don Rafa is a gruff man, but he insisted on riding back to the highway with me so that I wouldn't get lost. There was a new crop of Ayotzis at the toll booth, exacting fares "for the revolution." The GU was gone, the Rojos were diminished, and rival groups had eclipsed them. In Chilpancingo, a new mayor had been filmed having breakfast at a restaurant with a new drug boss. Don Rafa generally struck me as a harsh realist, but he told me that the boy's godmother, recently deceased, had come to his daughter in a dream. "She had looked for Julio César everywhere on the other side," Don Rafa said, "and found no sign of him. She said we should keep looking for him in this world." He told me to stop the car just before we reached the military checkpoint at the edge of town. "I used to roll his little sarape around him at night when he was a baby so he wouldn't be cold, and watch him sleep " he said, mostly to himself. "What a thing, huh?" he added as he got out of the car. "We care for and nurture our children so that the government can rip them away from us."

POSTSCRIPT. On July 10, 2023, an estimated two thousand people stormed down the stretch of the Mexico-Acapulco highway that has been the scene of so many protests over the years. Under a blazing noonday sun, carrying banners, the crowd lynched five men, swarmed over a police armored truck, drove it into town, crashed it through the gates of the Chilpancingo state administrative building, and rampaged through the city, setting cars on fire. Many of the demonstrators had come from the surrounding villages to demand attention to their situation—no farm credits, no rain for months, no crops, no way to survive—but it turned out that the more violent ones at the front of the march had a different demand: the release of two men, bus drivers associated with the new local leaders of the drug trade, who had been arrested earlier that week. What with all the other conflict and drama that took place that month, and every month, throughout the country, the deadly narco-march in Guerrero came and went without much consequence, but for those who noticed, it marked a radical swerve in organized crime's confrontation with the state. The drug clans have learned something from the endless campaign by the parents of the Ayotzinapa Forty-Three to find their sons and have now taught their support populations how to march. A few weeks later, in the southern Chiapas city Frontera Comalapa, crowds lined the highway to greet a parade of the Sinaloa mafia, moving slowly through the town in jeeps and pickup trucks, waving machine guns in the air. The Sinaloans had just routed their rivals from Jalisco, who are known to be particularly cruel rulers wherever they take over a town. In the northern state of Sonora, a leader of the Rarámuri people begged the leadership of the local drug group to replace the leader in their area with someone not quite as vicious. In Guerrero as in other states, priests are quietly acting as intermediaries between drug lords and victim populations, to see if less punishing living conditions can be established. In every case, the Mexican state is not taken into account. Mexico now faces a nationwide plague of murderous drug clans, which is a criminal problem; the takeover of numerous small towns, which is a sovereignty issue; and an enormous public safety problem everywhere, which it has so far been unable to solve or even abate. But by restructuring the corrupt federal police as a new National Guard—under the nominal jurisdiction of the Public Security Ministry, but officially administered and operated by the Defense Ministry—the government of Andrés Manuel López Obrador created a new conundrum for itself. From now on, if a criminal group orders its subject population to stage a march, does the National Guard/Army open fire on the citizenry? And if it doesn't, what happens next? This is perhaps the most fraught issue the incoming president, Claudia Sheinbaum, will have to face.

NOTE

An abbreviated version of this chapter was published in the *New Yorker*, March 11, 2024.

Acknowledgments

In a book of such geographical span, with so many different types of stories, it's impossible to give individual thanks to the many, many people who gave their time, and sometimes took terrible risks, in order to help me understand. I cherish the names of a few interviewees in particular: the Nicaraguan hero Dora María Tellez, who spent nearly two years in a dark isolation cell, courtesy of the Ortega–Murillo regime; the brilliant Venezuelan former guerrilla, newsman, militant, and wit Teodoro Petkoff, hounded to his very grave by Nicolás Maduro and his bureaucrats and goons; Zoilamérica Narváez, who has survived with wisdom and grace the many grotesque crimes inflicted on her by her mother and stepfather and the Nicaraguan state. Lastly, the brave jokester and great Mexican reporter, my friend Javier Valdez, shot down in his prime by murderers whose names no one will ever remember. Javier's writings will be read by generations.

There is no reason why any sensible human being might ever want to speak to a reporter, and yet people consistently spoke to me, generously, patiently for these stories. My deepest gratitude to every person mentioned in this collection, and to the many others whose names do not appear here, but who contributed their knowledge and/or profound experience of life in Latin America to these pages. Names pulled from my notebooks at random of people without whom these stories would not exist: Malú Aguilar, Santiago Aguirre, Enrique García, Kau Sirenio, Eduardo Guerrero, Elías Jaramillo, the late Esther Chávez, Carol Kiecker, Marcela Turati and Periodistas de a Pie, Gustavo de la Rosa, Davíd Carrasco, Jason Berry, Froylan Enciso, Carol Pires, Luz Mely Reyes, Raúl Peñaranda, Alonso Salazar, Claudia García, Pedro Abramovay, Emmanuel del Real, David Holiday, Nicole Bravo, the brothers Carlos and

Óscar Martínez. If I have misinterpreted what they told me or otherwise failed to do justice to their time and patience, the blame is mine alone.

Former president Juan Manuel Santos made me welcome in Colombia, and I owe him immense thanks.

There are dear friends who over the years have provided meals and drinks and a sympathetic ear, and shared their privileged knowledge with me. Brian Nissen, Rafael Noboa, Salomón Kalmanovitz, Juanita León, Margarita Martínez, Karen de Young, Cynthia Arnson, Peggy Engel, Donald Donovan, and Jennifer Lake. Esther Allen and Nathaniel Wice, Elisa Jiménez, Patrick Iber, Adriana Martínez, Gloria Loomis and Walter Bernstein, Bertha Navarro, Fredy Florez, Mafe Márquez, and Mariclaire Acosta and John Burstein have been a source of comfort and help in the worst of times. Sergio and Tulita Ramírez, Carlos Dada, Ramón Jimeno, Mac Margolis, Carlos Fernando Chamorro, and Alvaro Jiménez always helped me take a story one step further. Guillermo Osorno, Damian Fraser, Jennifer Homans, and Ben Fountain have patiently read and commented on first versions and tenth drafts.

I travel and do my reporting alone, in order to keep myself as exposed as possible to the reality around me. But I've never worked alone; wherever I go fixers and researchers, brilliant young people like Luis Mendoza, Cristina Monsalve, Nicole Bravo, and Carlos Salinas Maldonado have refrained from laughing at my ignorance and helped me find my way. I can't think of any reporter and writer luckier than me throughout the decades I've spent working with editors at publications I cherish. At *National Geographic* magazine, that grand institution, Oliver Payne took my words and charmed them into the best stories I could ever hope to write, while the rest of the staff worked its usual magic with fact-checking and maps and glorious images. Some of the stories I'm happiest to have had the chance to report were written for the *New Yorker*. I'm in awe of the many people involved in turning a story into a *New Yorker* story—the late Martin Barron and his successor, Peter Canby, at the head of the fact-checking department, and their teams of brilliant checkers; the readers and okayers and illustrators and Comma Ladies—I can't thank them enough. David Remnick, editor of a magazine that is one of the greatest achievements in publishing, has always been there to offer support and welcome. More than half my reporting life has been spent at the *New York Review of Books*, and I can think of nothing that makes me prouder. Heartfelt thanks to Rea Hederman, publisher nonpareil, Hugh Eakin, Michael Shae, and Matt Seaton, who've brought a surgeon's skill and an artist's eye to the craft of editing, and to the heroic Emily Greenhouse, who has brought new life to a unique and indispensable publication.

This book would not exist without the kind and always generous support of Gil Joseph, who shepherded a bundle of stories over to Duke University Press. At Duke, Gisela Fosado proved to have in spades the enthusiasm, discernment, and efficiency all writers h ope to find in an editor, and shaped the stories into a book. Huge thanks to her for her alegría, siempre, y su gran corazón, and to the entire editorial staff, in particular Livia Tenzer, for the delicate attention paid to every word and every page.

This book is dedicated to the memory of the three editors who turned me into a writer and, I hope, a better person: Robert Silvers, Bob Gottlieb, and John Bennet. Their like will never be seen again.

And to Néstor, who, I hope, somewhere has found peace.